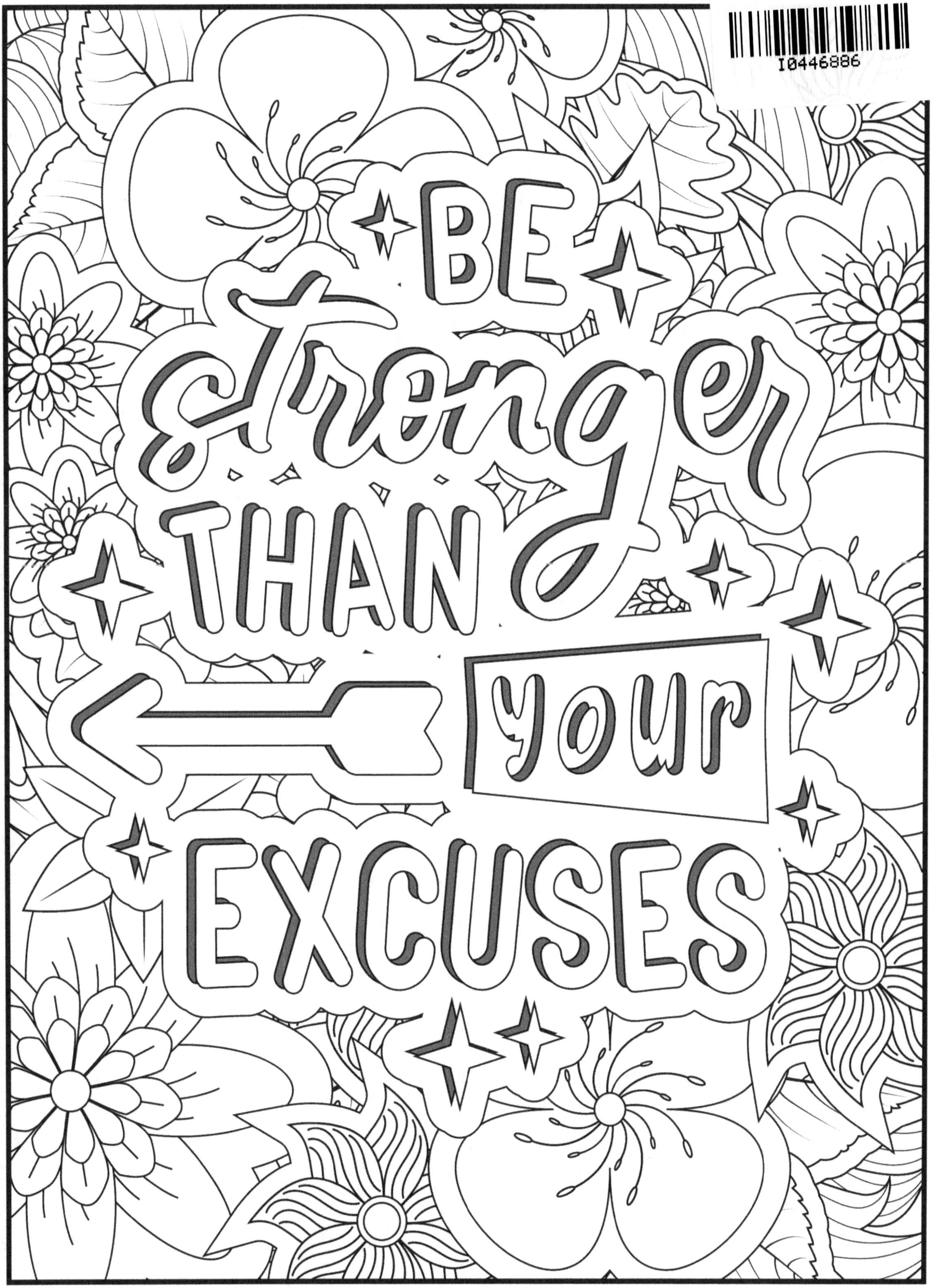
BE
Stronger
THAN
your
EXCUSES

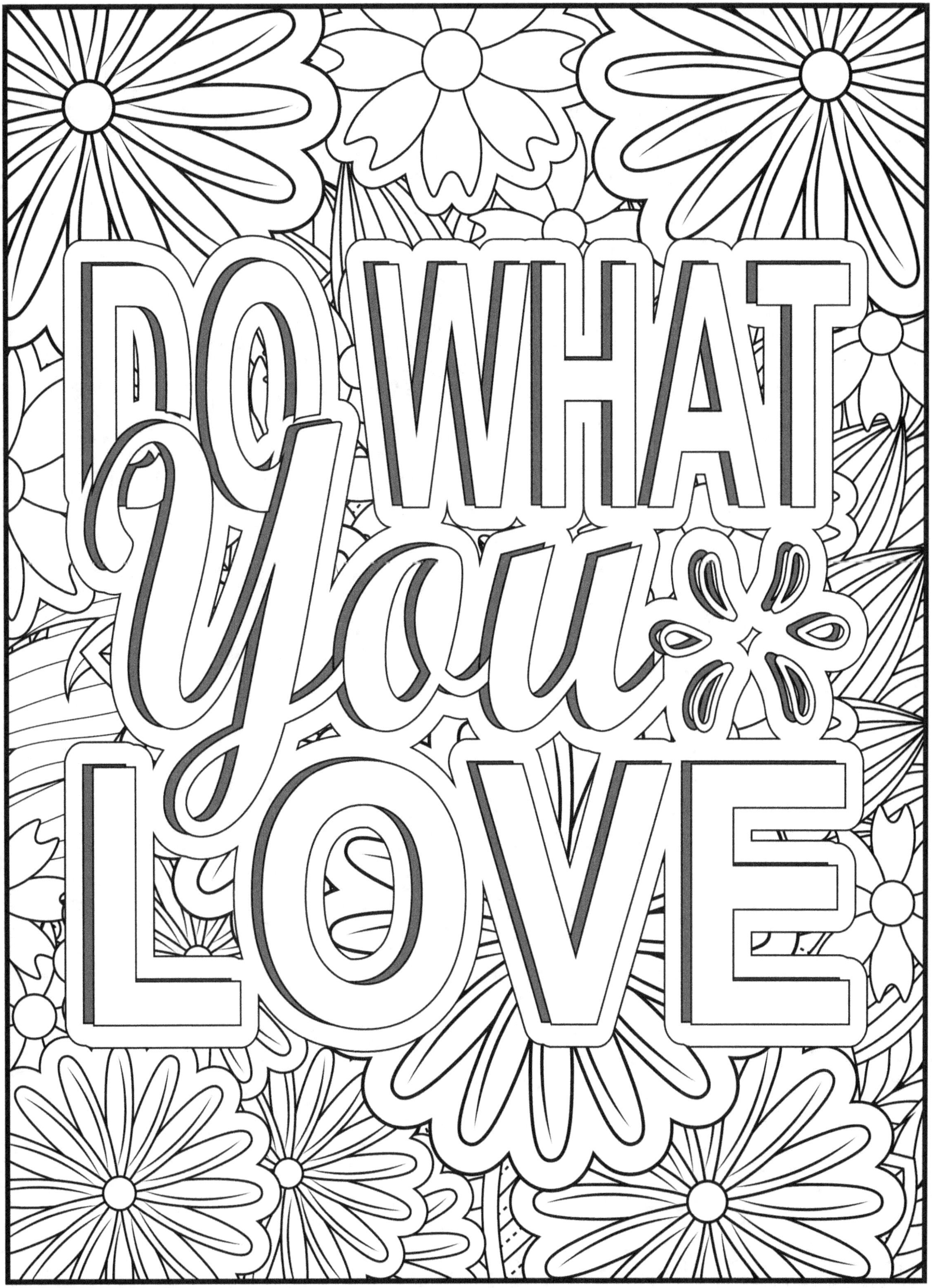
DO WHAT
You
LOVE

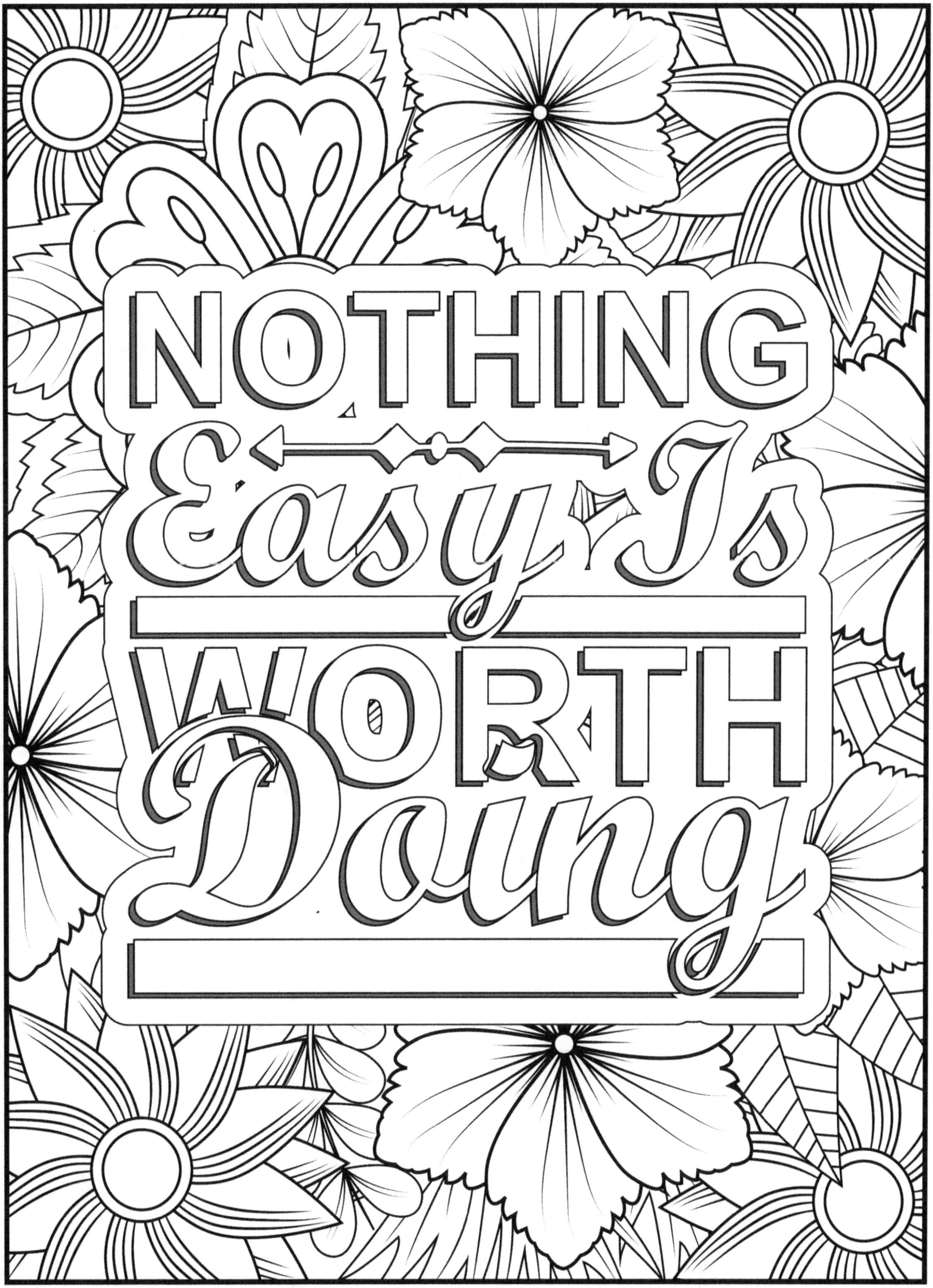
NOTHING
Easy Is
WORTH
Doing

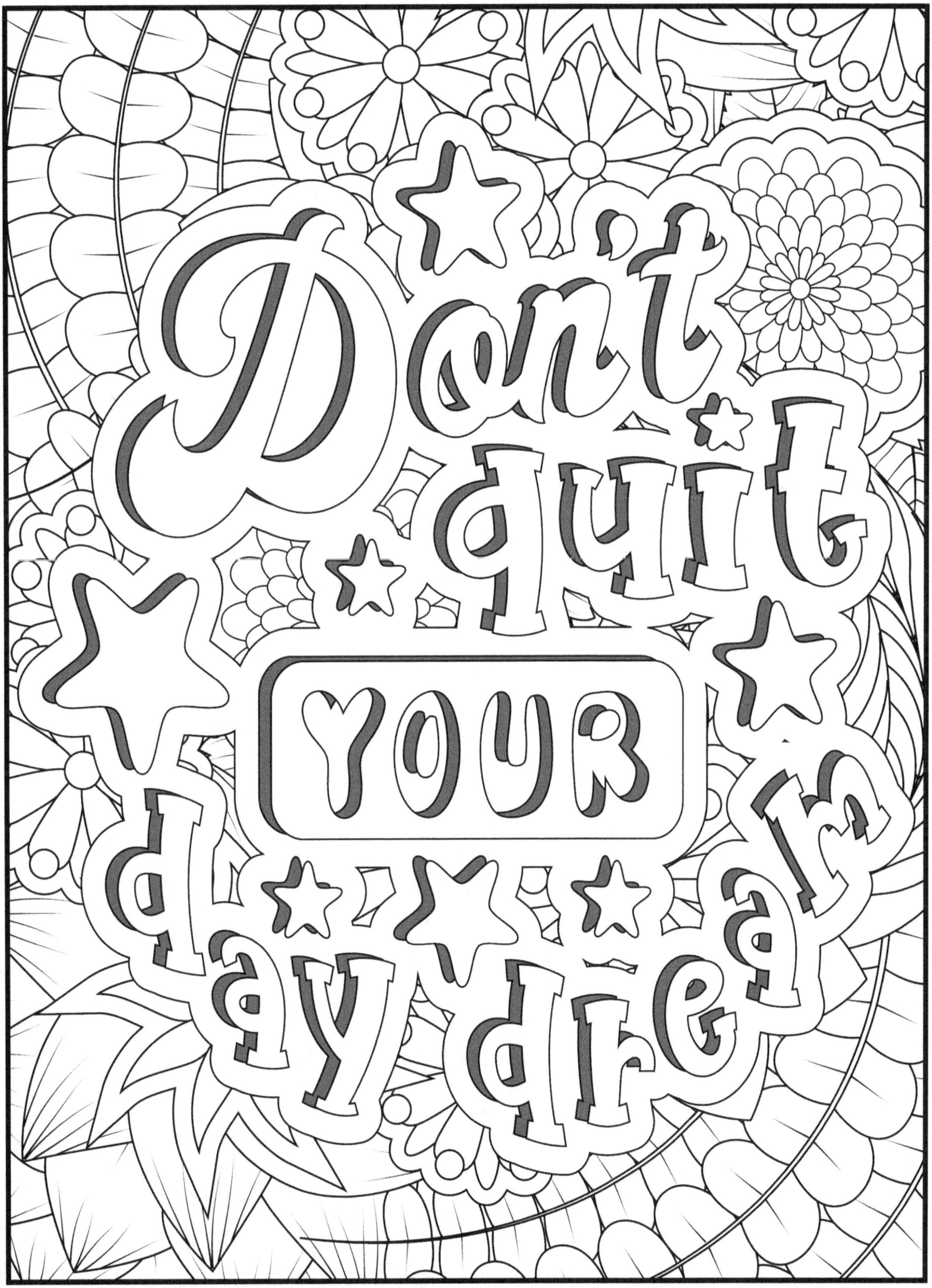
Don't quit
YOUR
day dream

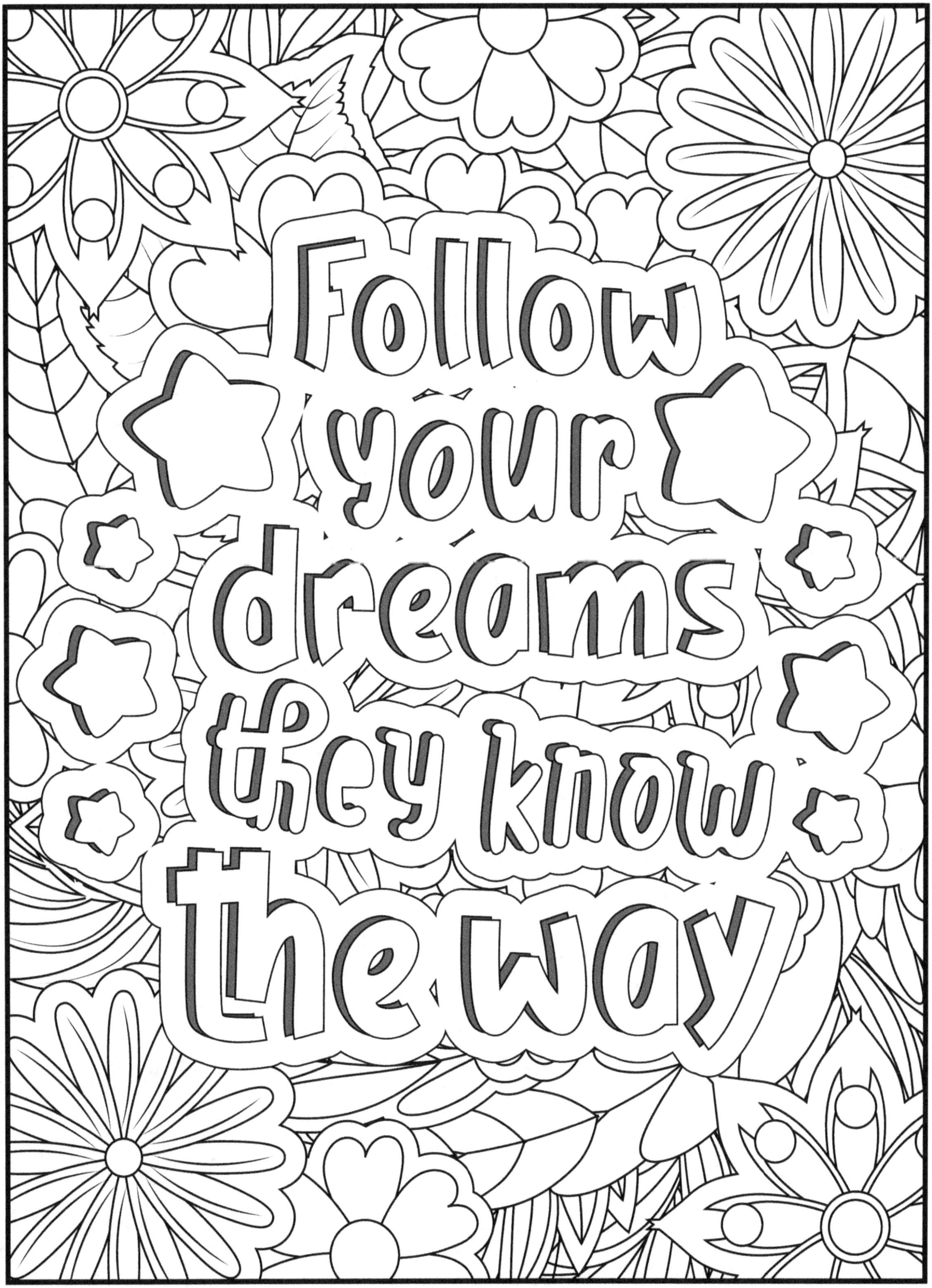
Follow your dreams they know the way

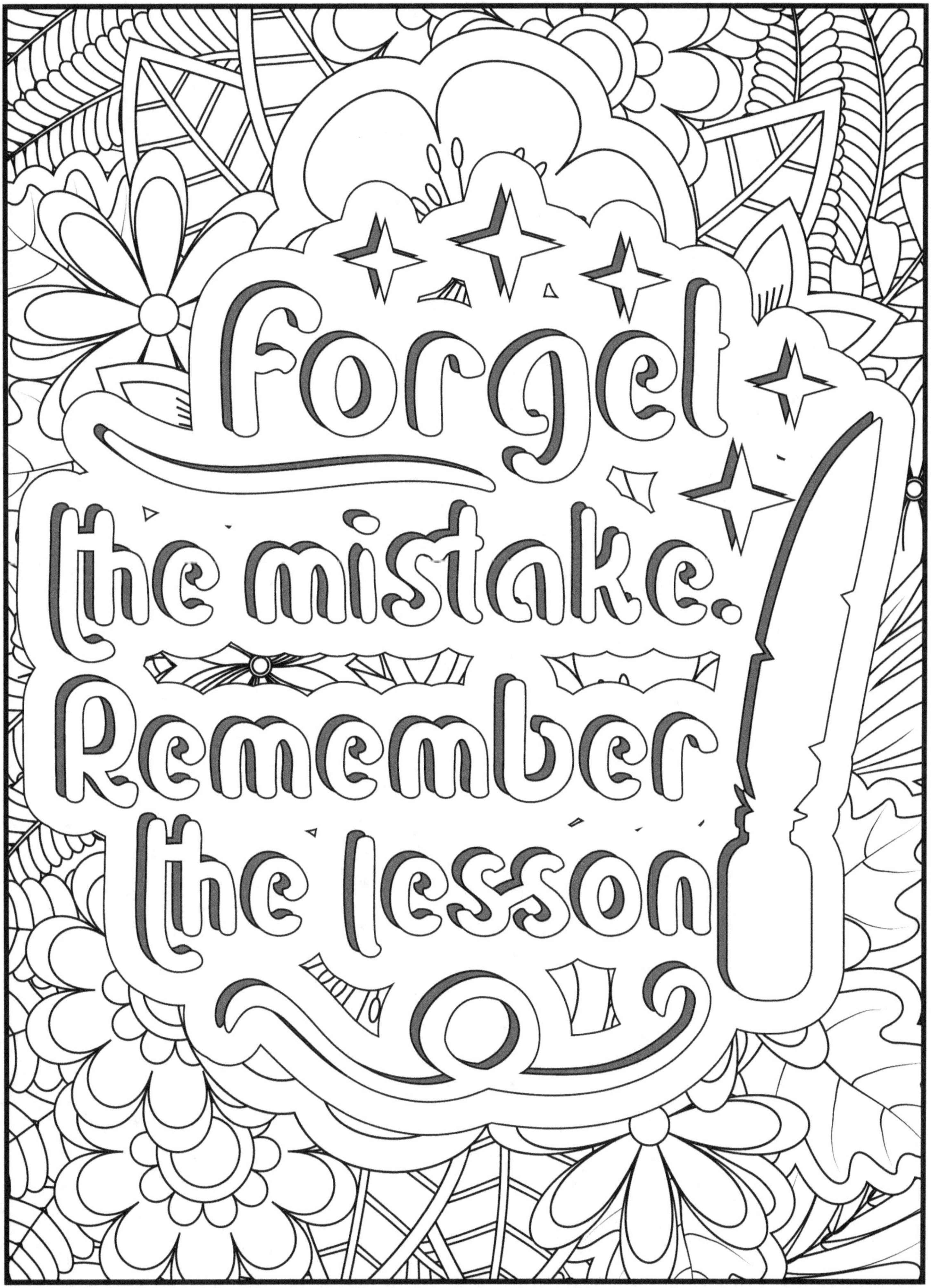
Forget
the mistake.
Remember
the lesson

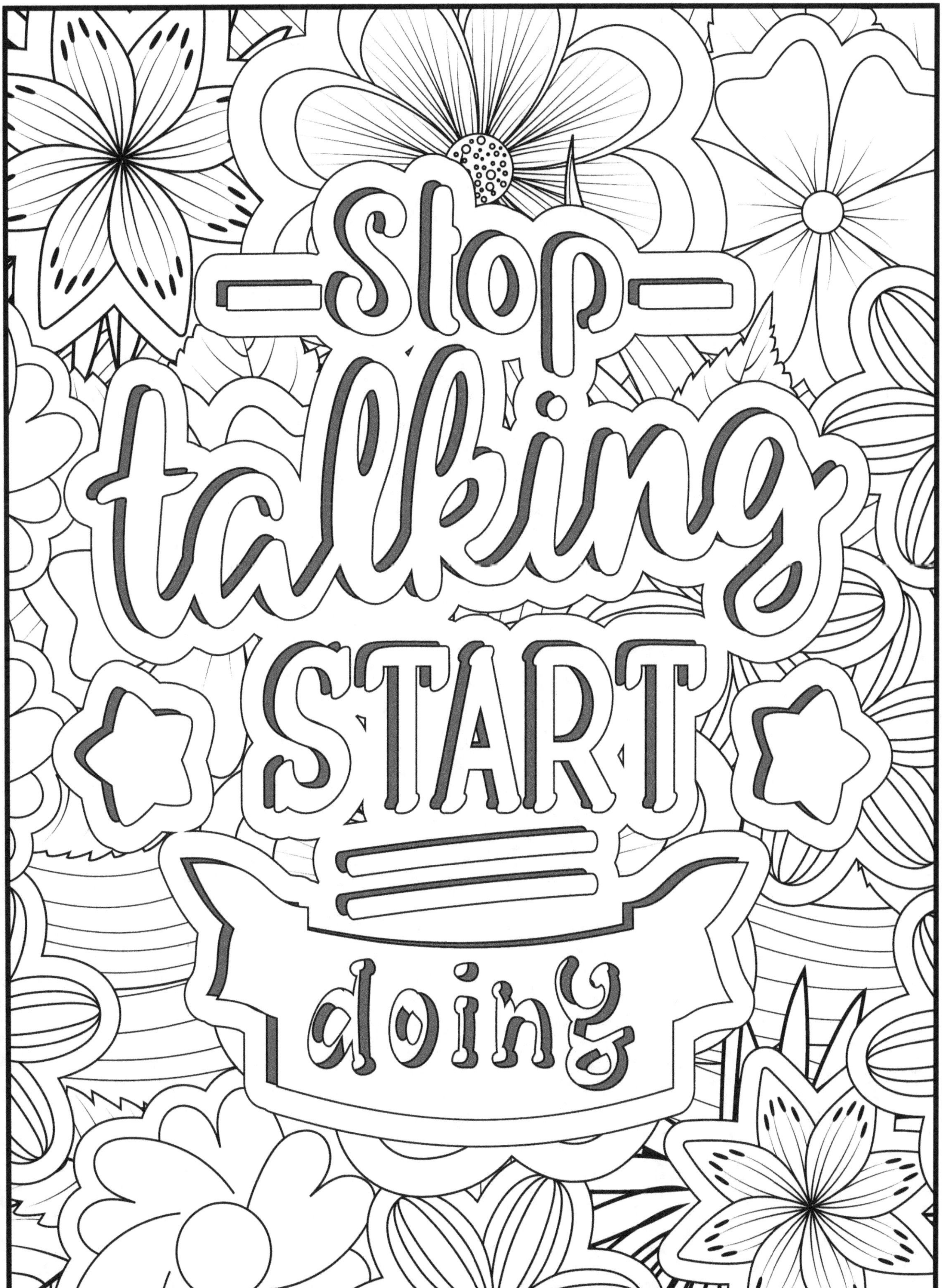
Stop talking
START
doing

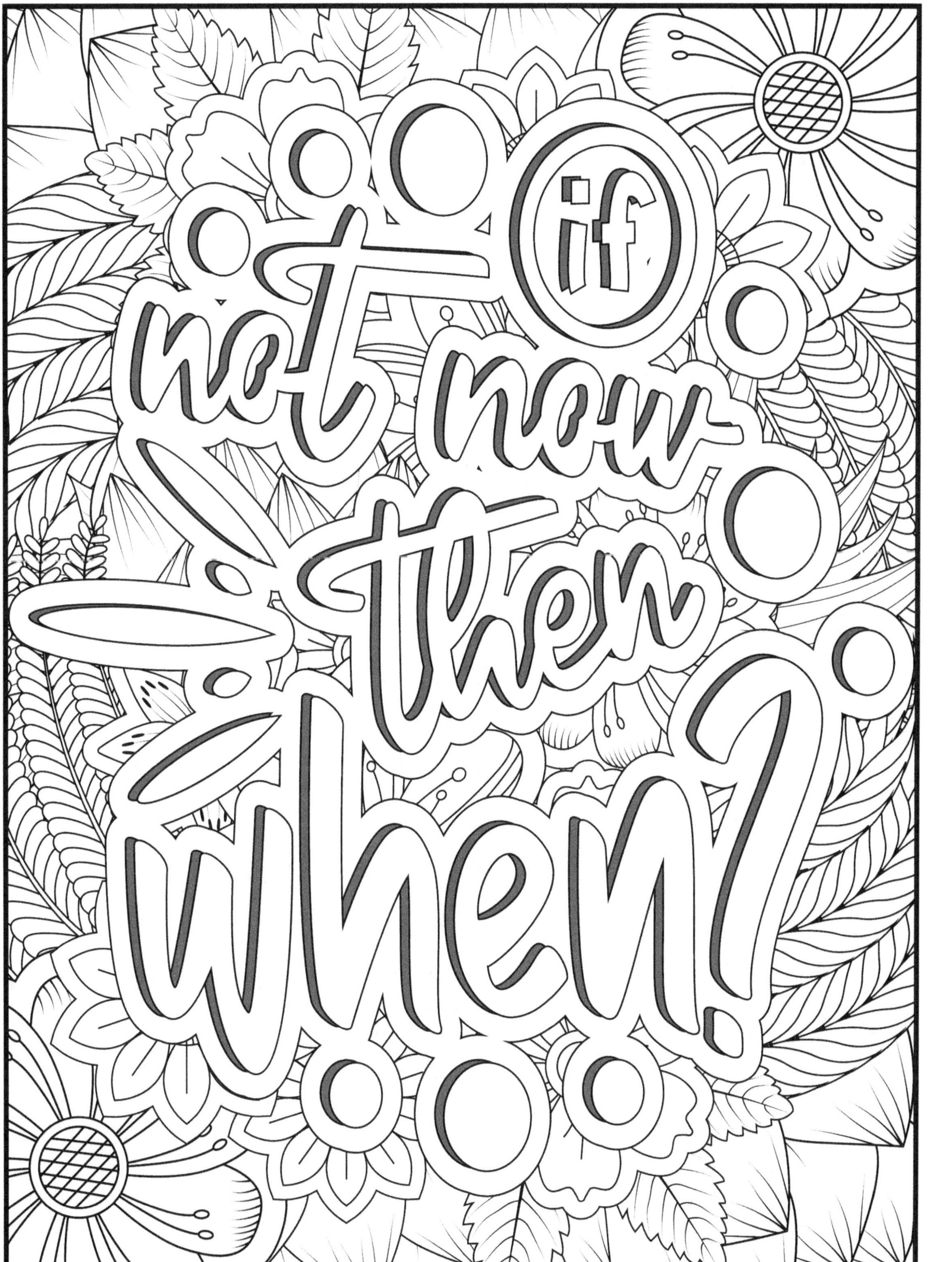
if
not now
then
when?

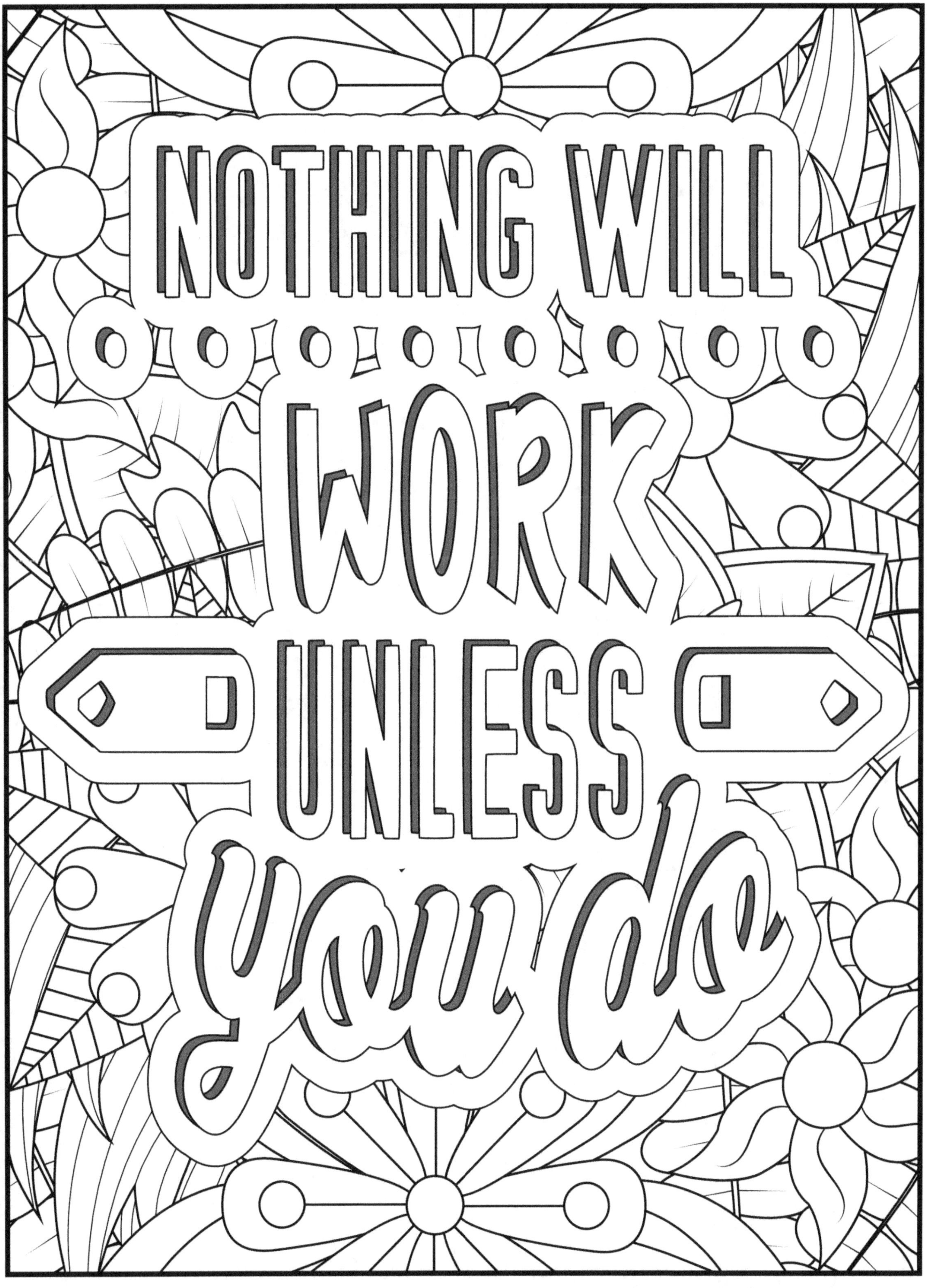
NOTHING WILL
WORK
UNLESS
you do

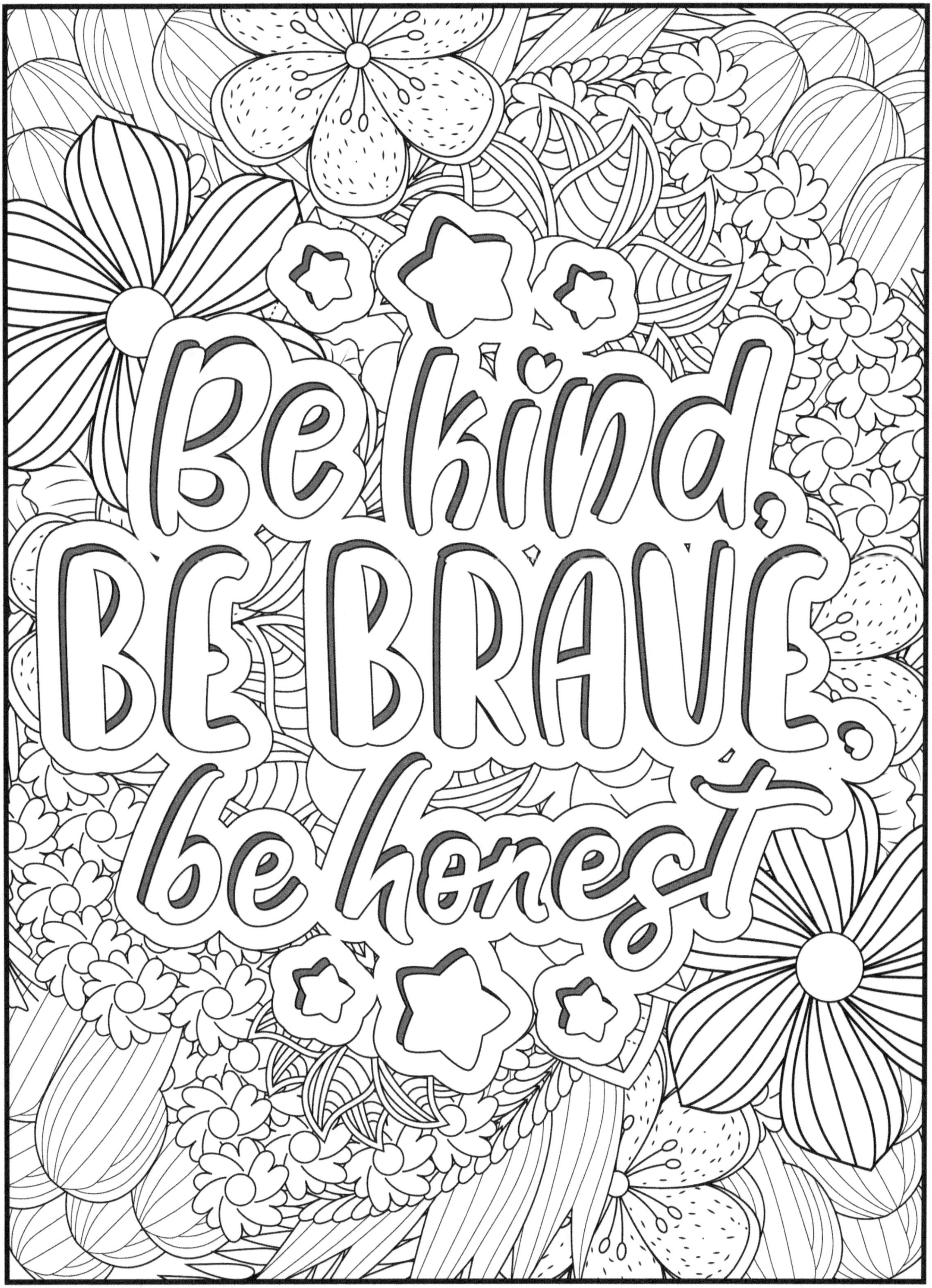
Be kind,
BE BRAVE,
be honest

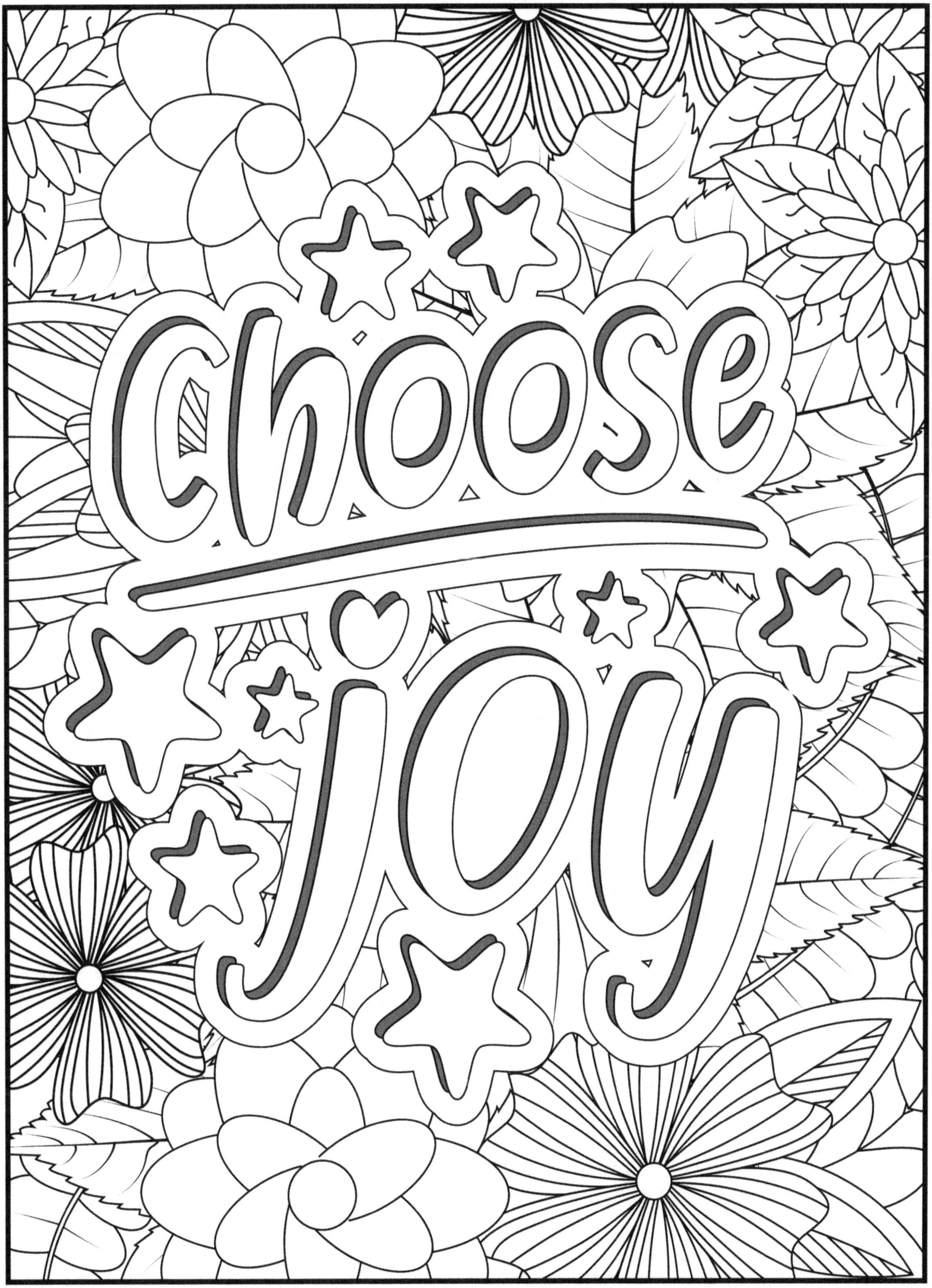
Choose
joy

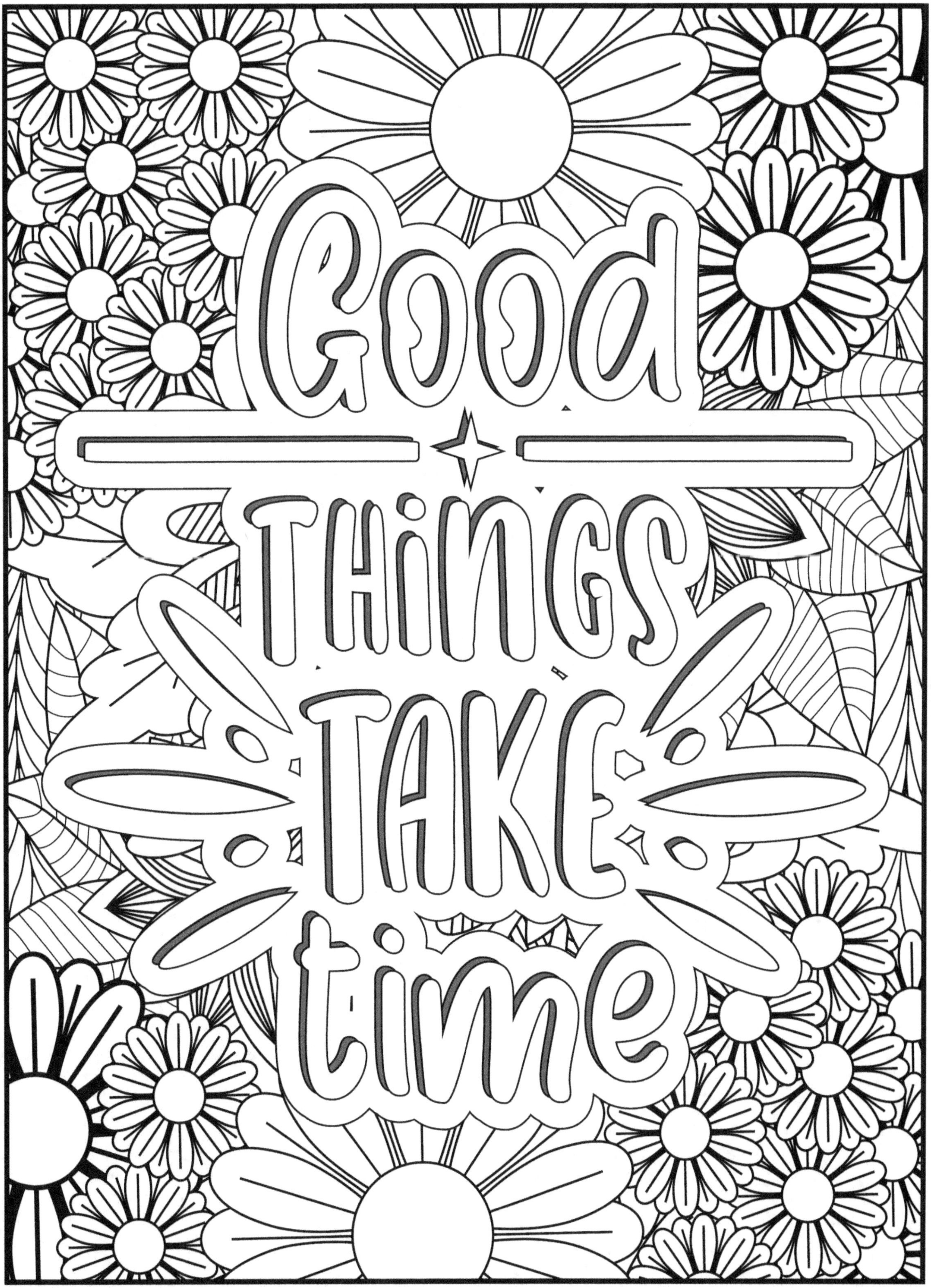
Good
Things
Take
time

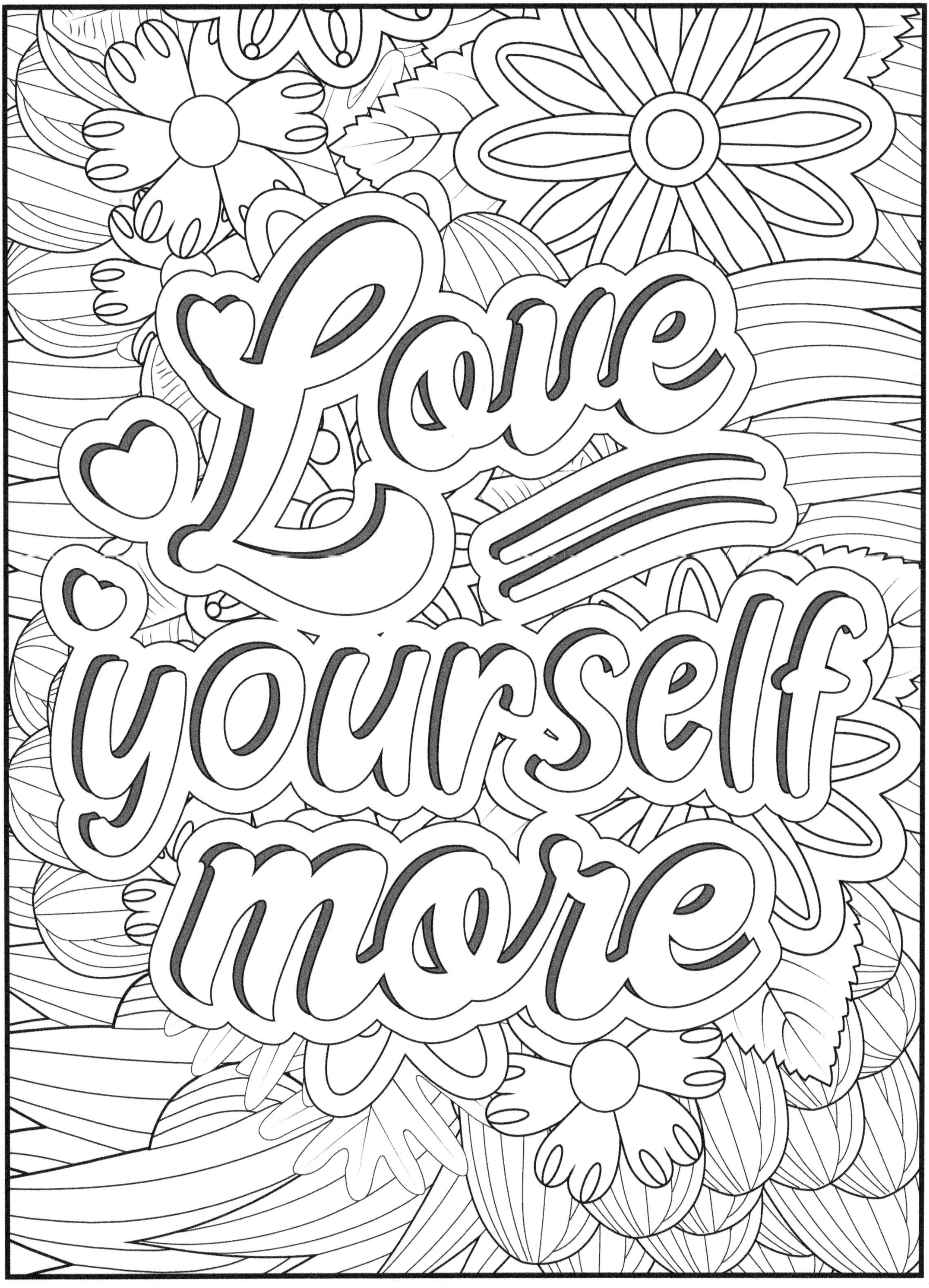
Love
yourself
more

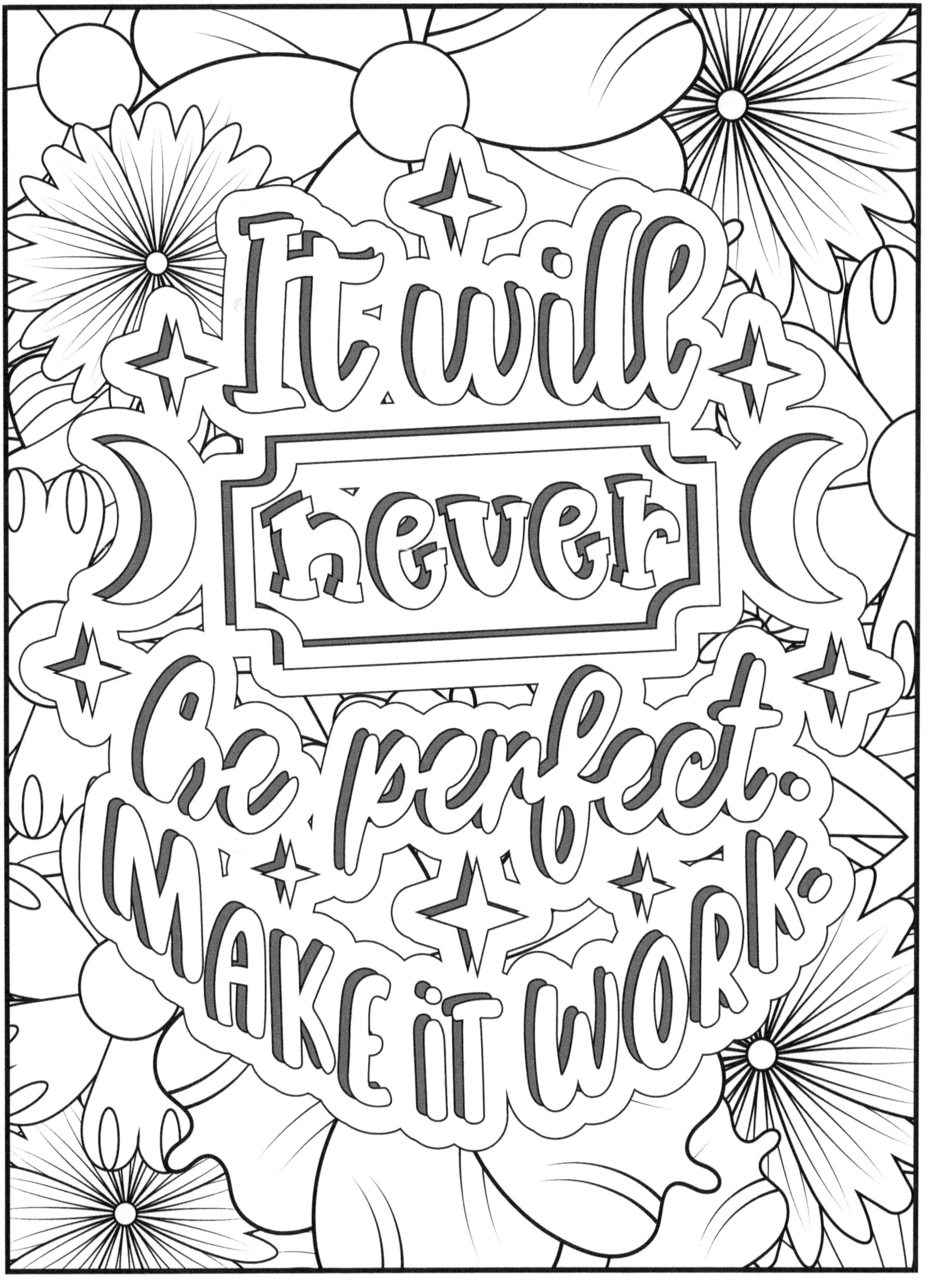
It will
never
be perfect.
MAKE IT WORK.

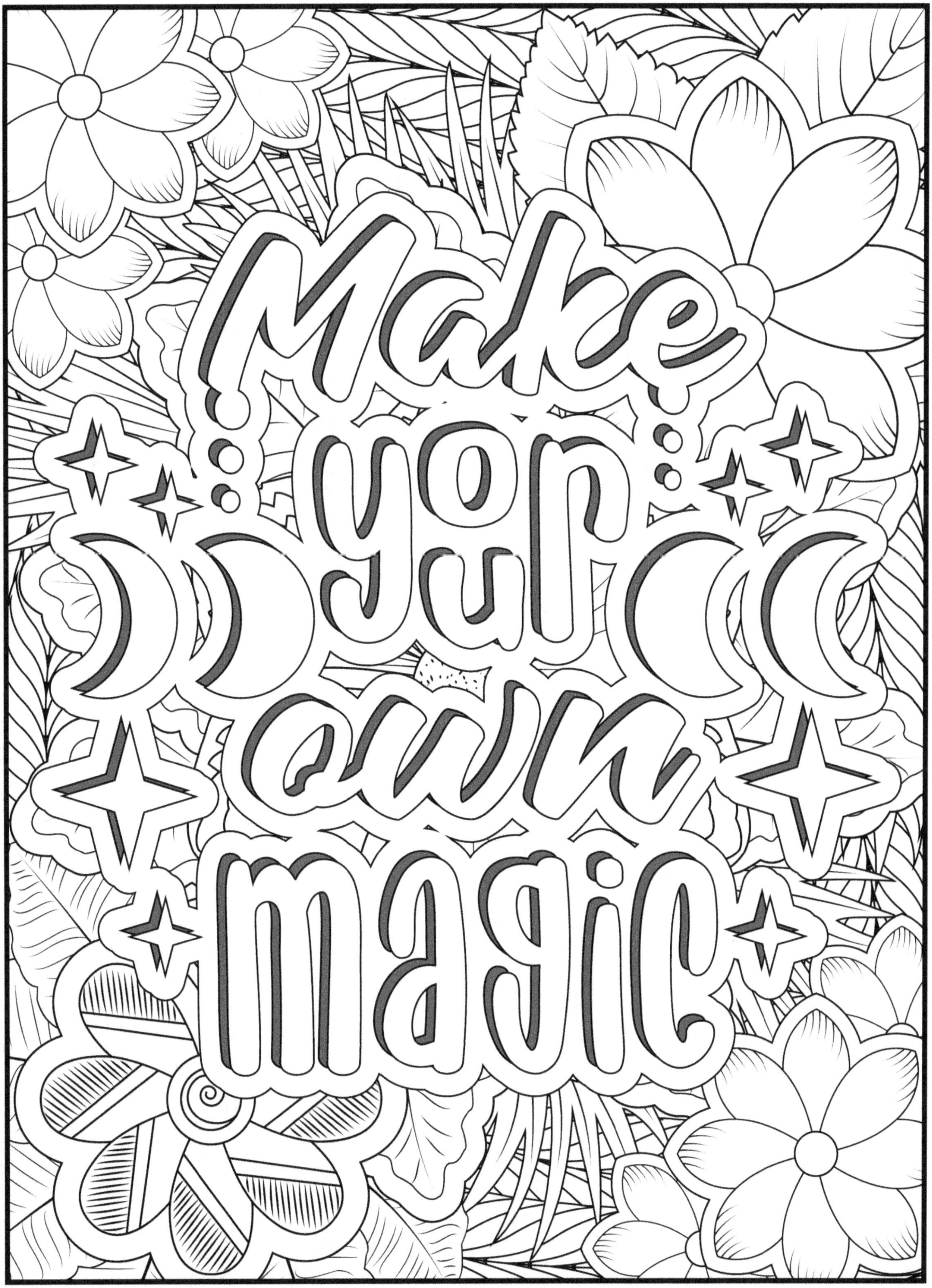
Make your own magic

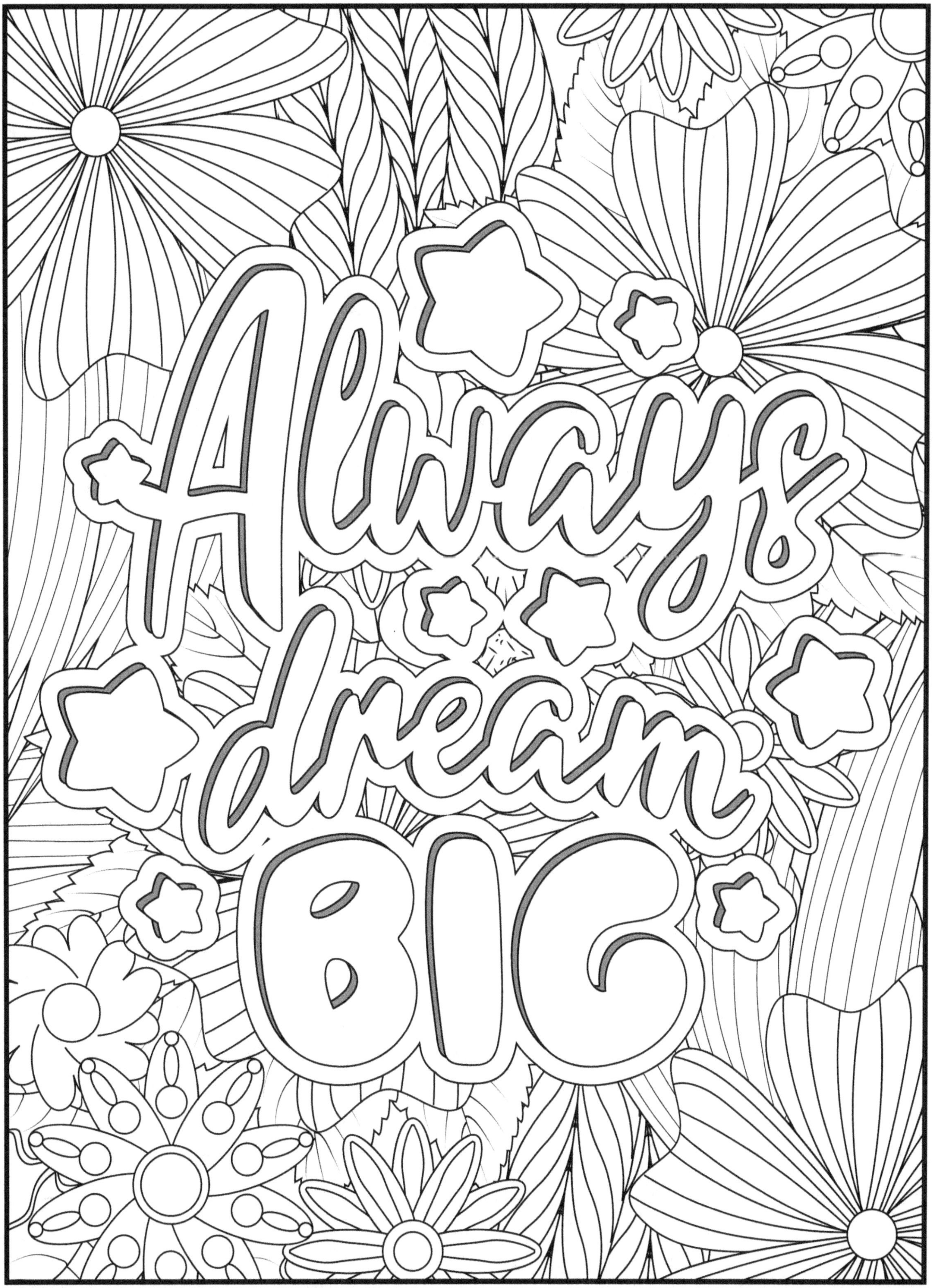
Always dream BIG

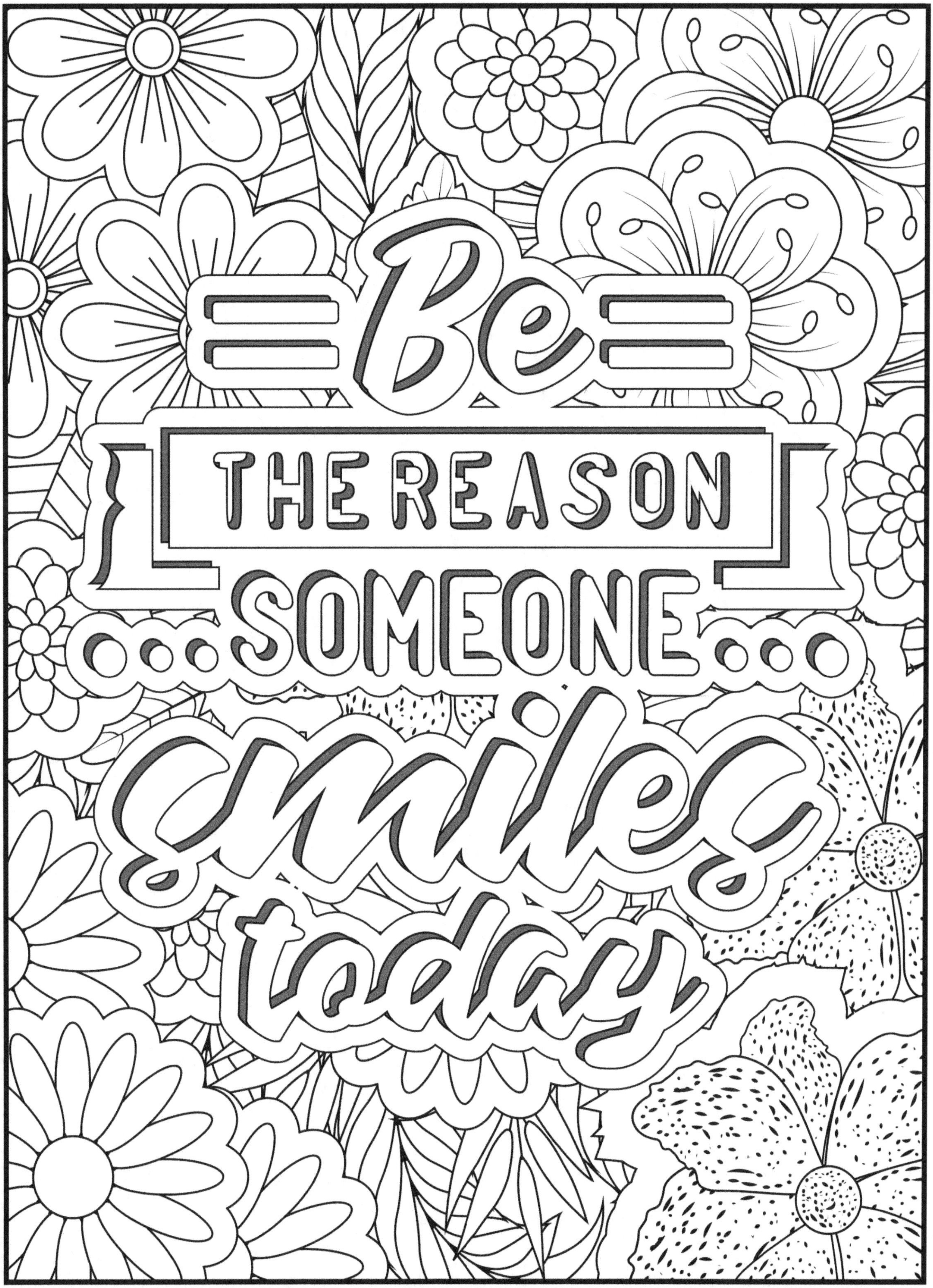
Be
THE REASON
SOMEONE
smiles
today

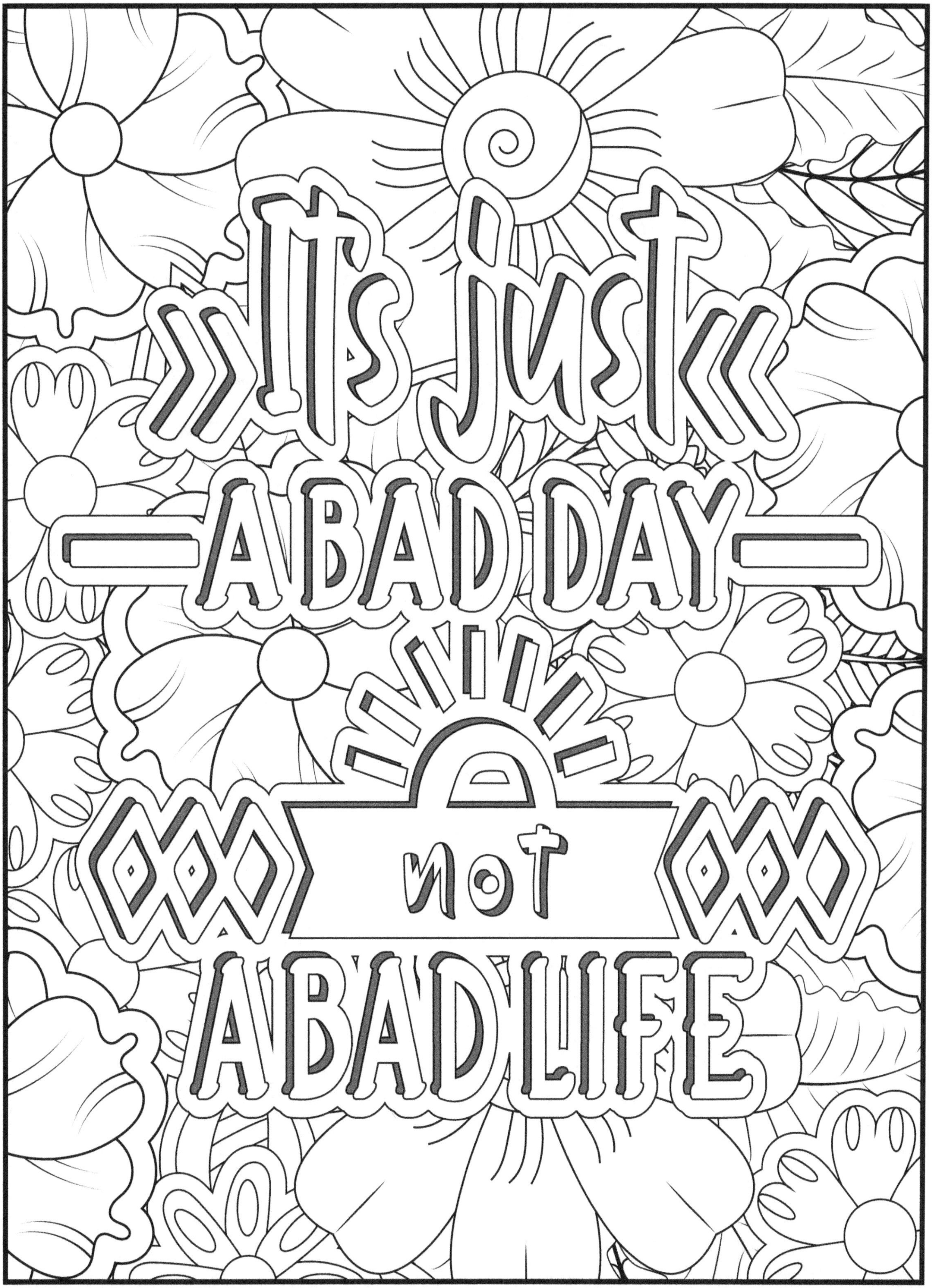
It's just
A BAD DAY
not
A BAD LIFE

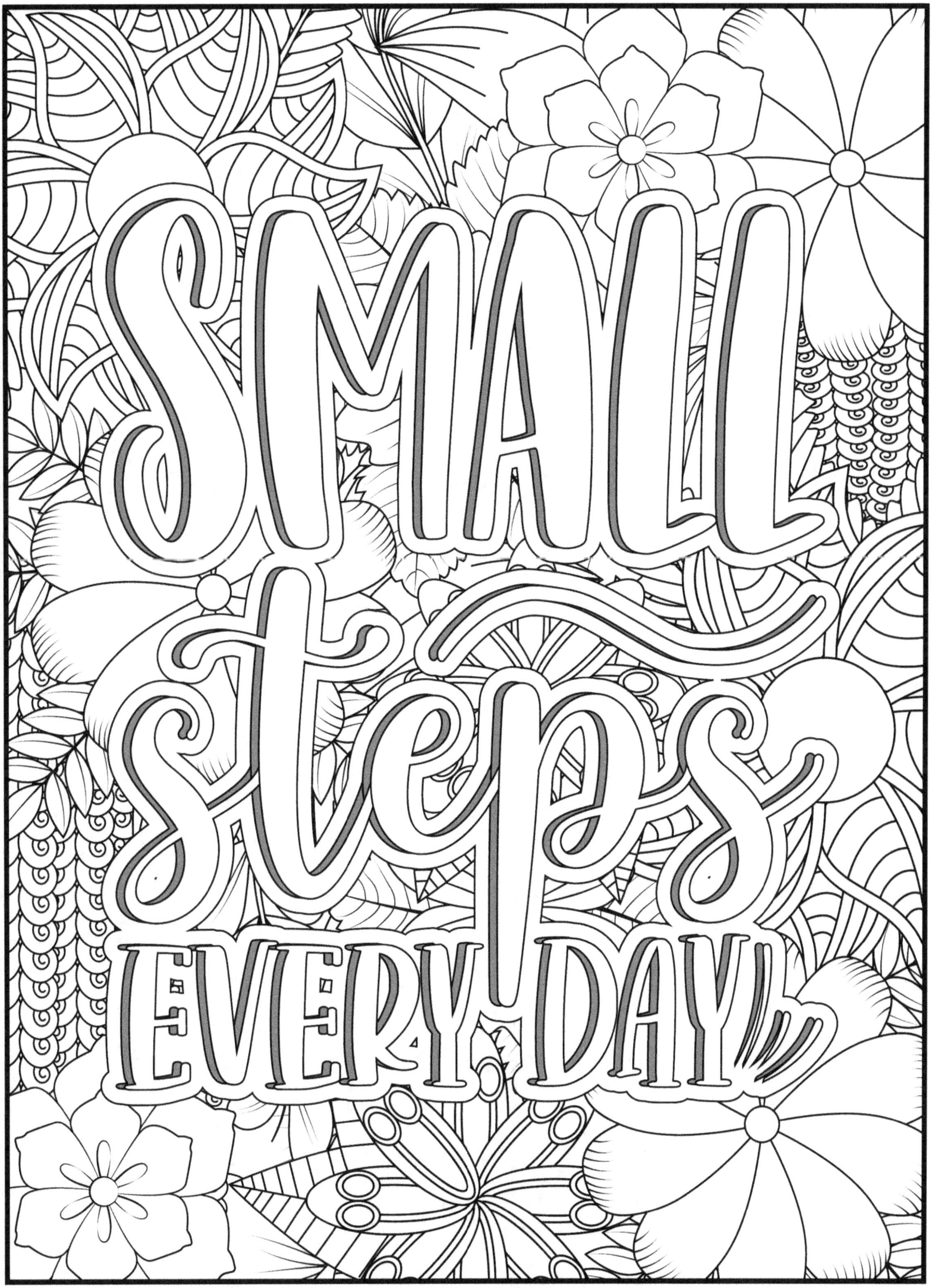
SMALL
steps
EVERY DAY

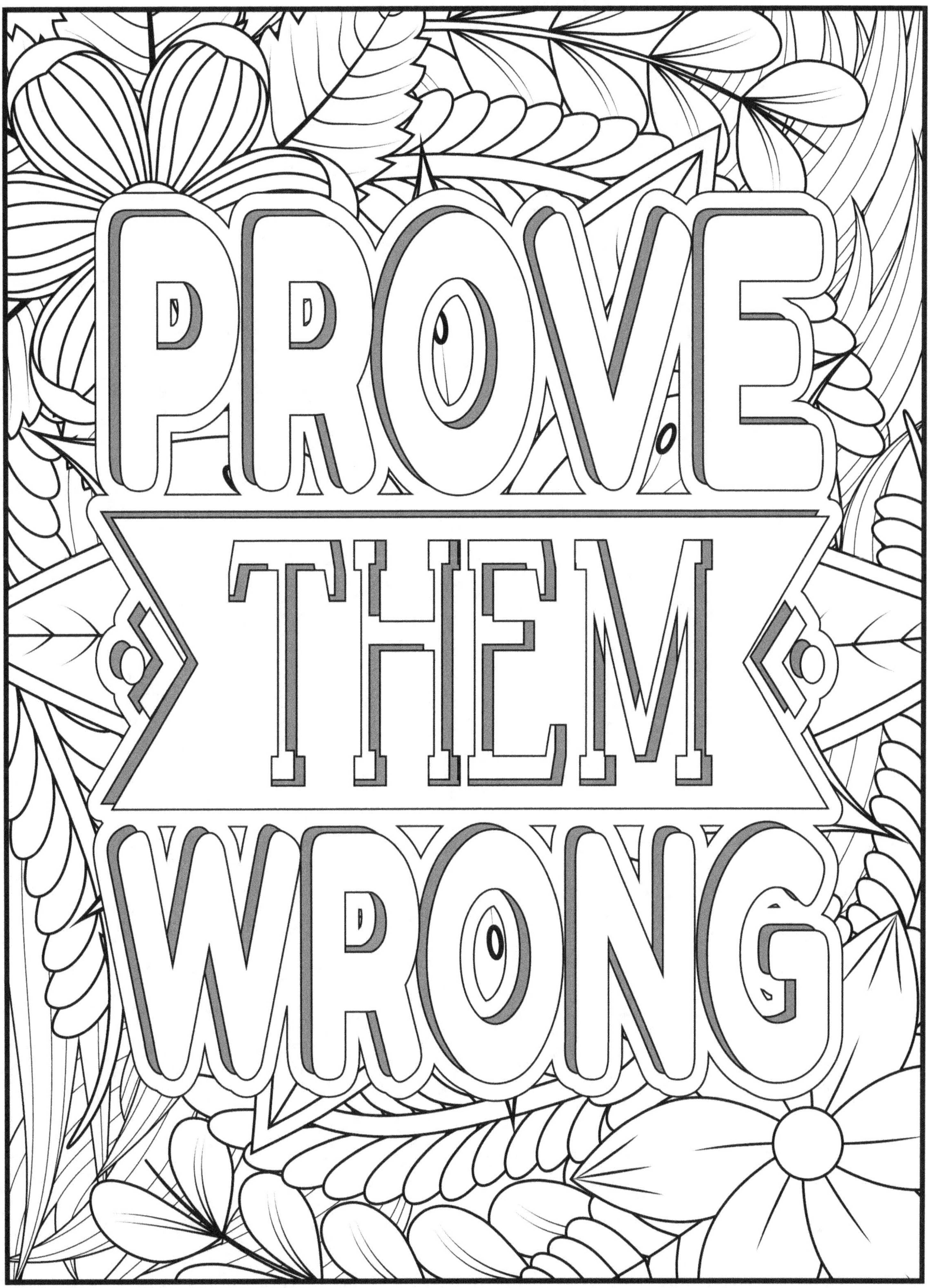
PROVE
THEM
WRONG

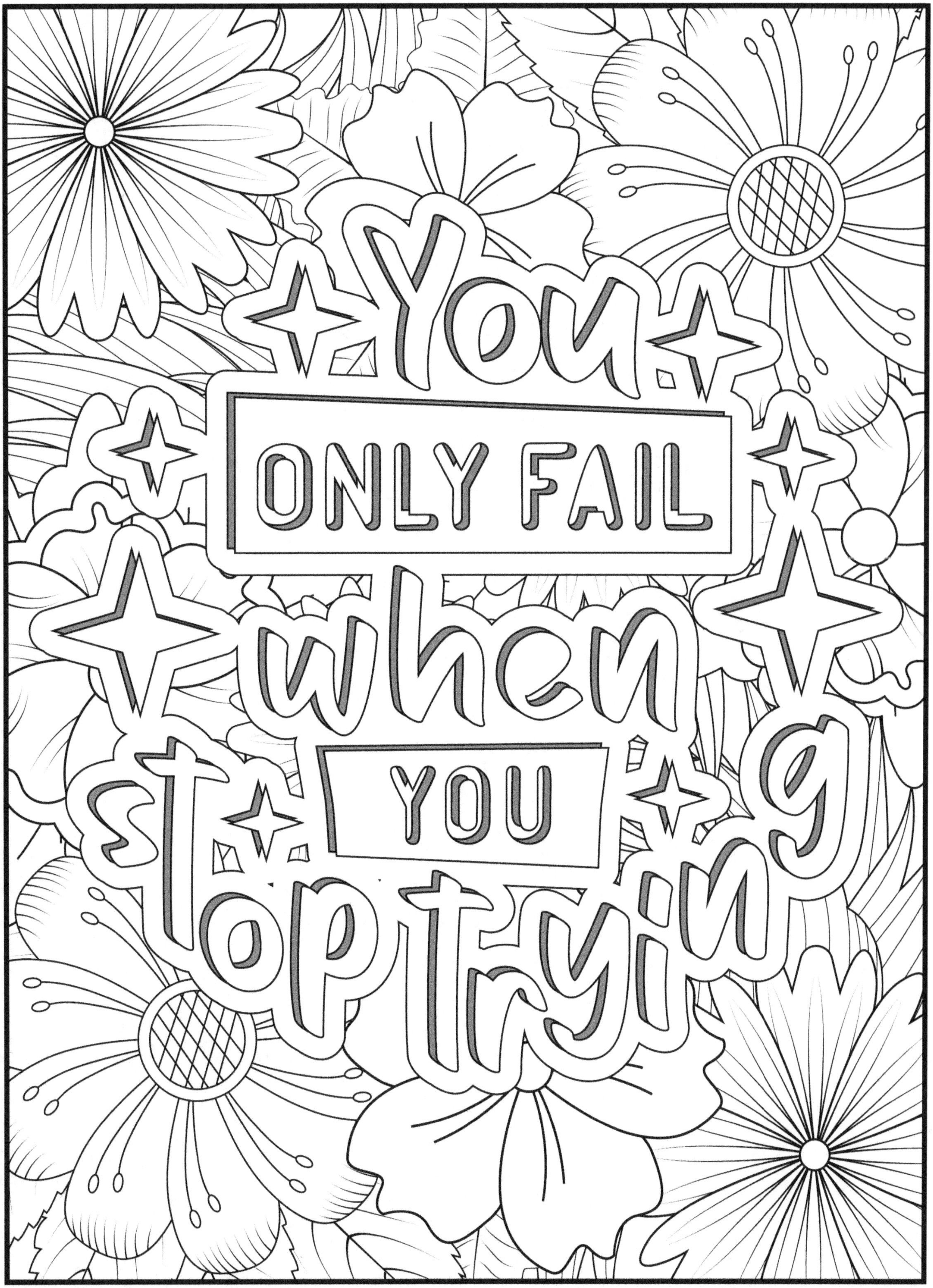
You
ONLY FAIL
when
YOU
stop trying

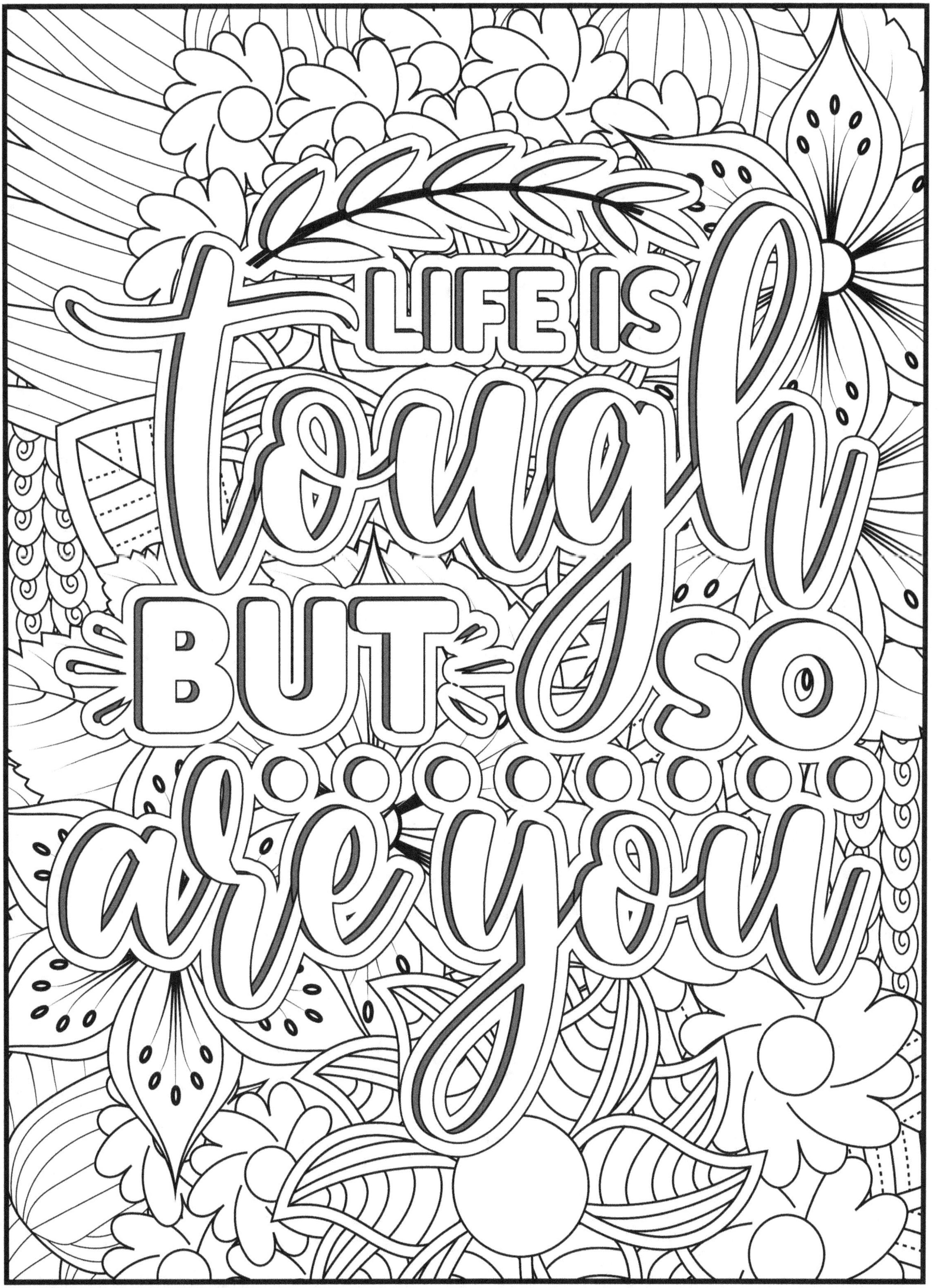
LIFE IS
tough
BUT SO
are you

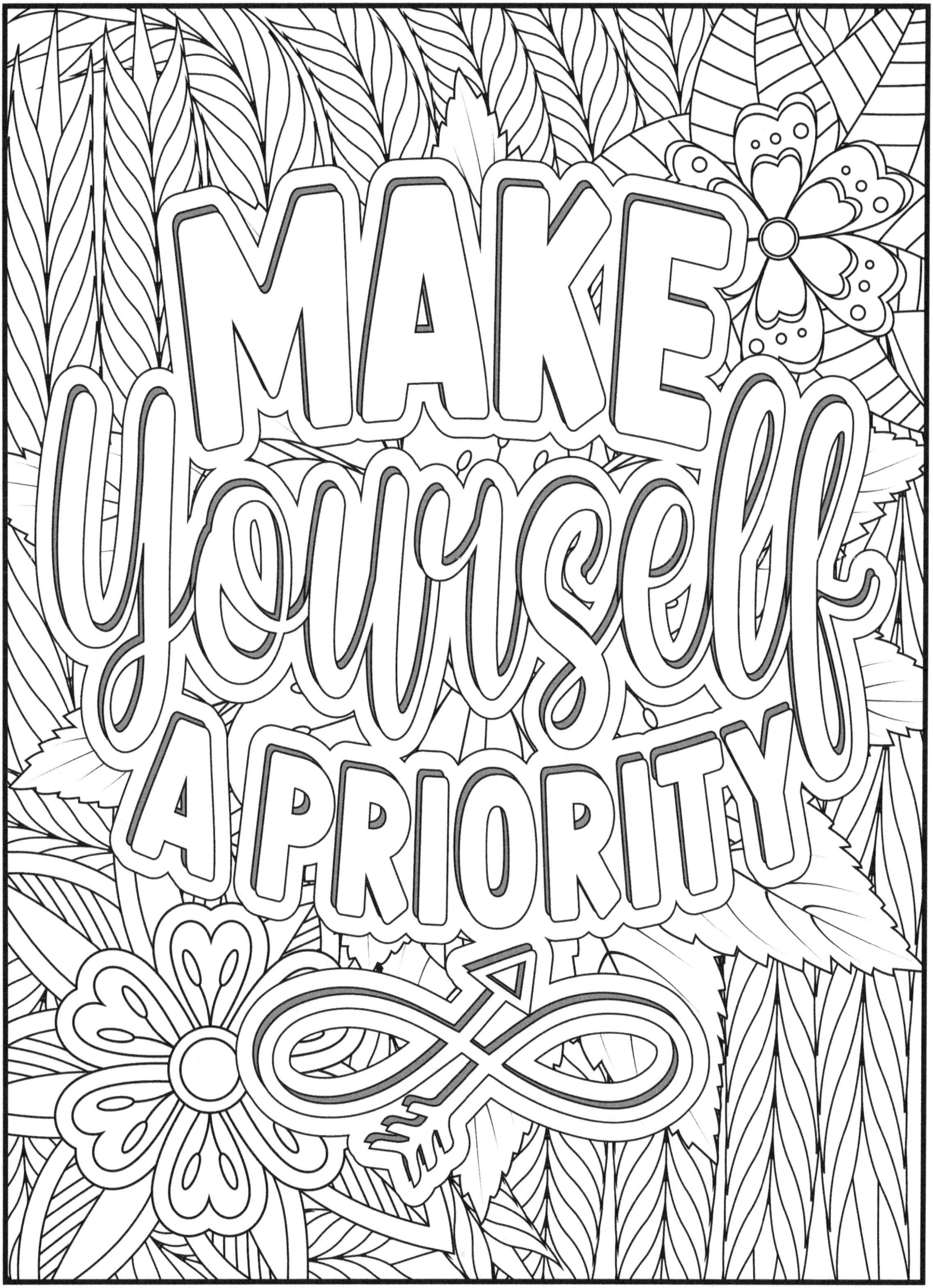
MAKE
yourself
A PRIORITY

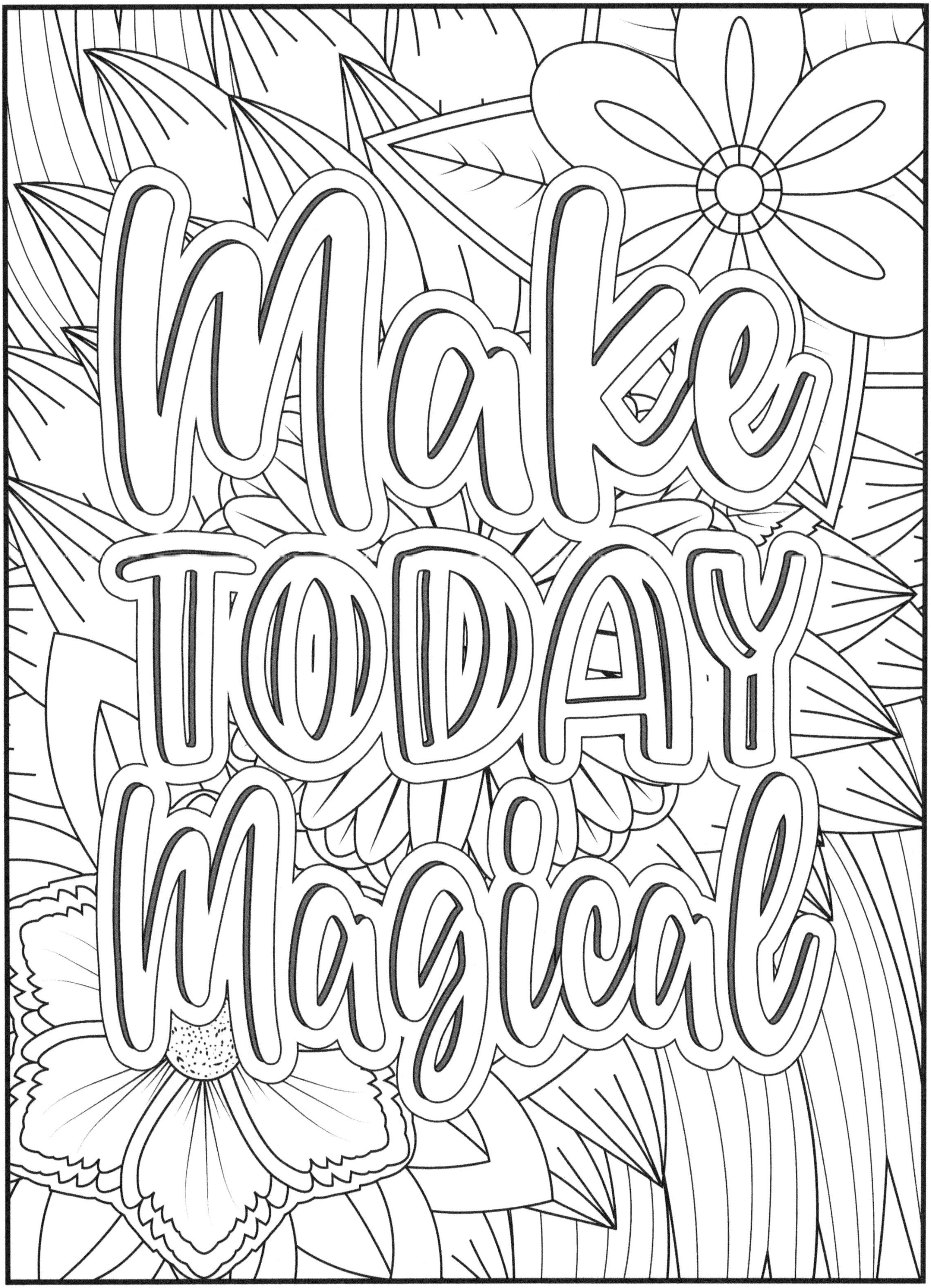
Make
TODAY
Magical

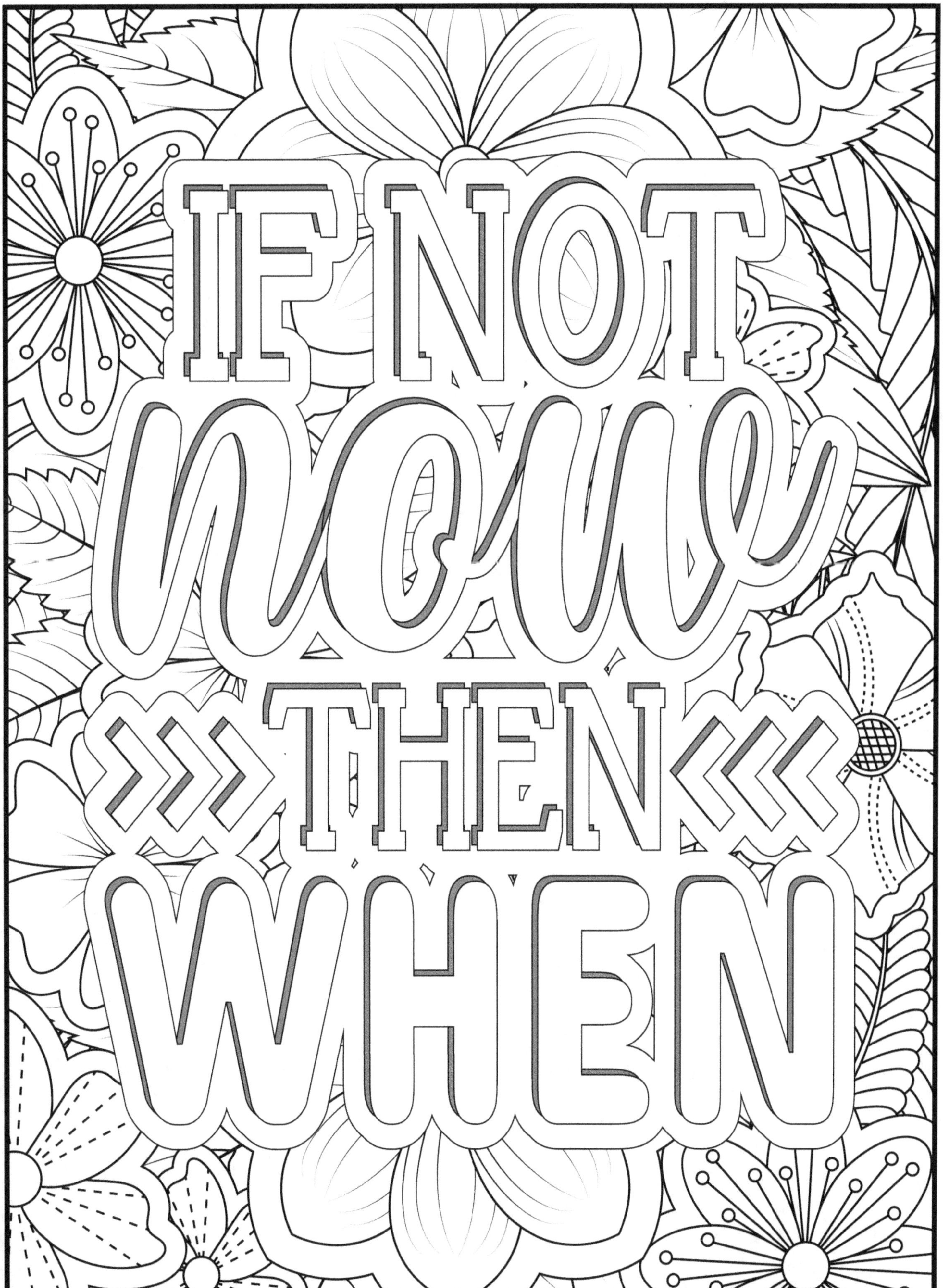
IF NOT
now
THEN
WHEN

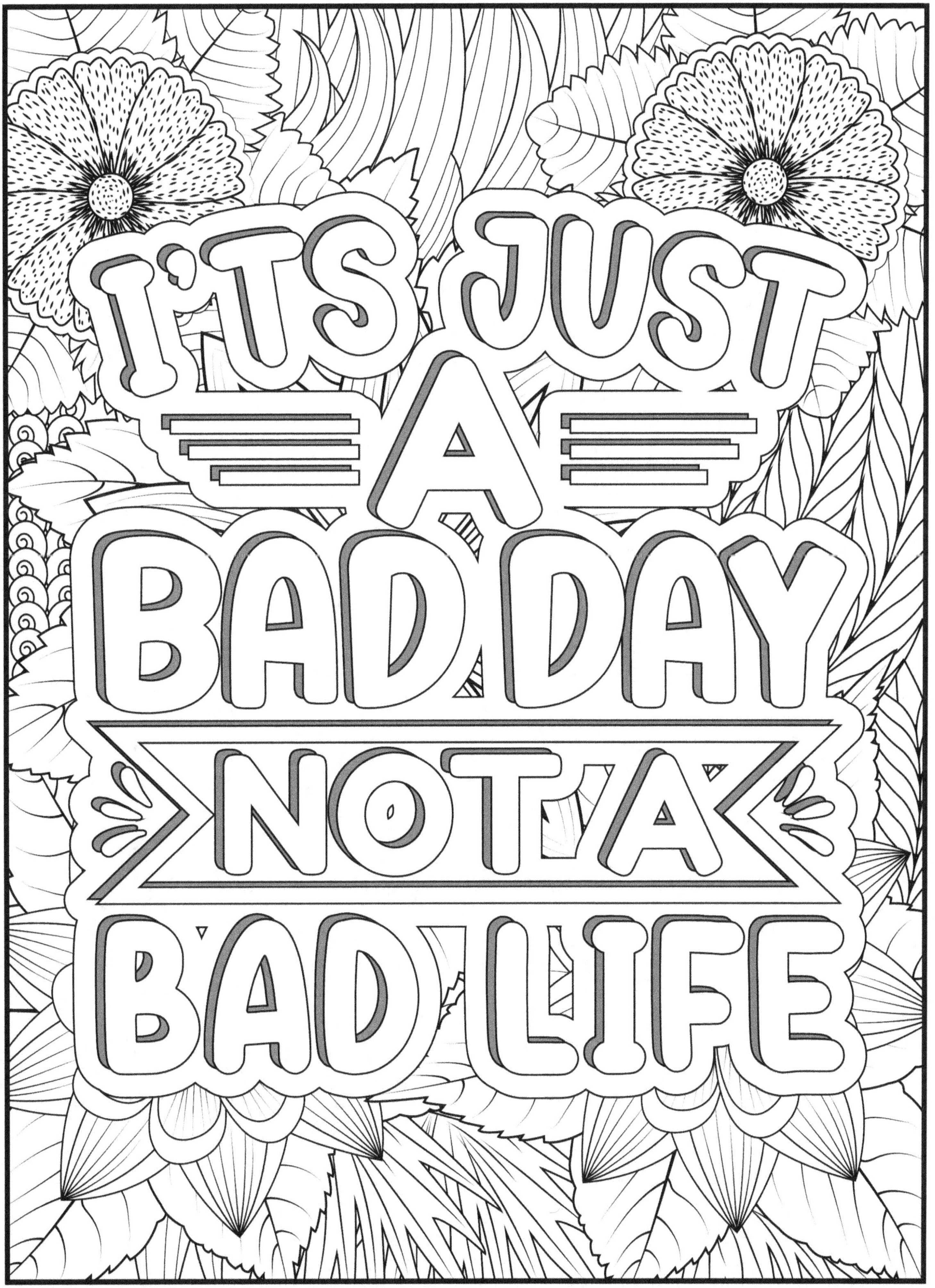
I'TS JUST
A
BAD DAY
NOT A
BAD LIFE

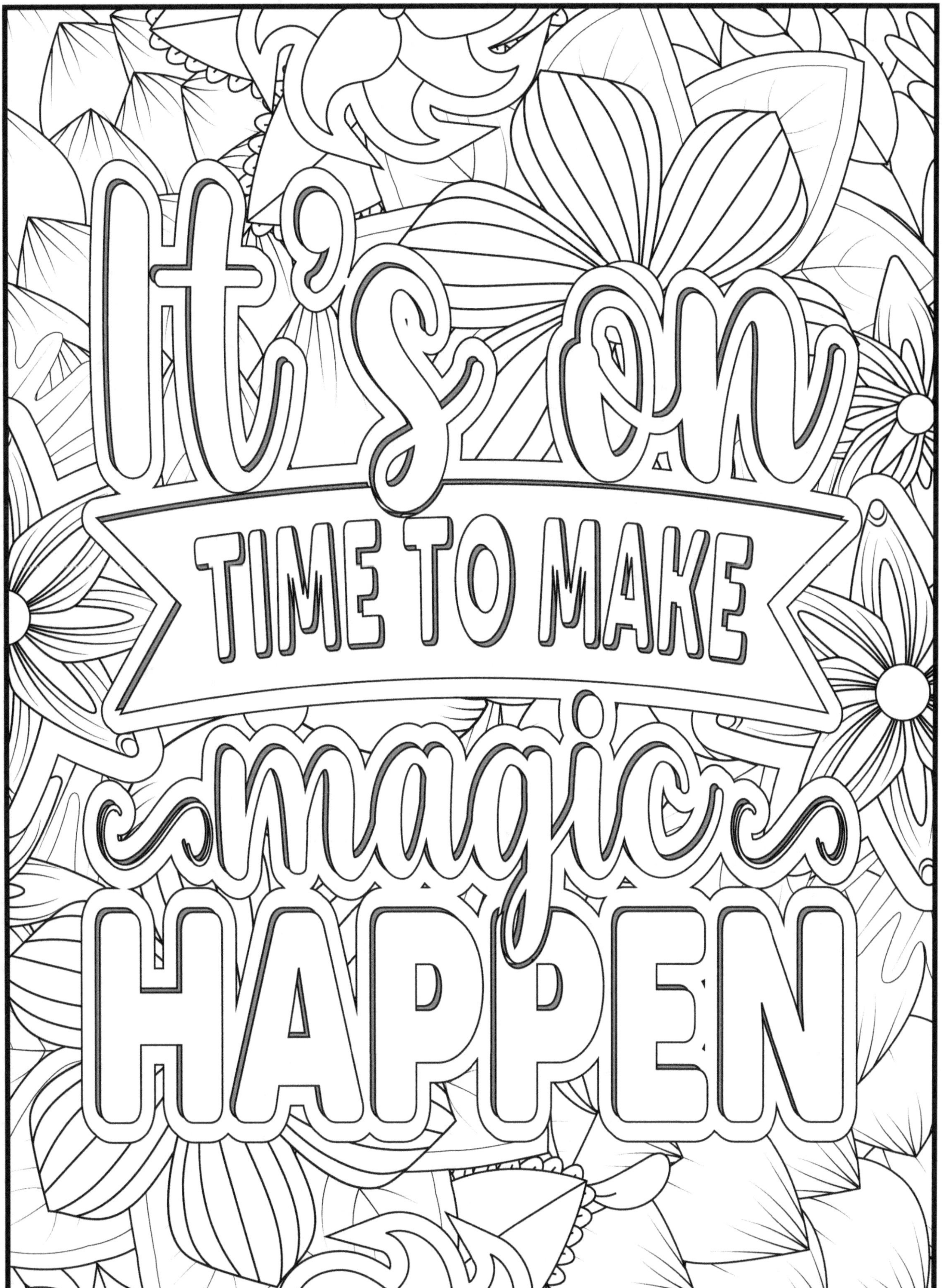
It's on
TIME TO MAKE
magic
HAPPEN

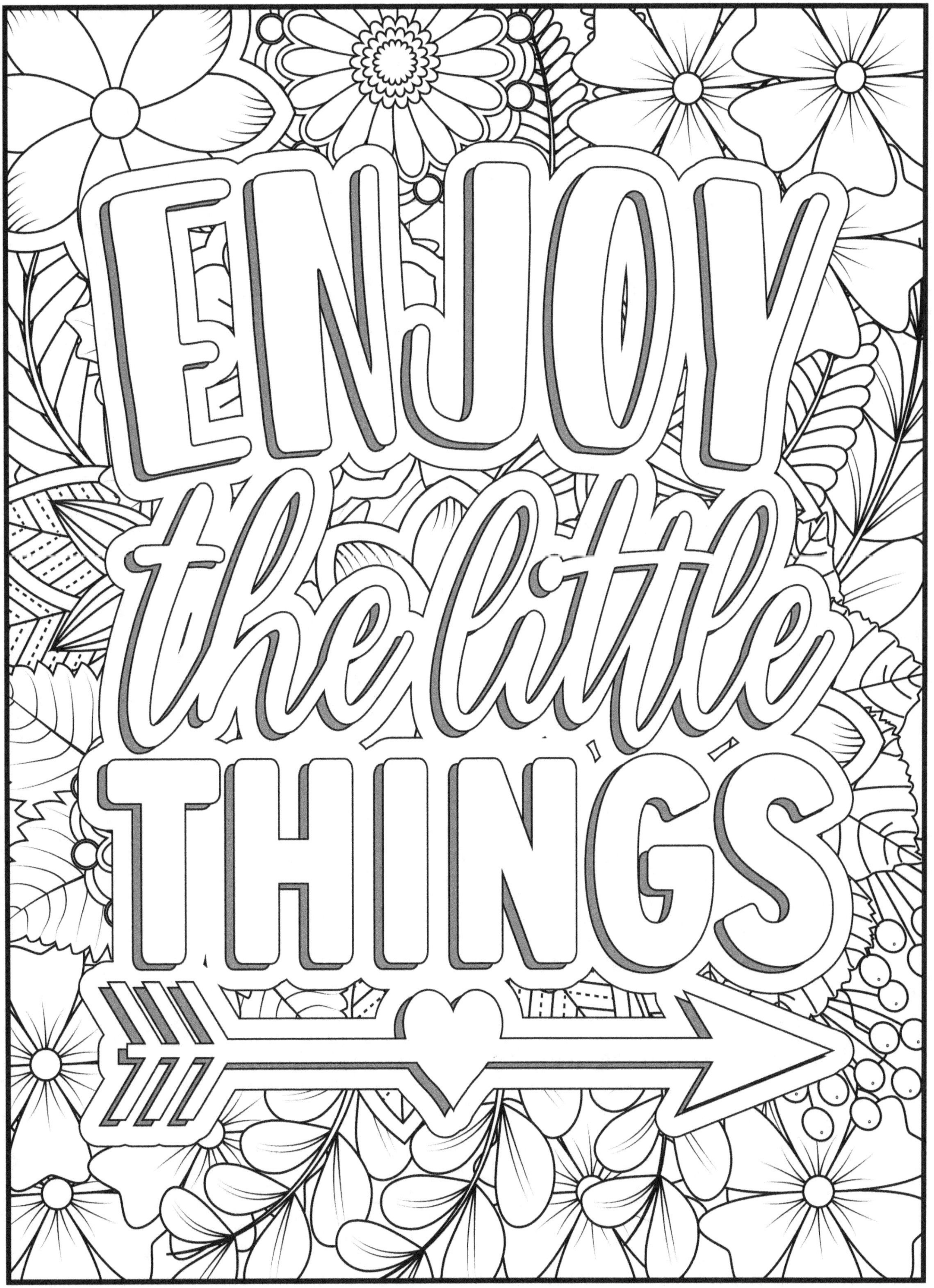
ENJOY
the little
THINGS

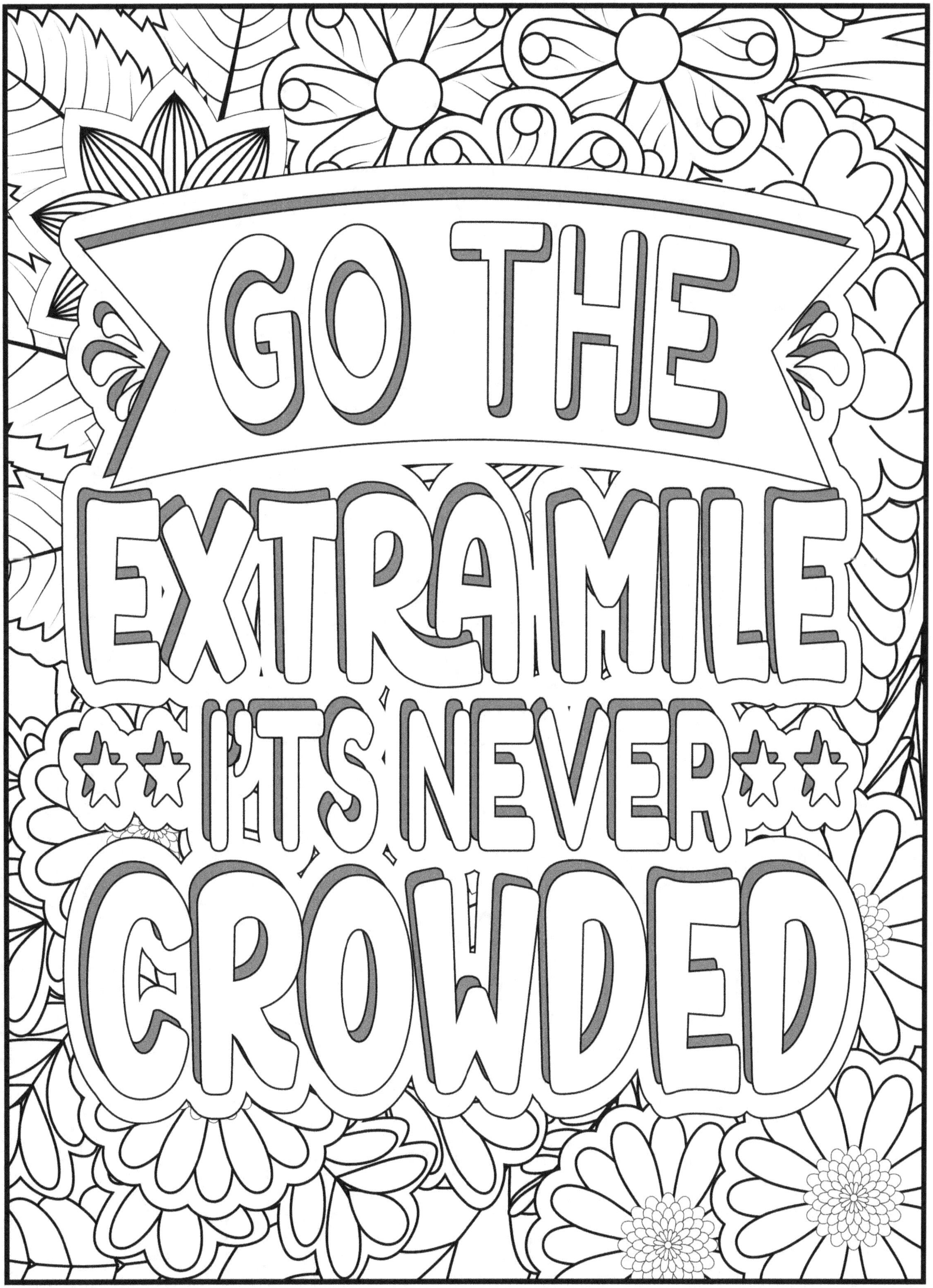
GO THE
EXTRA MILE
IT'S NEVER
CROWDED

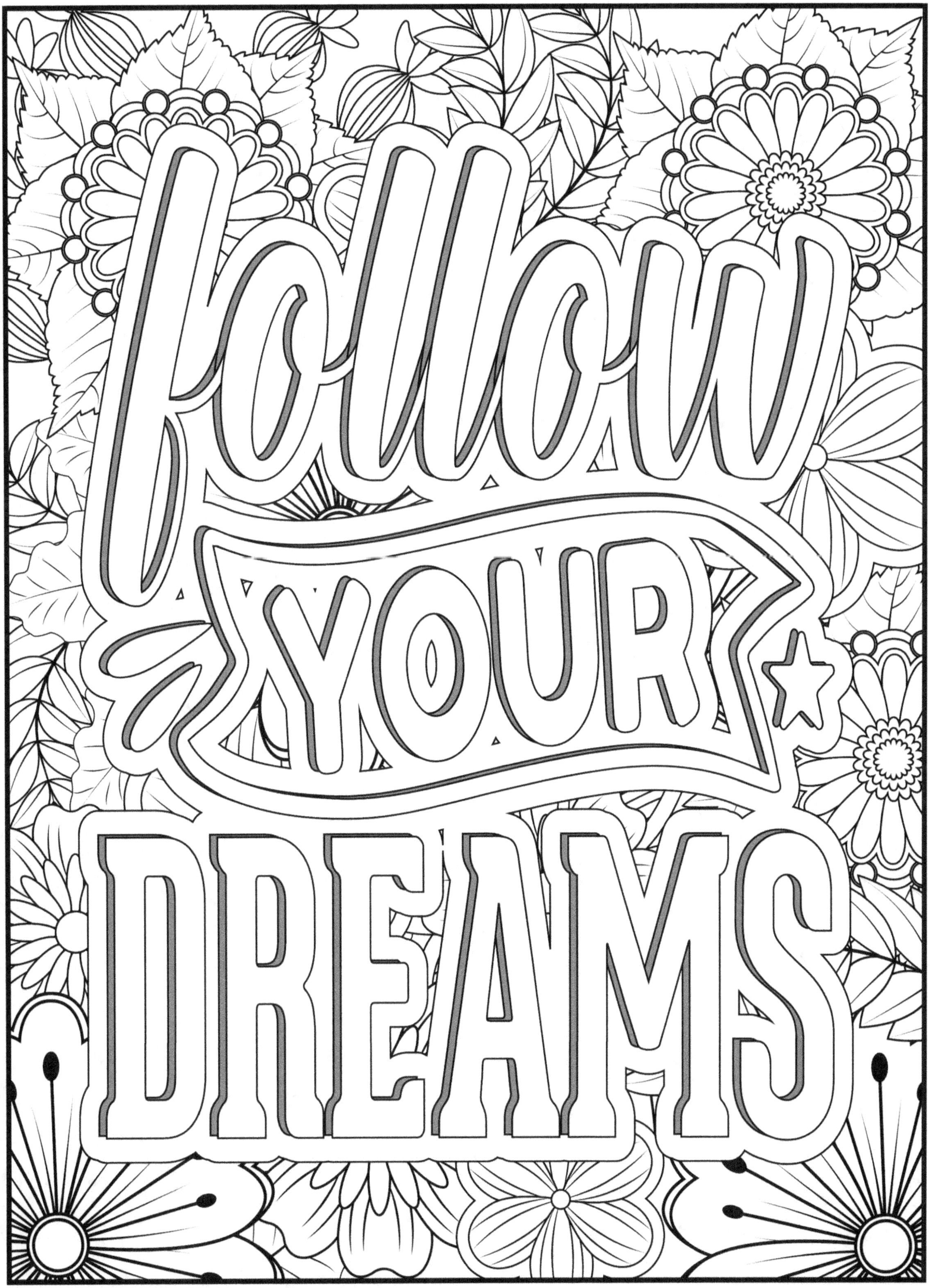
follow
YOUR
DREAMS

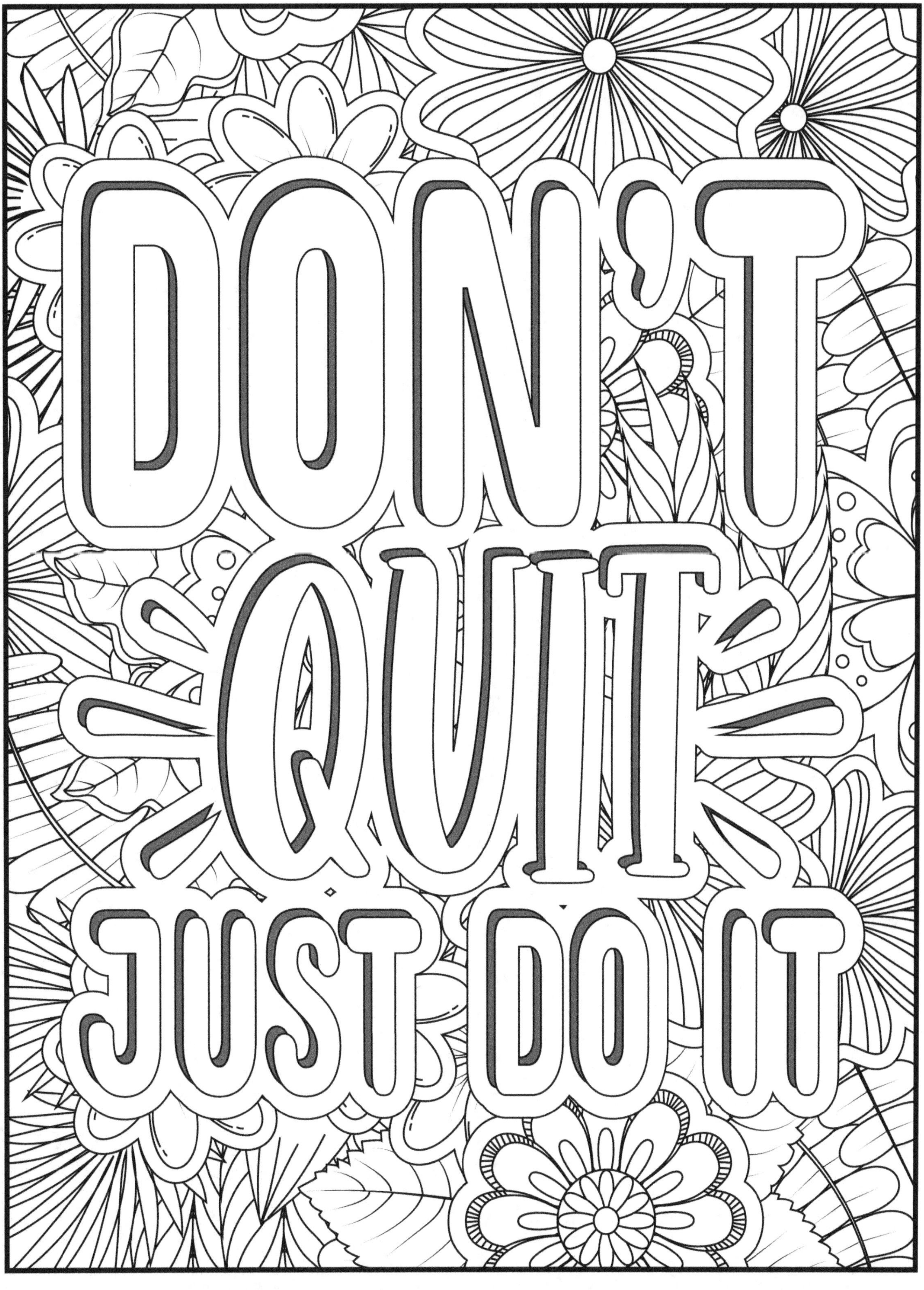
DON'T
QUIT
JUST DO IT

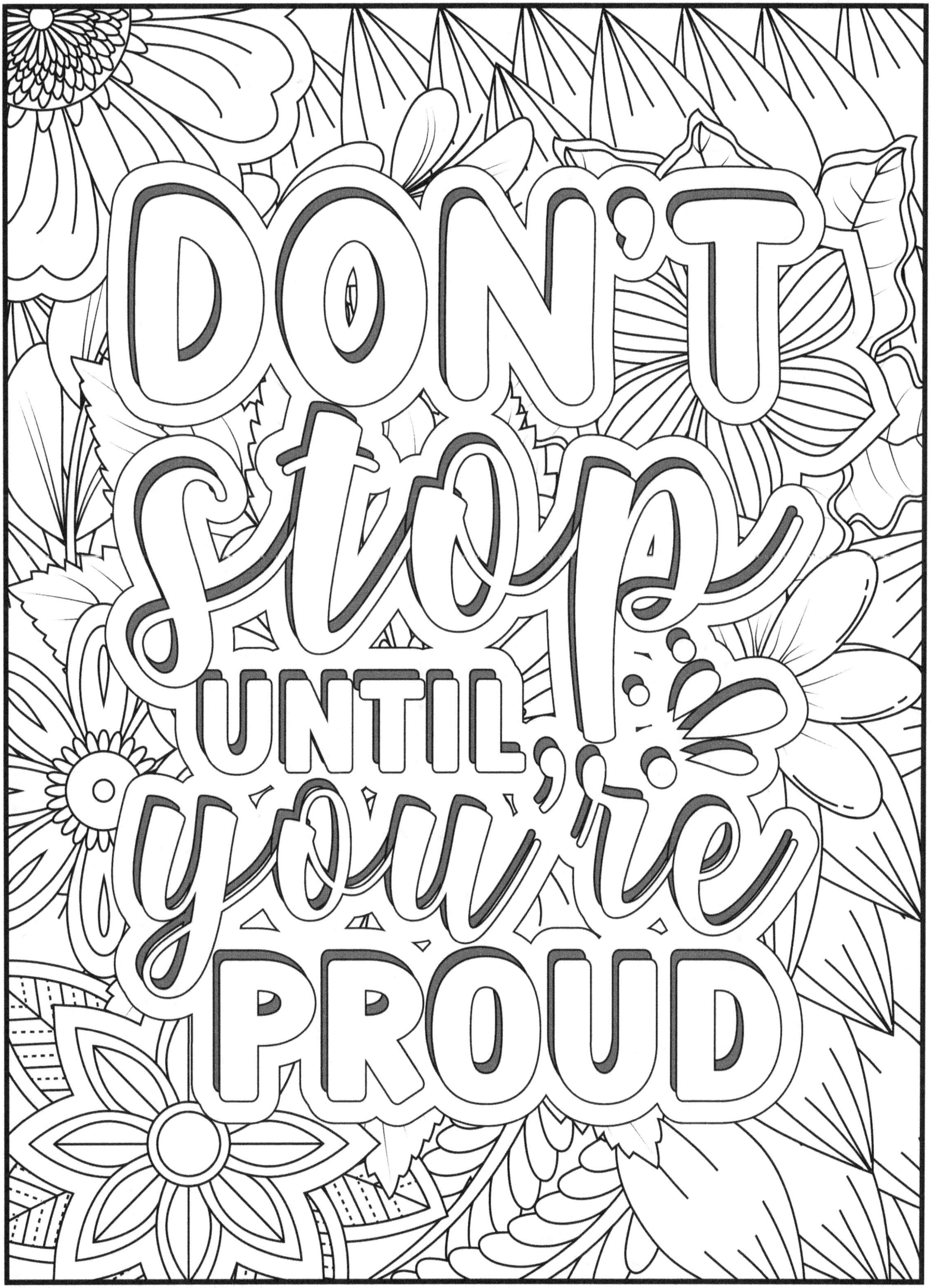
DON'T
stop
UNTIL
you're
PROUD

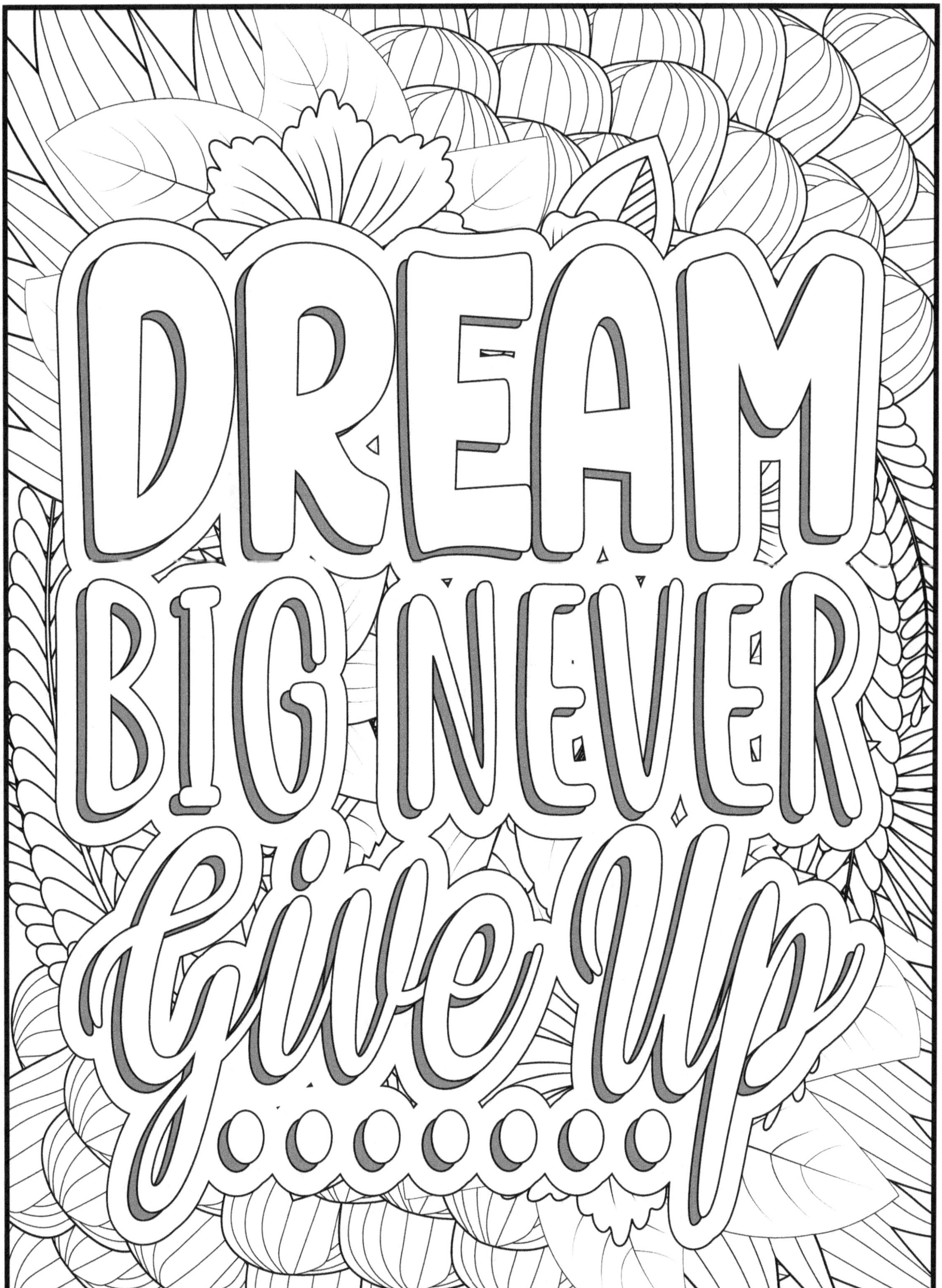
DREAM
BIG NEVER
Give Up

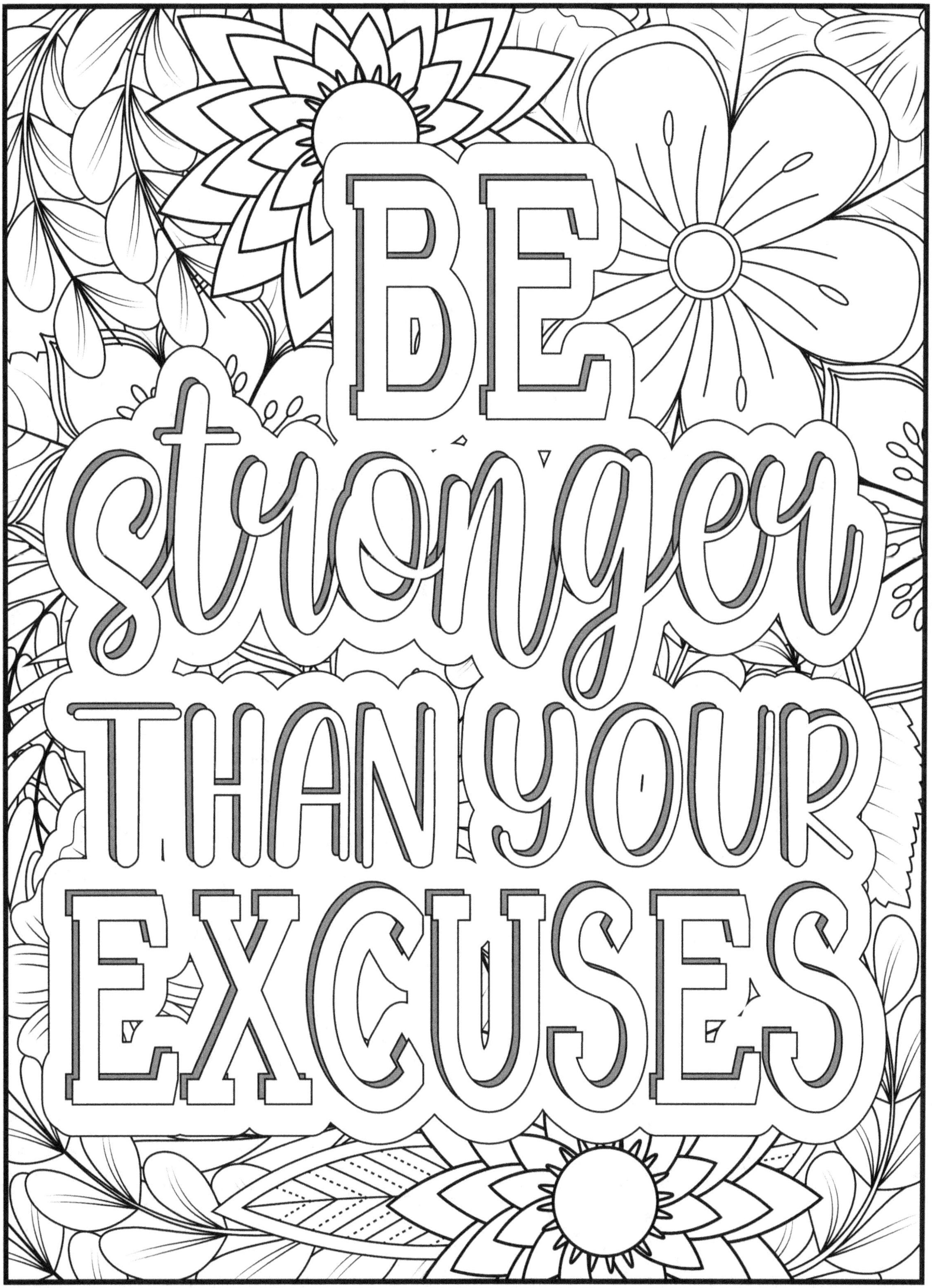
BE
stronger
THAN YOUR
EXCUSES

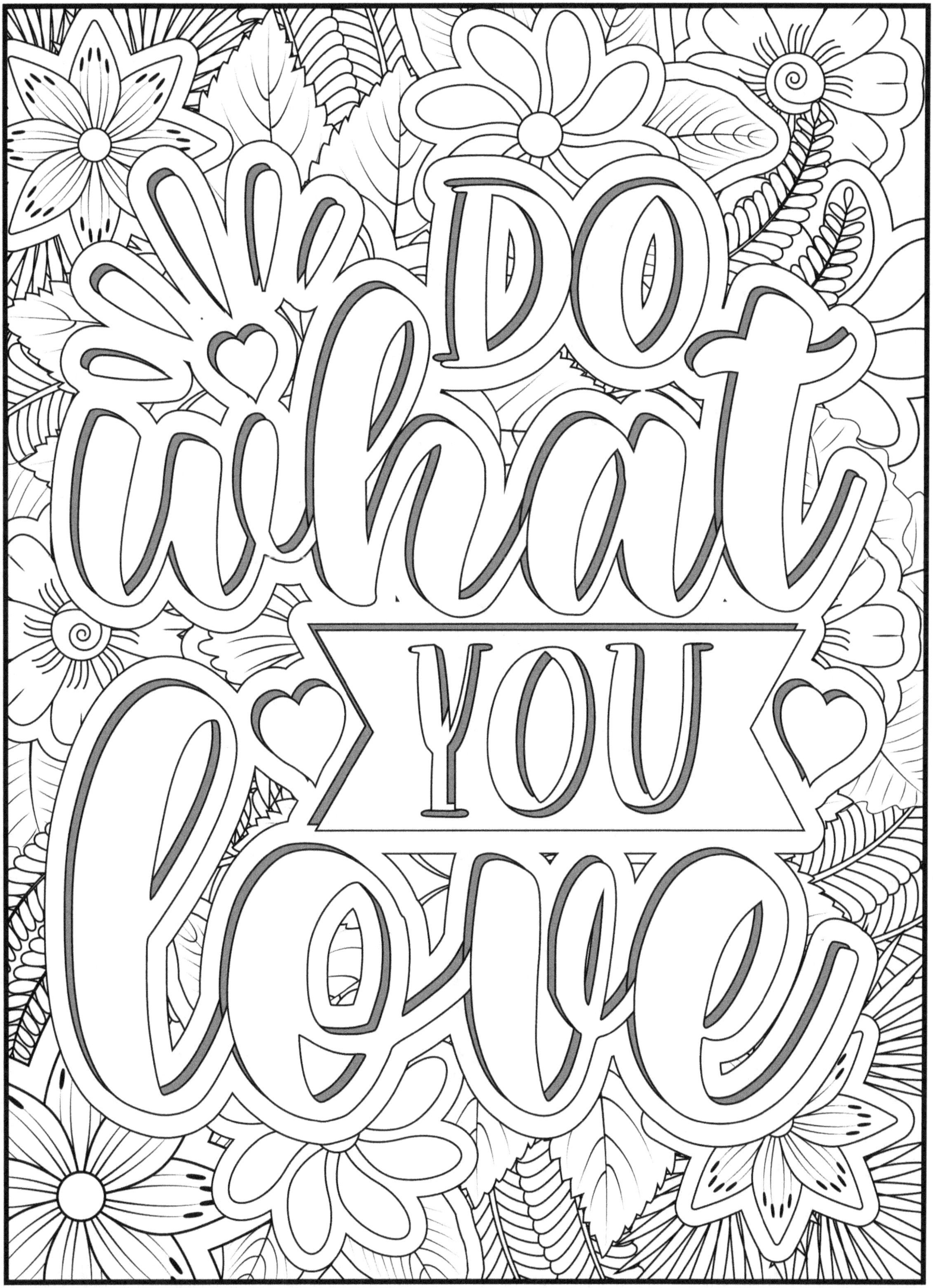
DO
what
YOU
love

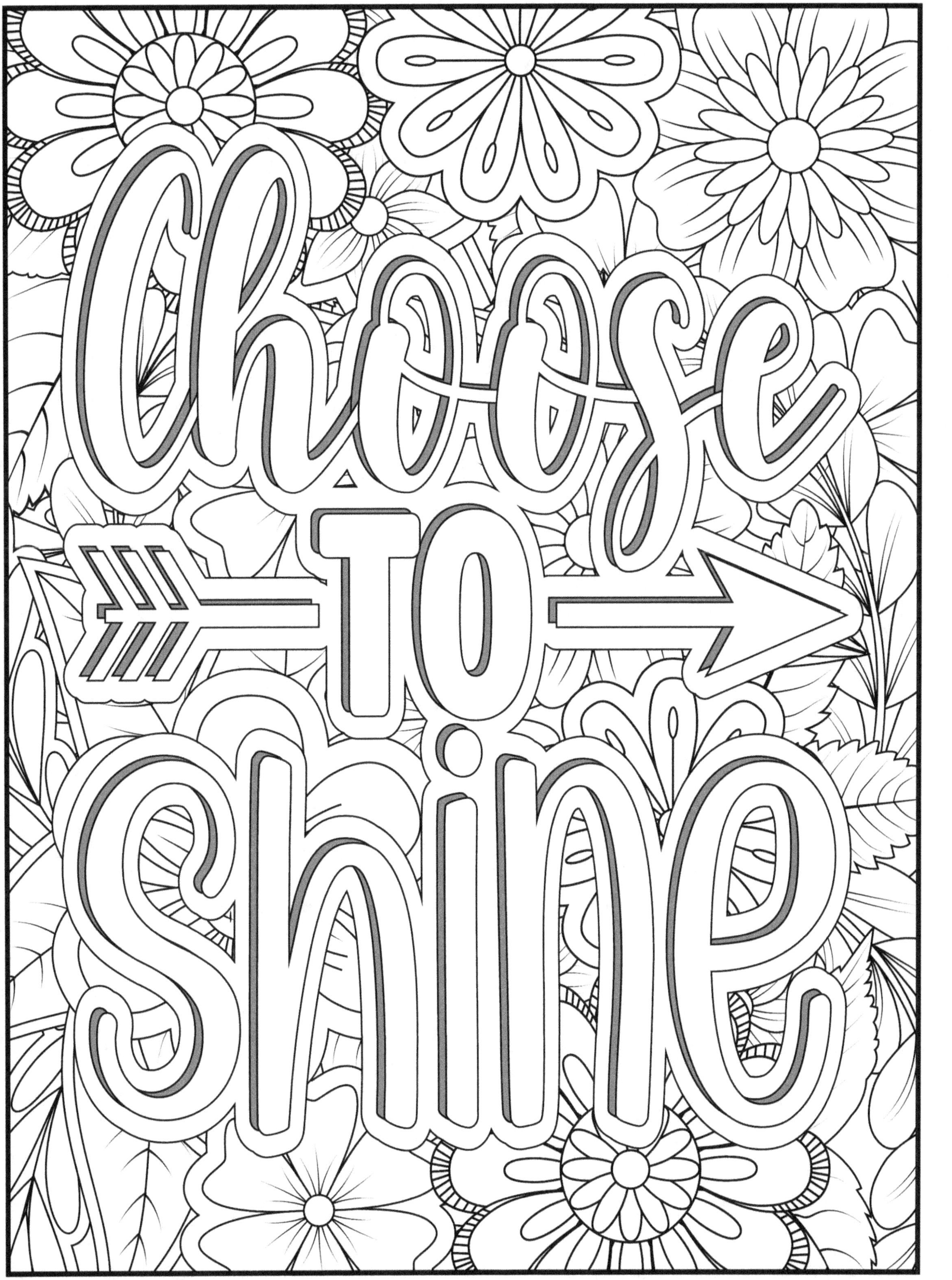
Choose
TO
Shine

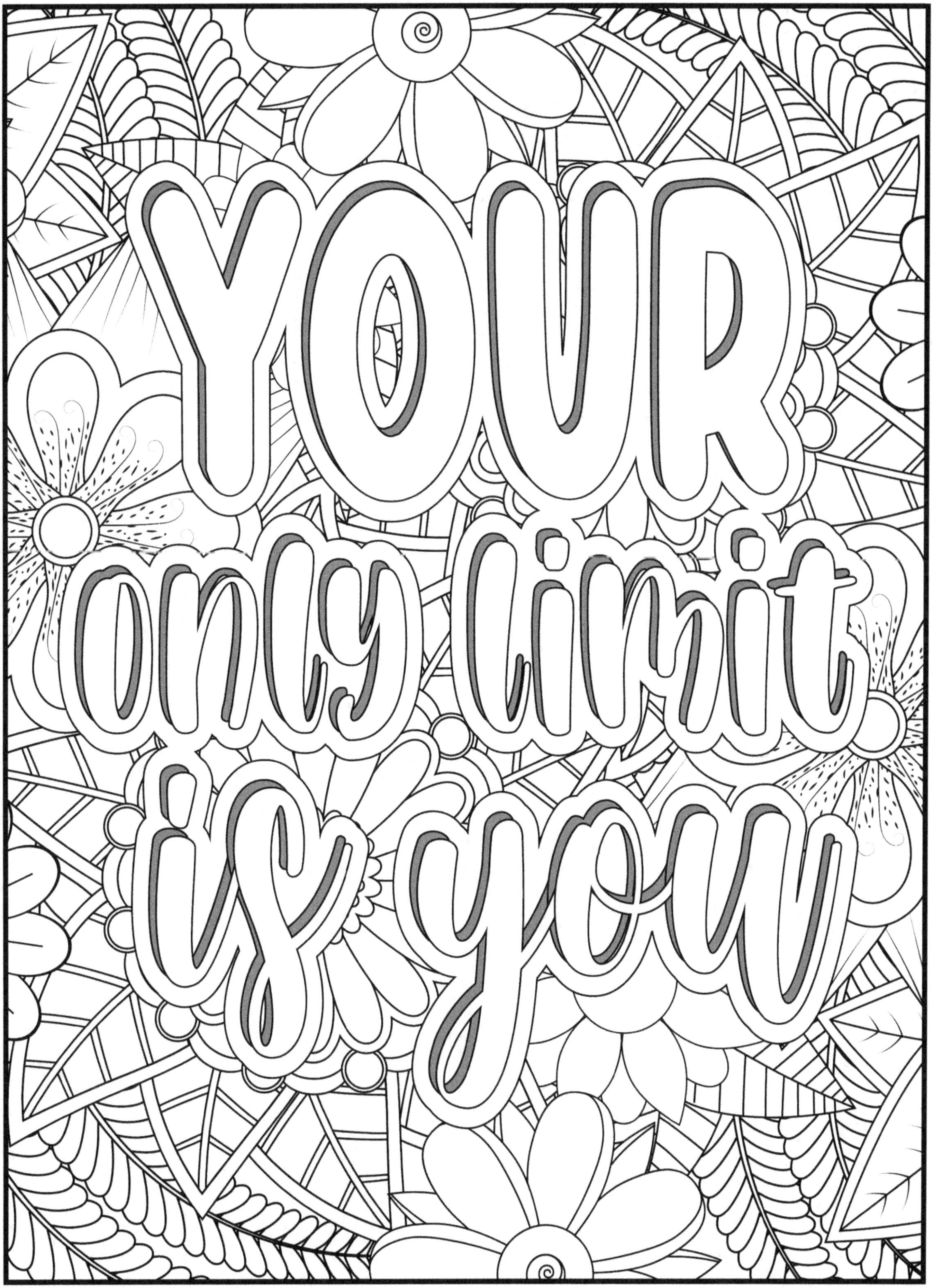
YOUR
only limit
is you

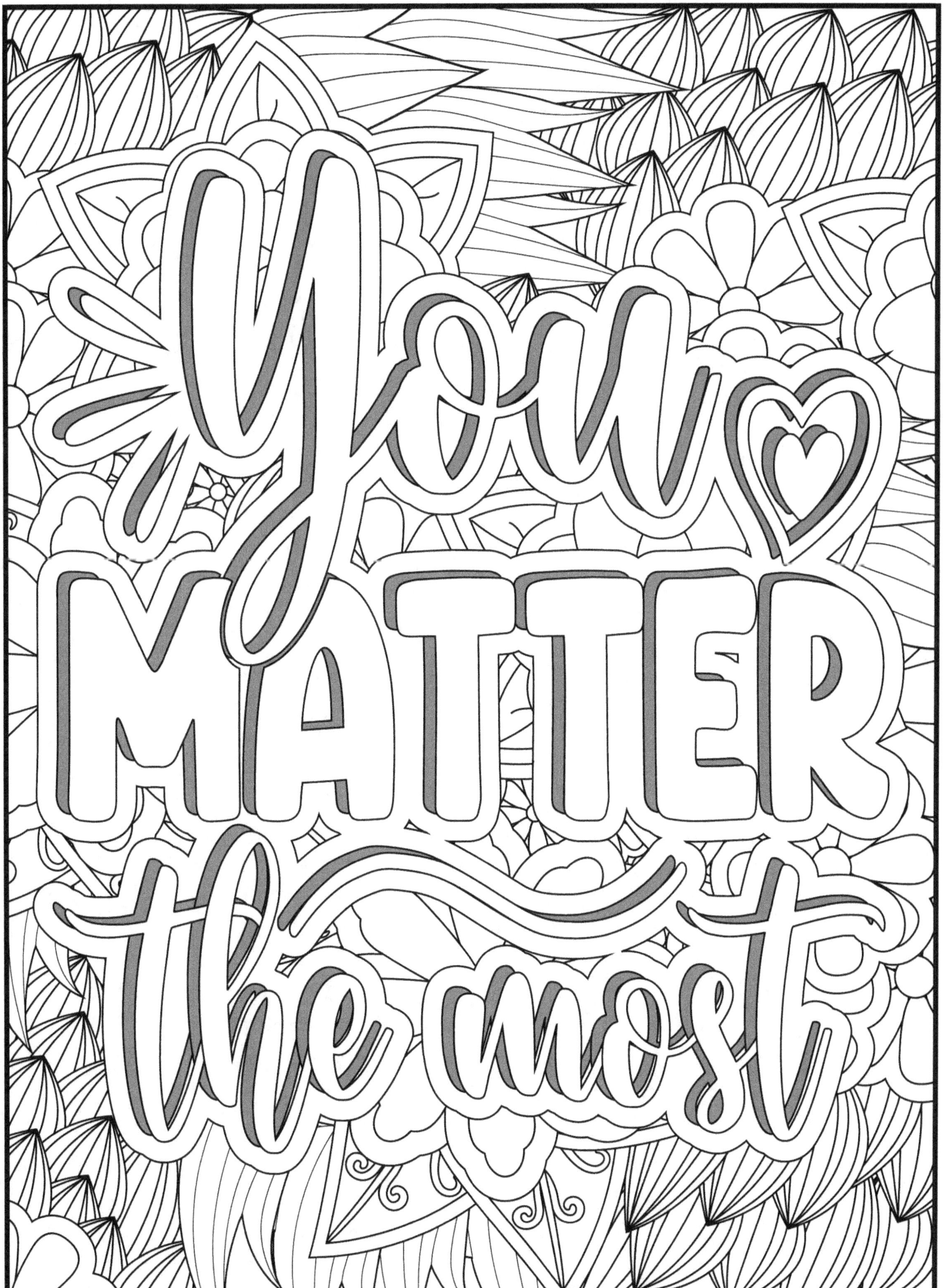
You
MATTER
the most

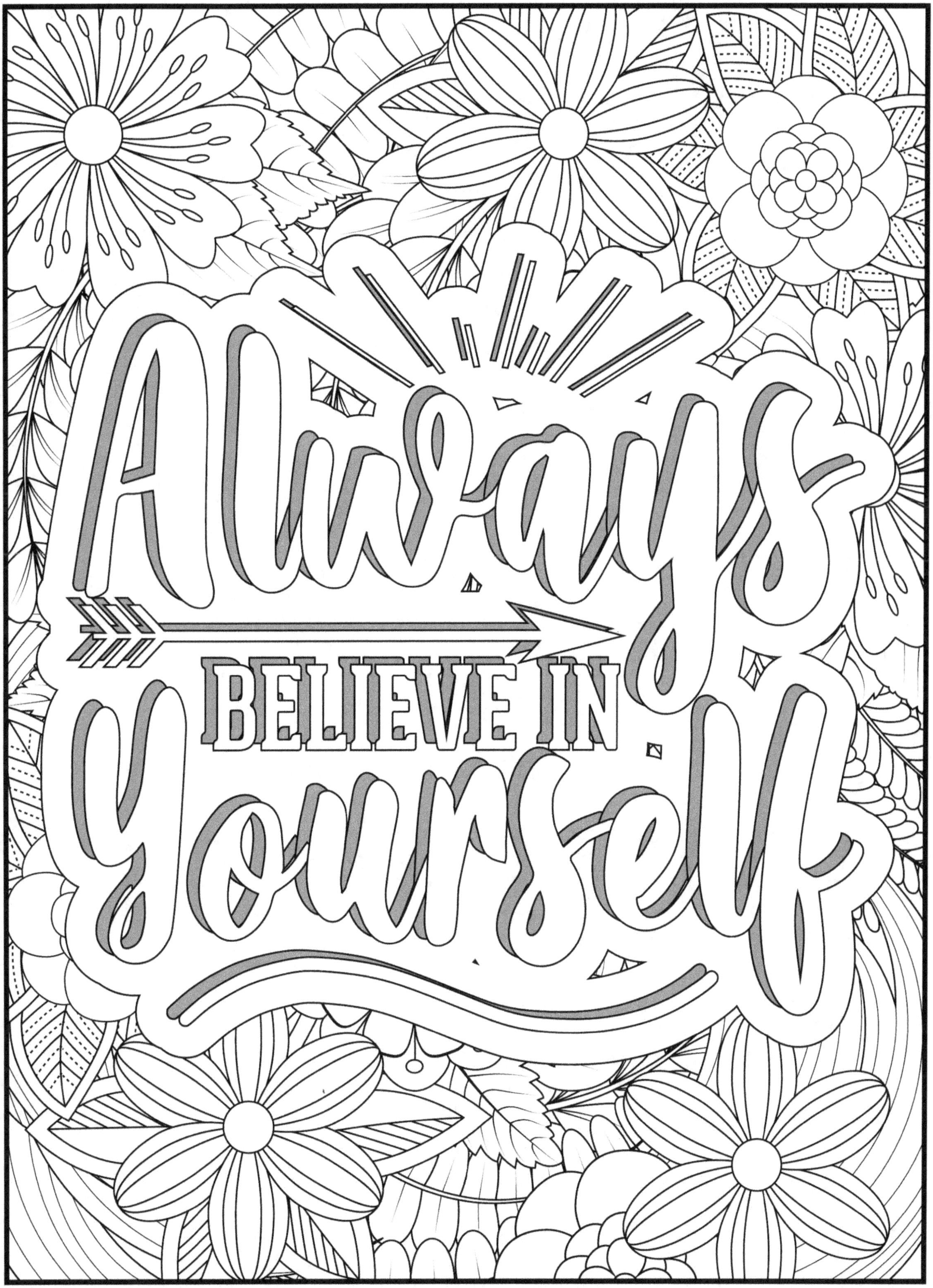
Always
BELIEVE IN
Yourself

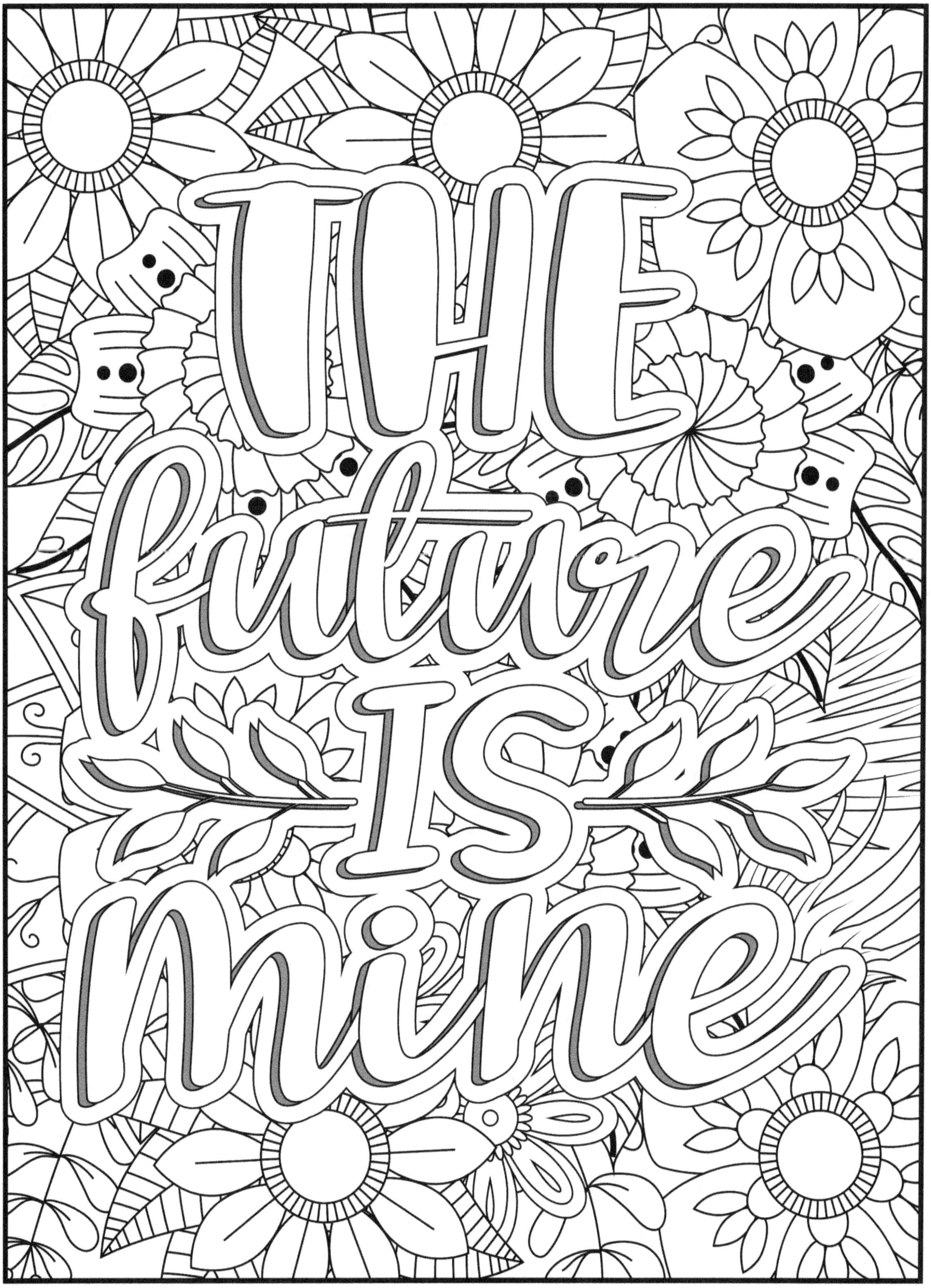
THE future IS mine

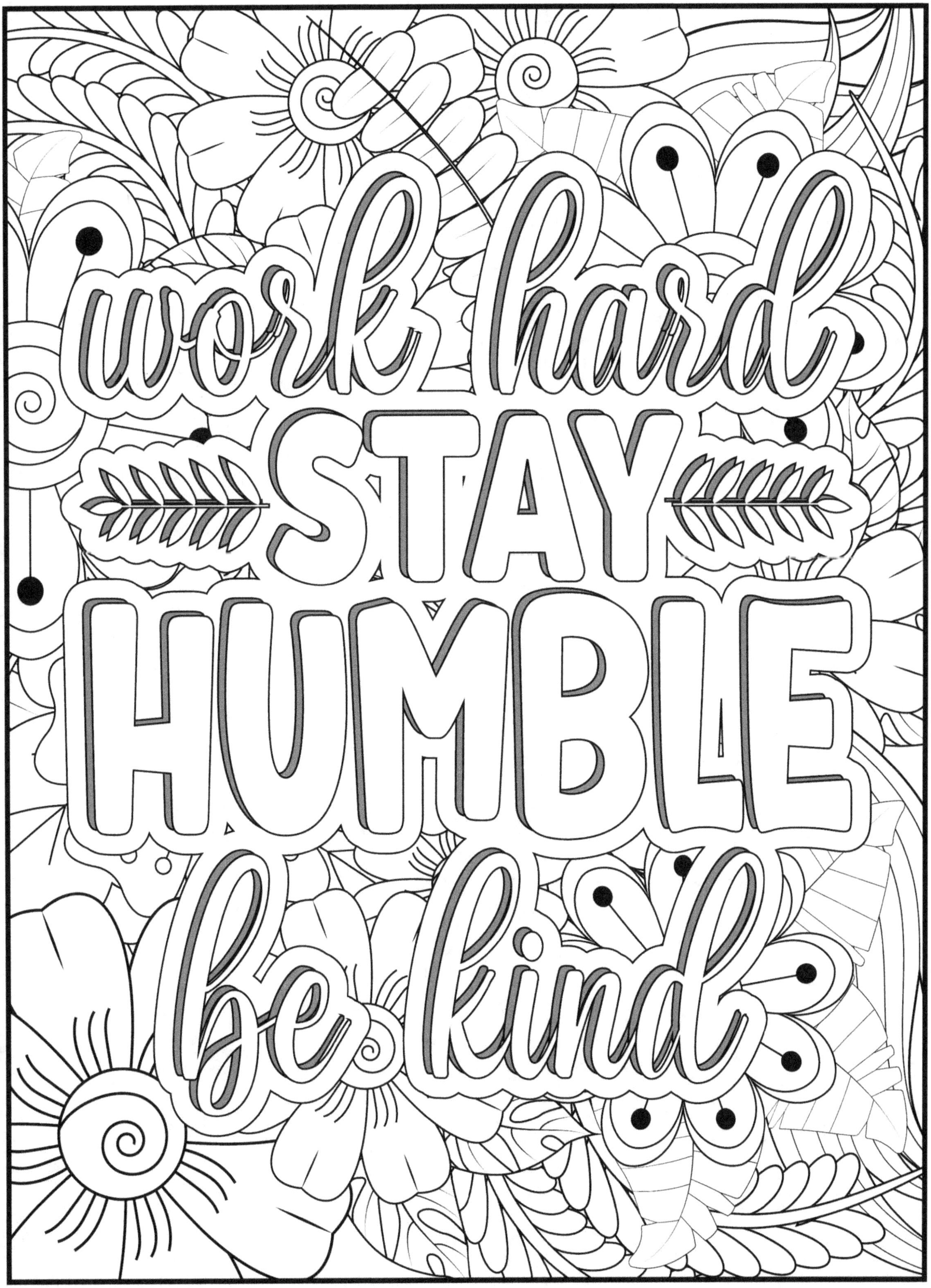
work hard
STAY
HUMBLE
be kind

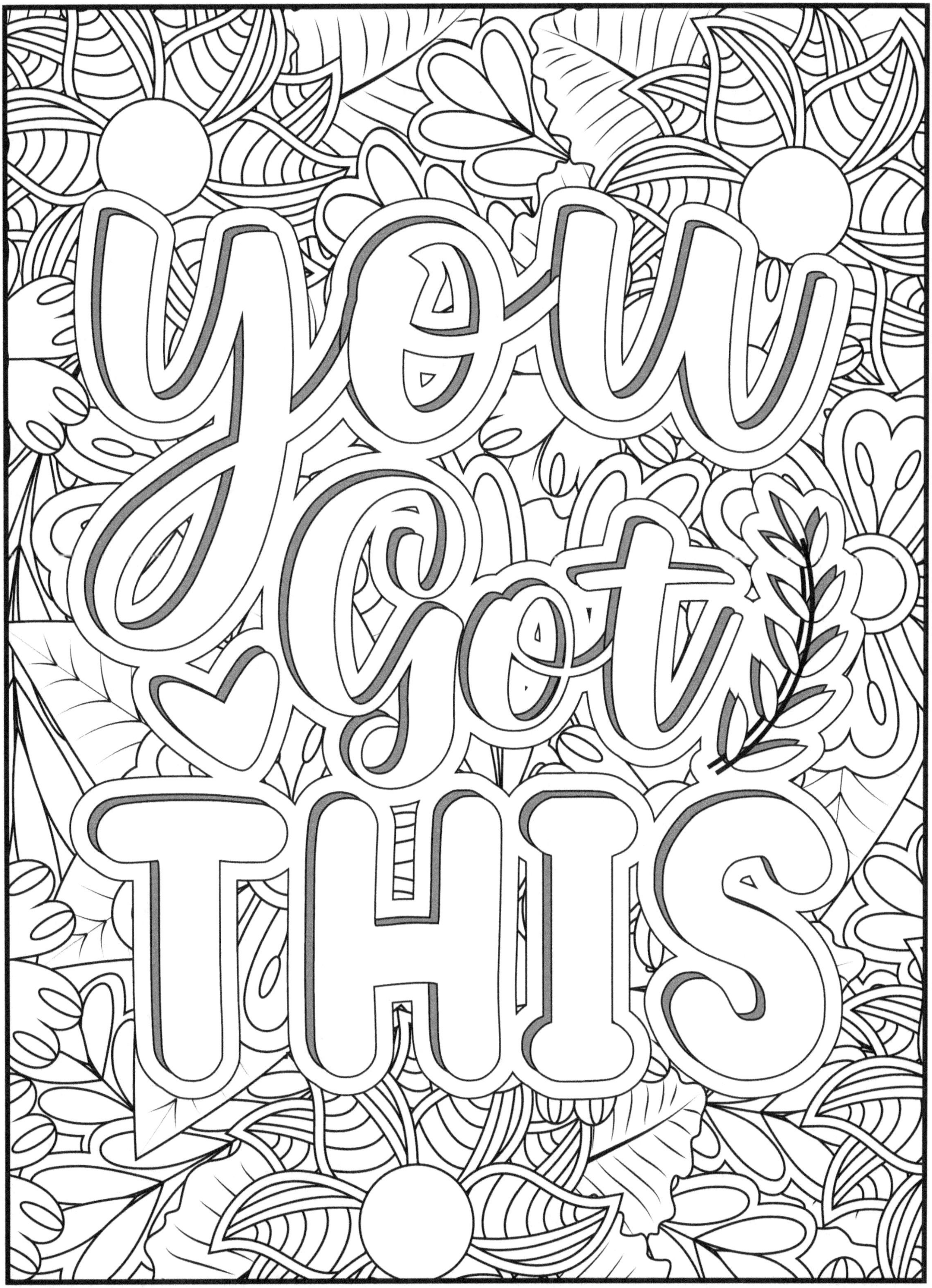
you
got
THIS

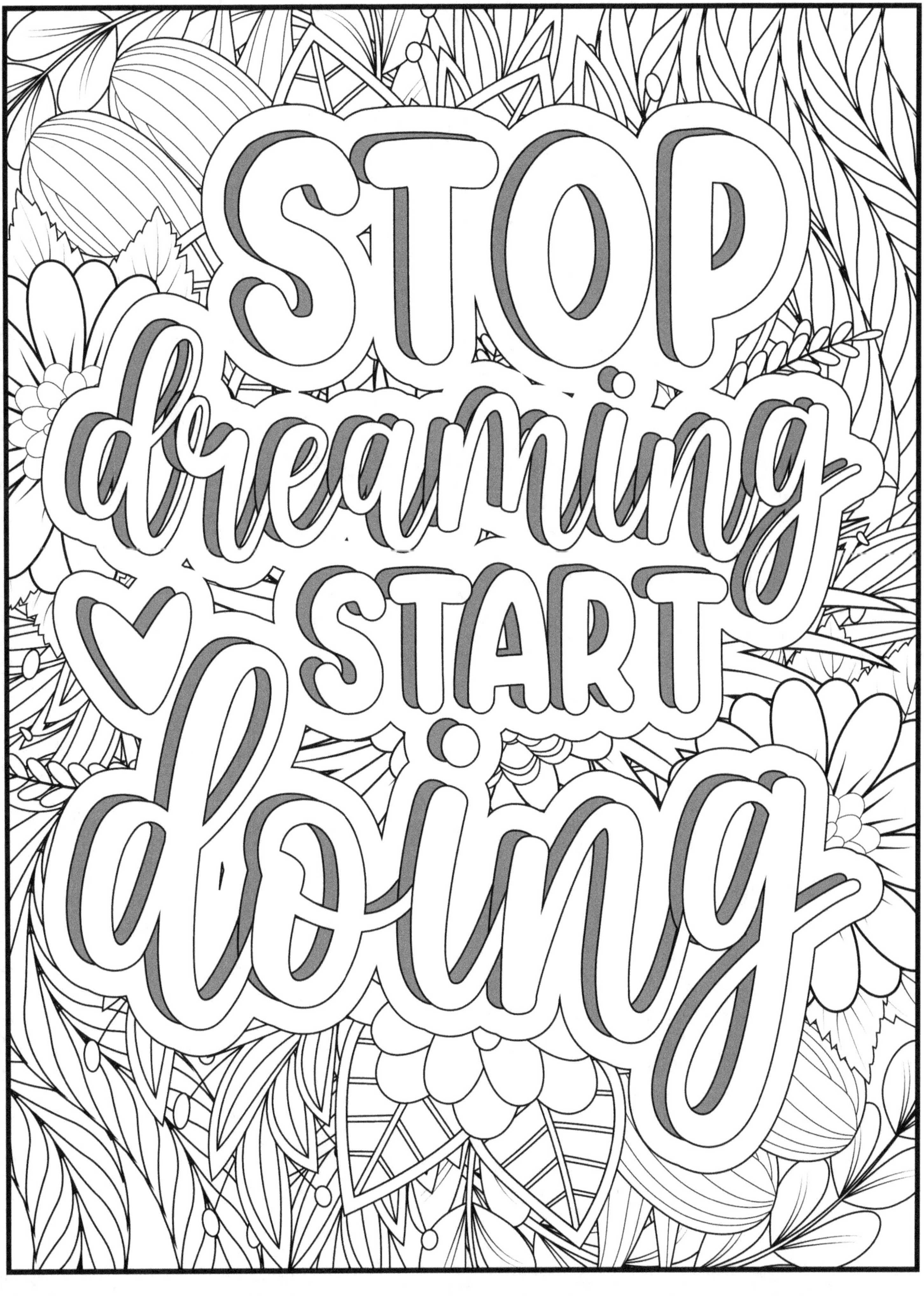
STOP
dreaming
START
doing

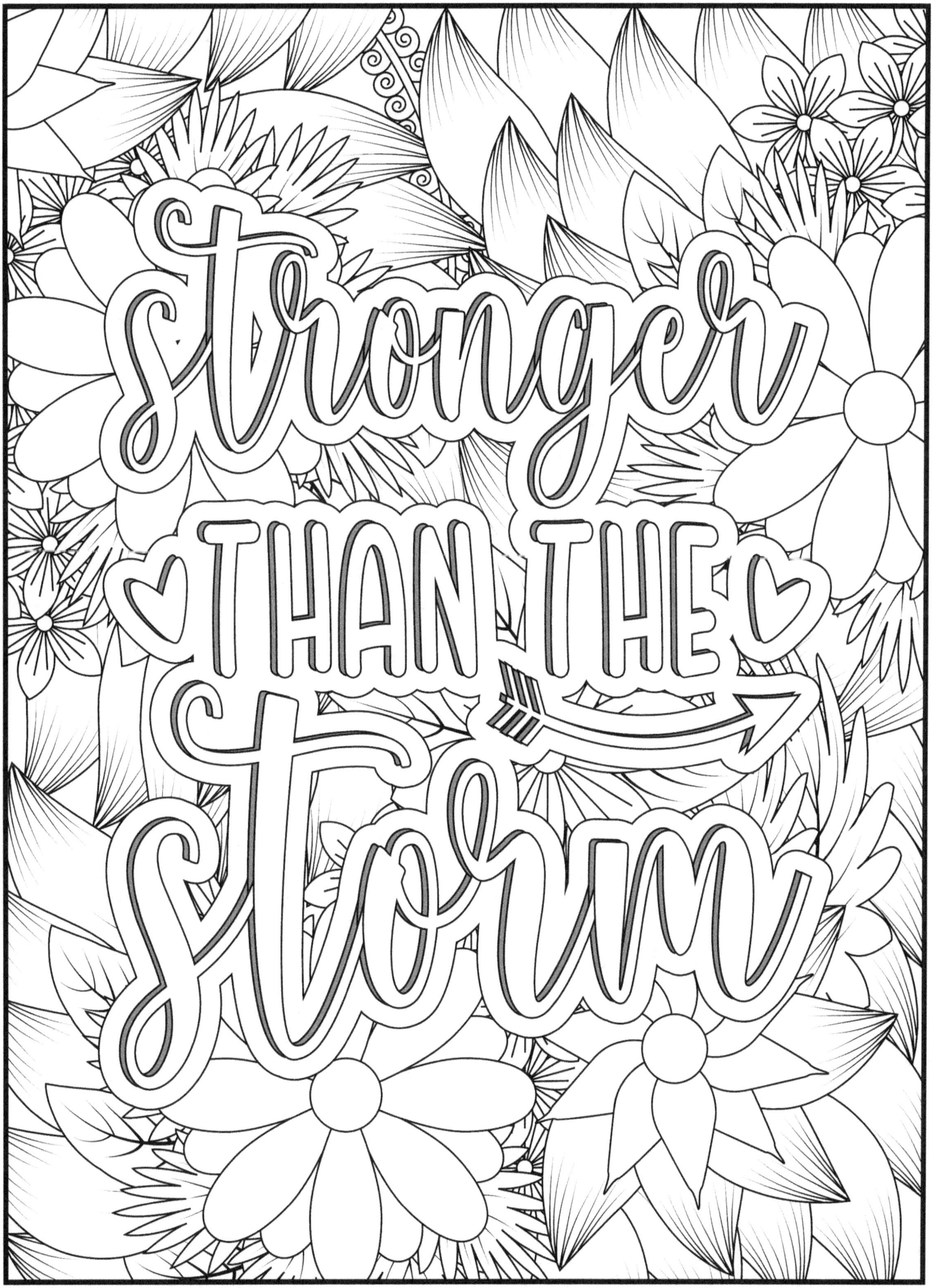
Stronger
THAN THE
Storm

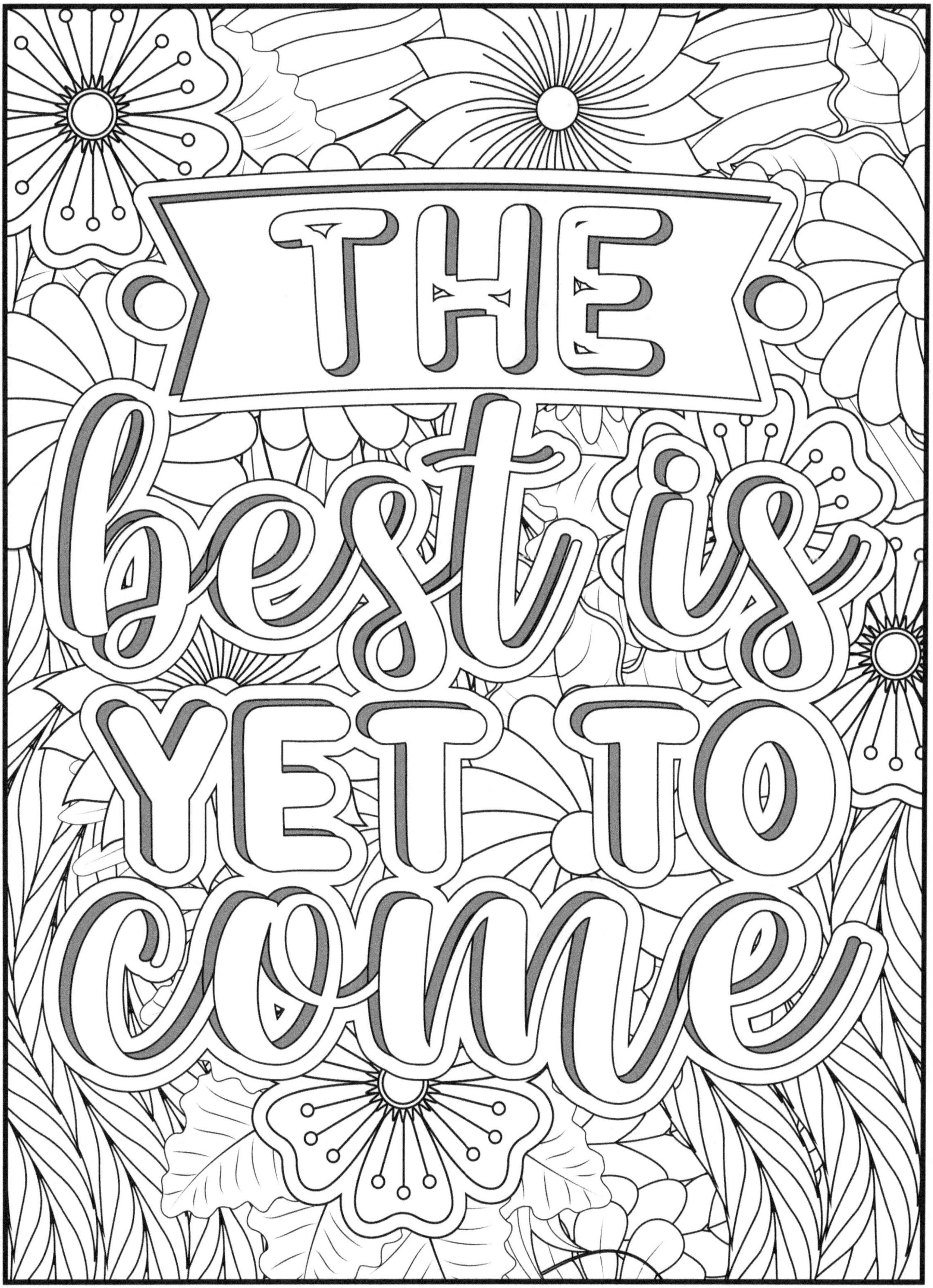
THE
best is
YET TO
come

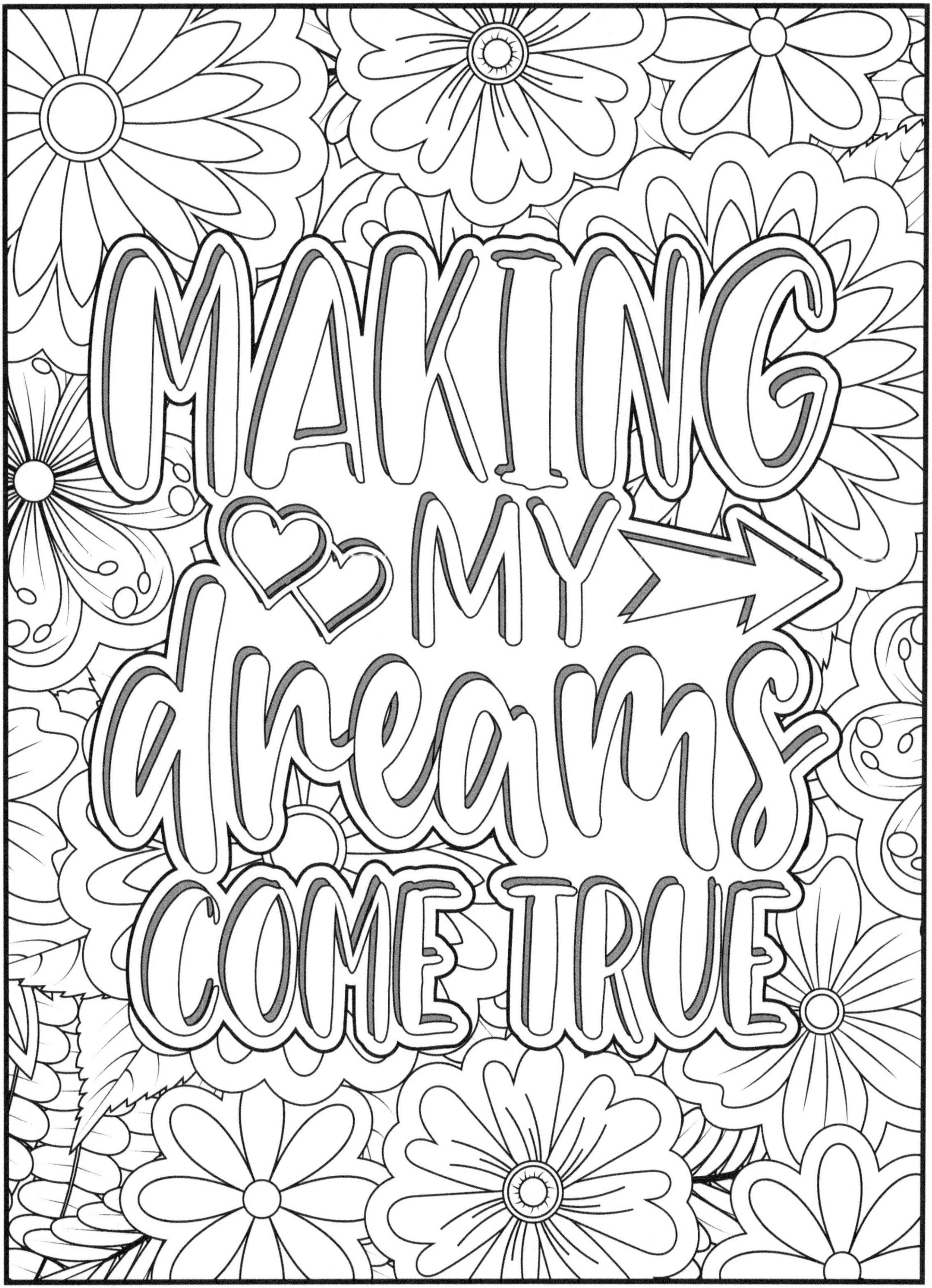
MAKING
MY
dreams
COME TRUE

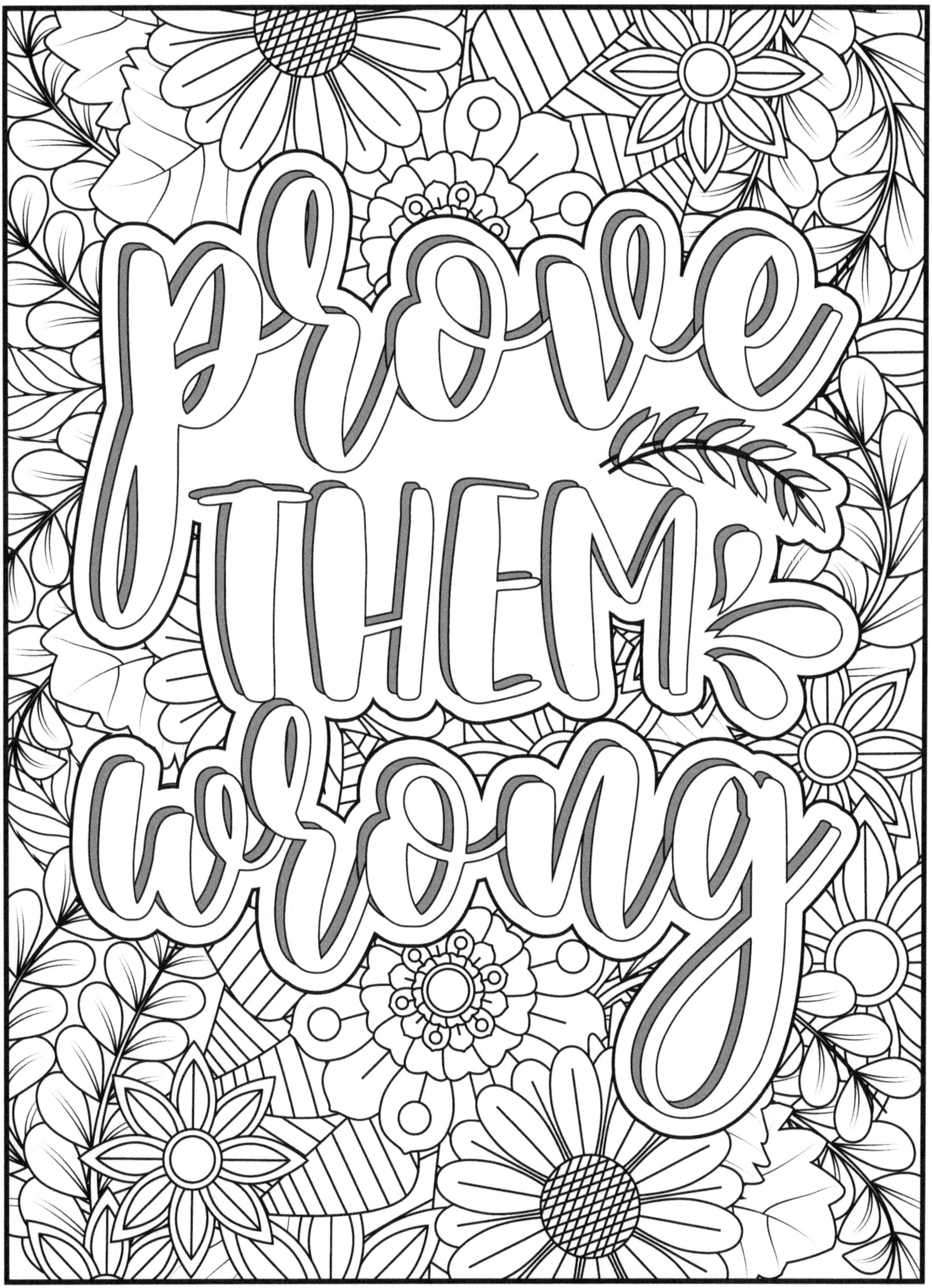
prove
THEM
wrong

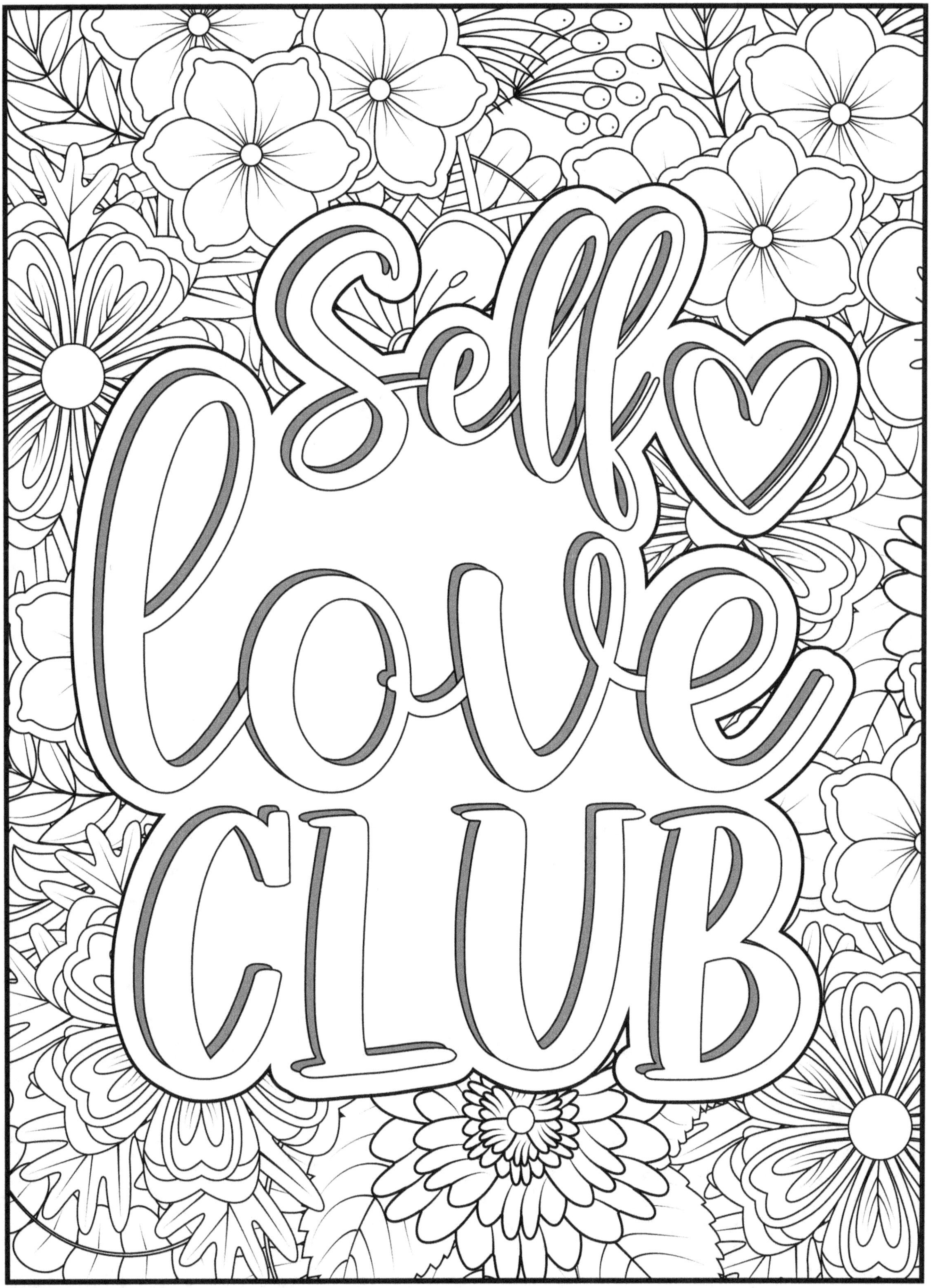
Self love
CLUB

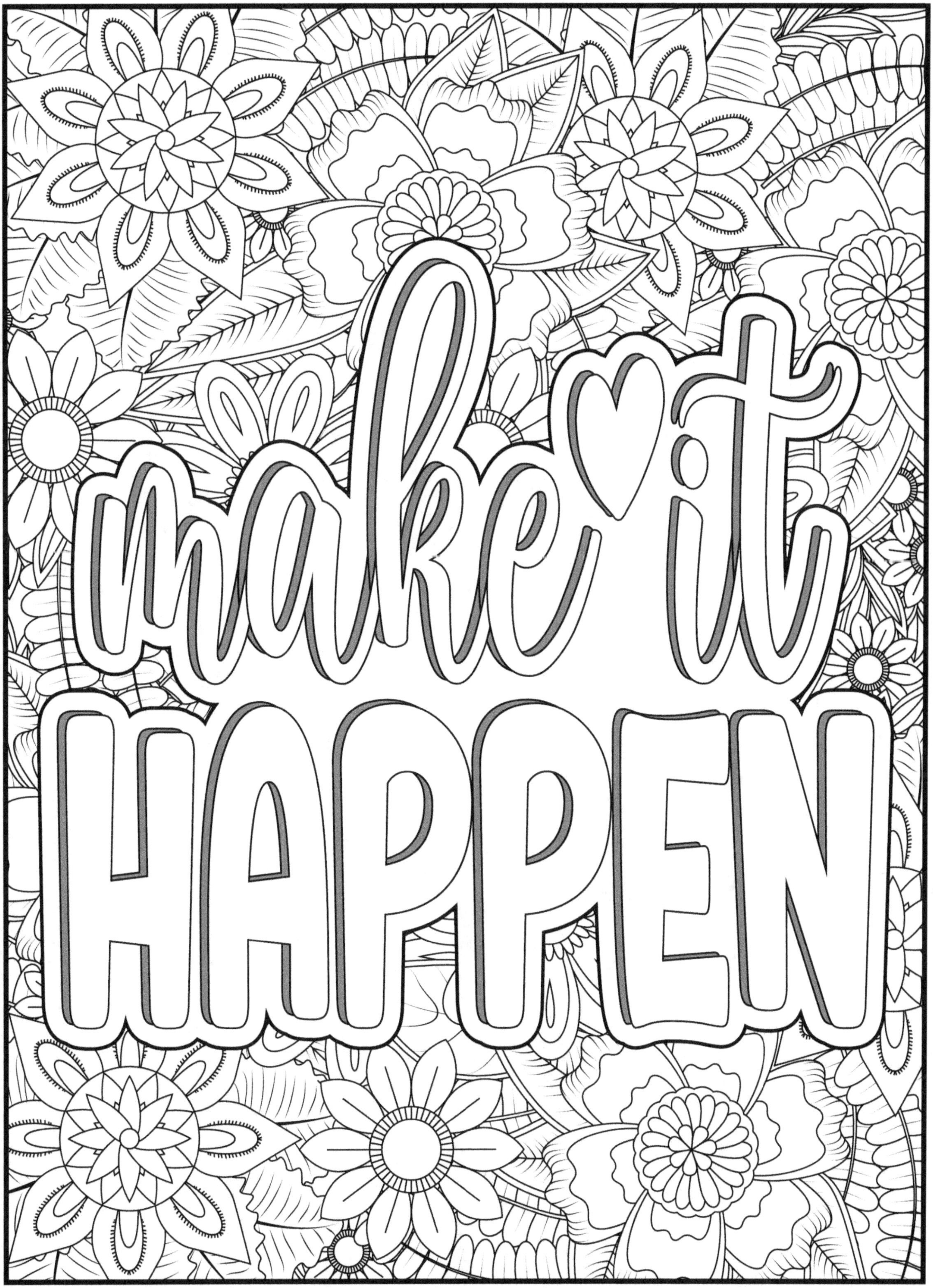
make it
HAPPEN

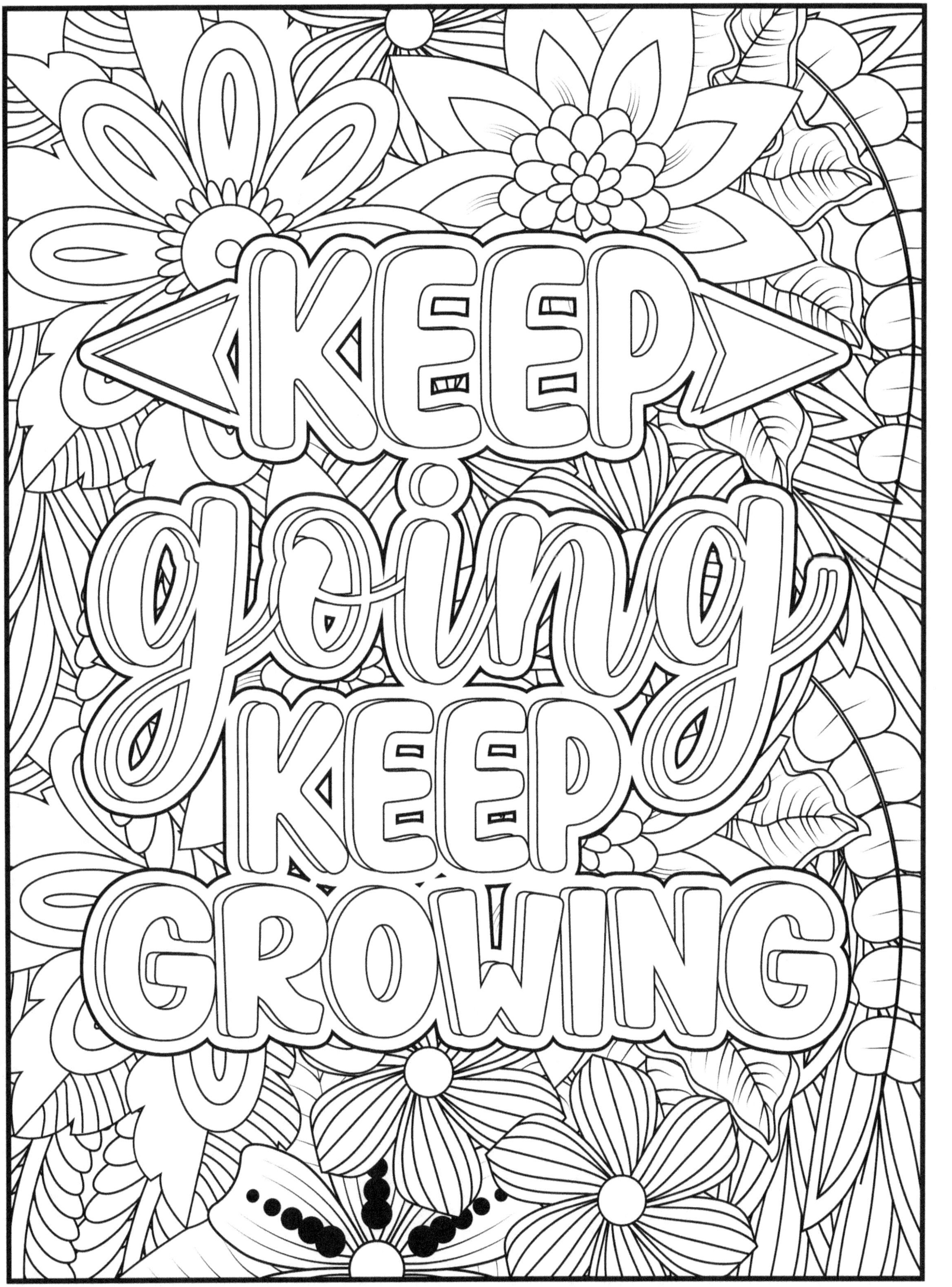
KEEP
going
KEEP
GROWING

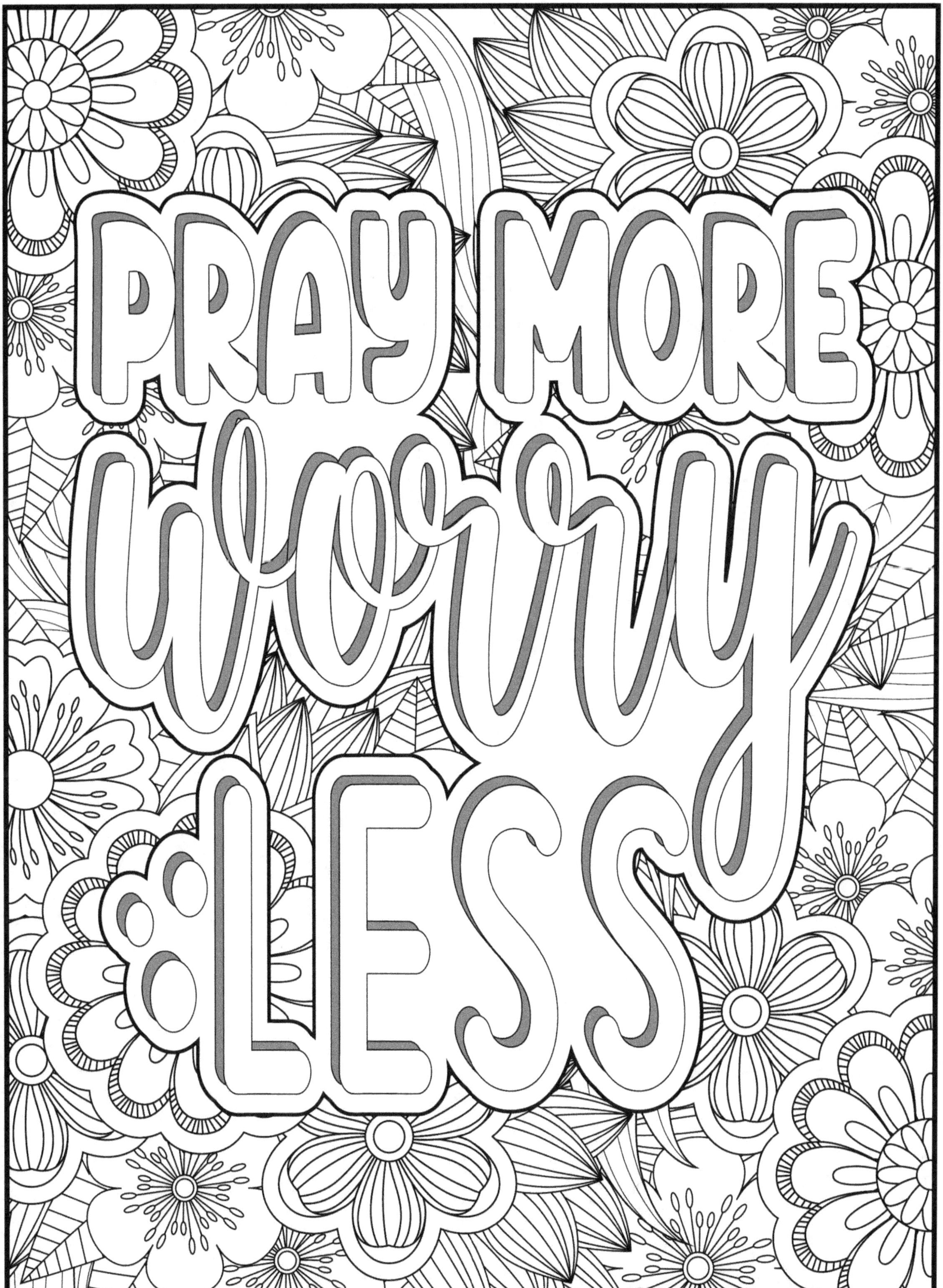
PRAY MORE
worry
LESS

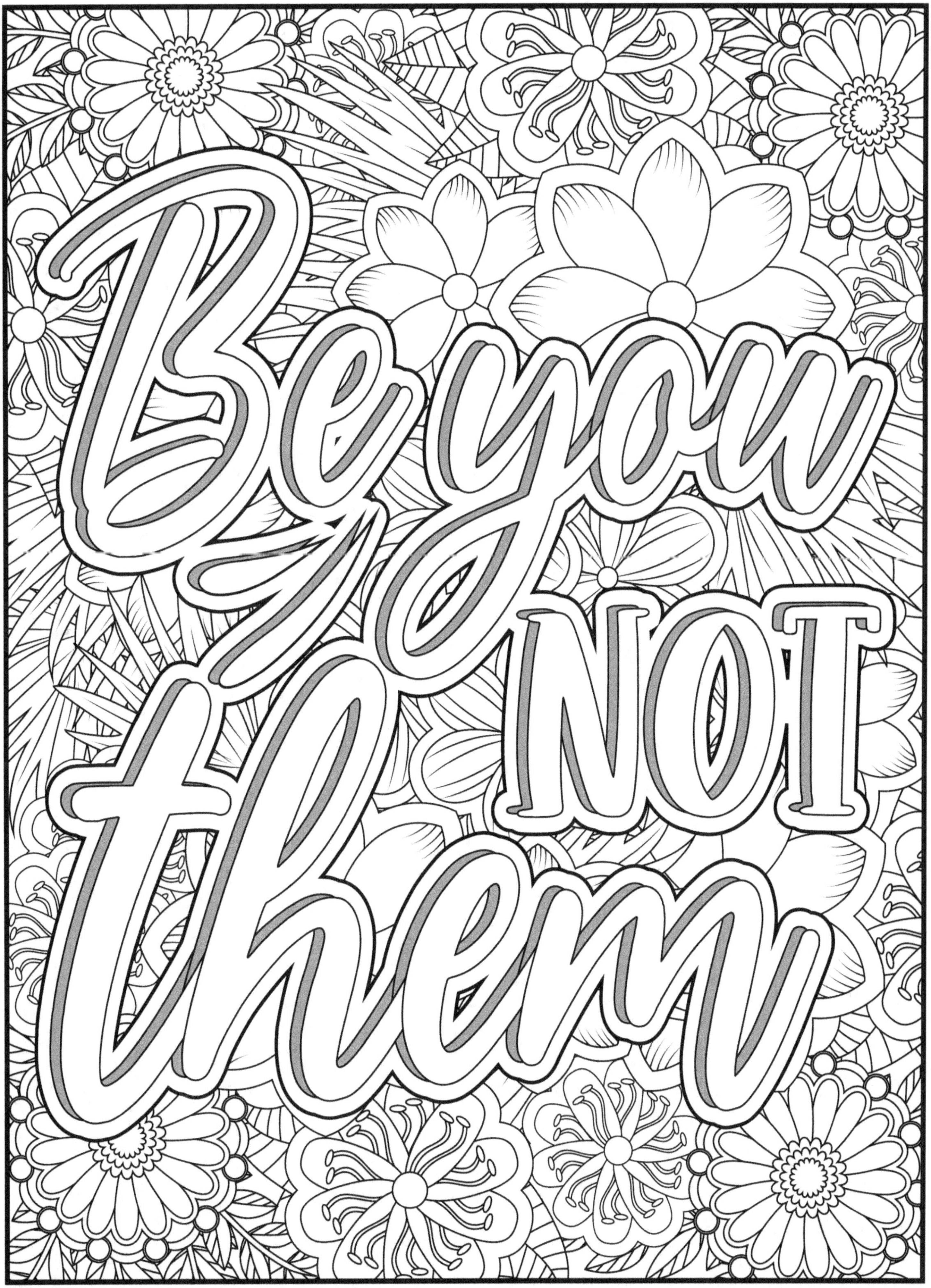
Be you
NOT
them

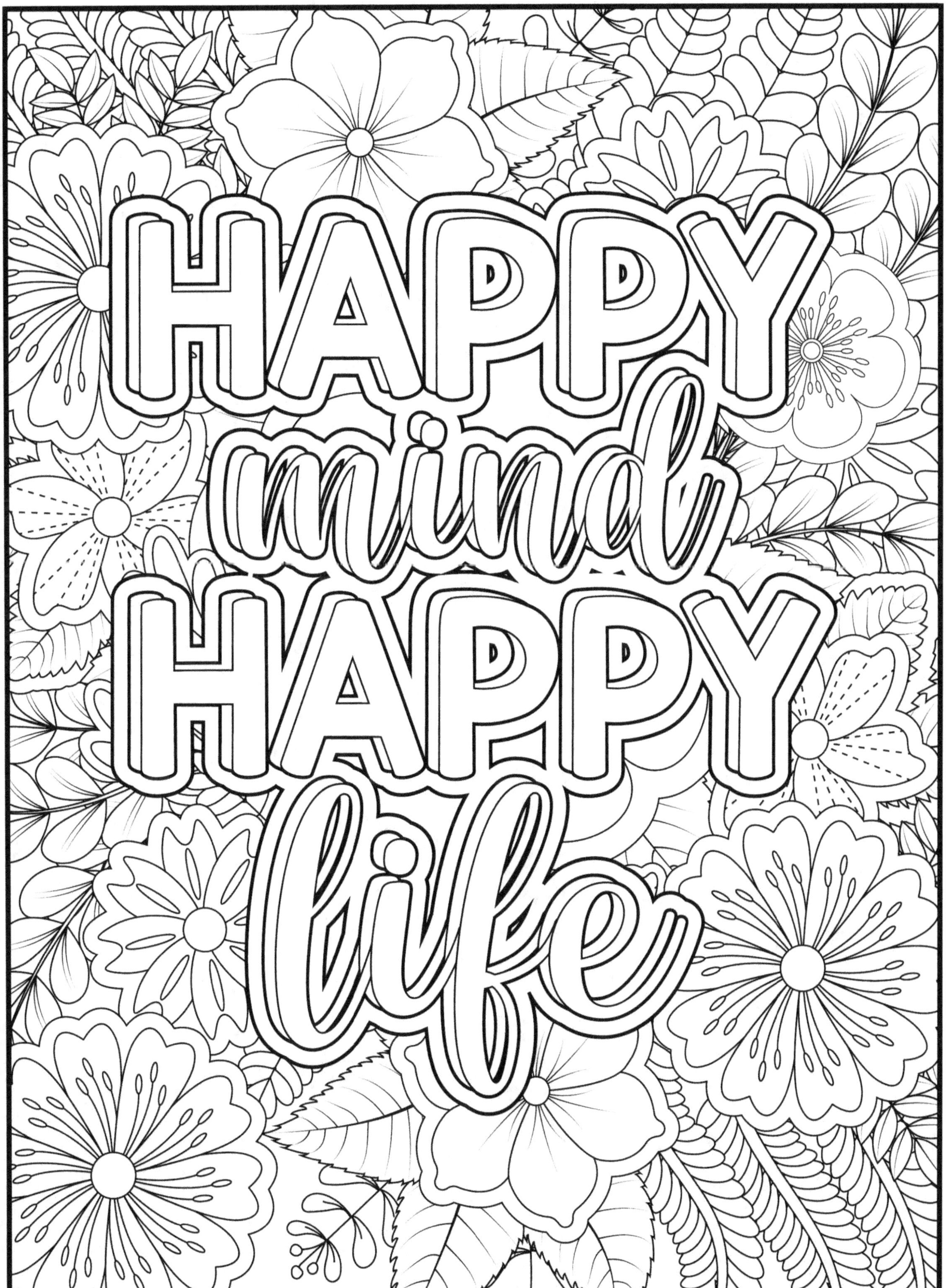
HAPPY
mind
HAPPY
life

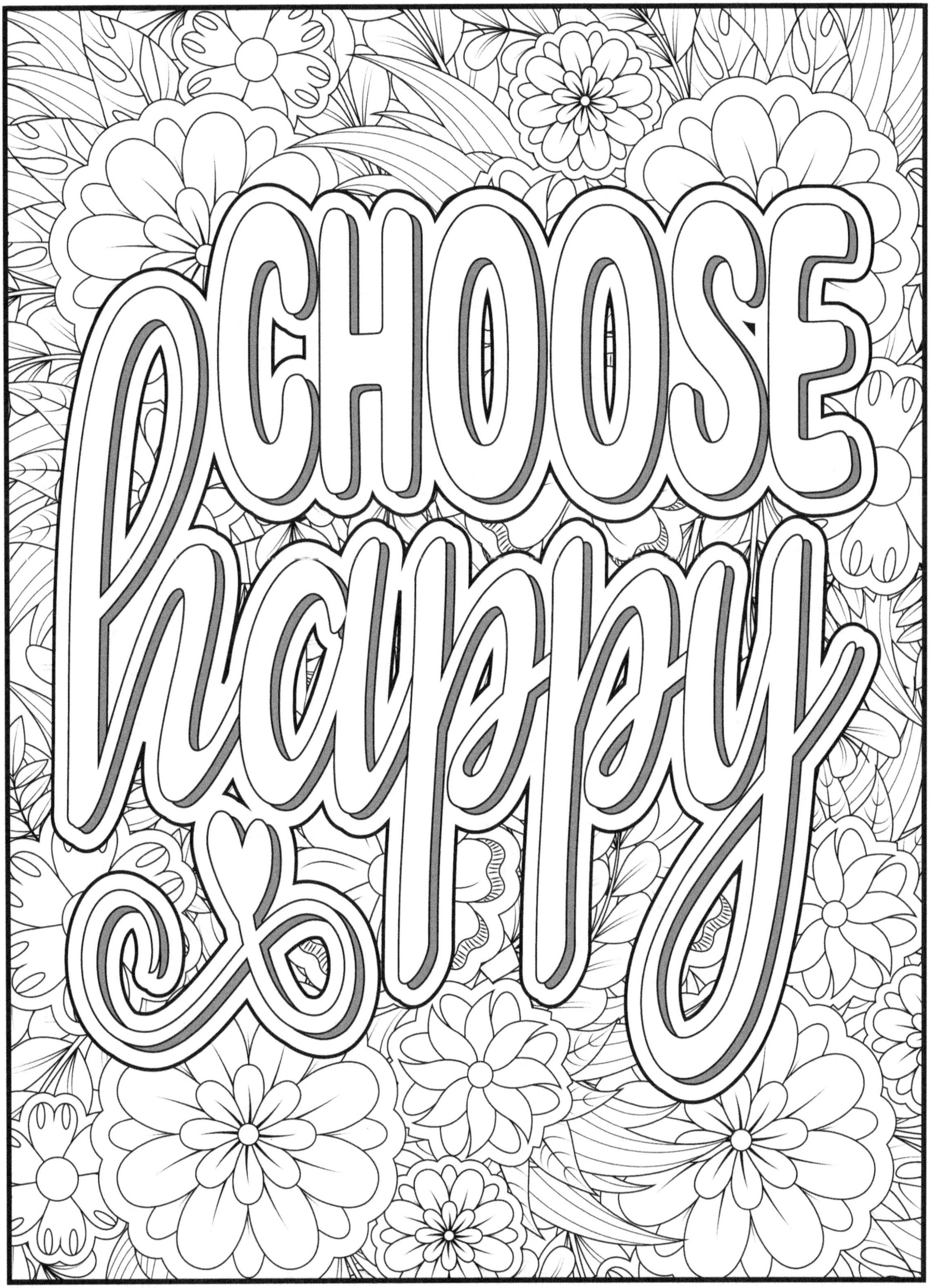
CHOOSE
happy

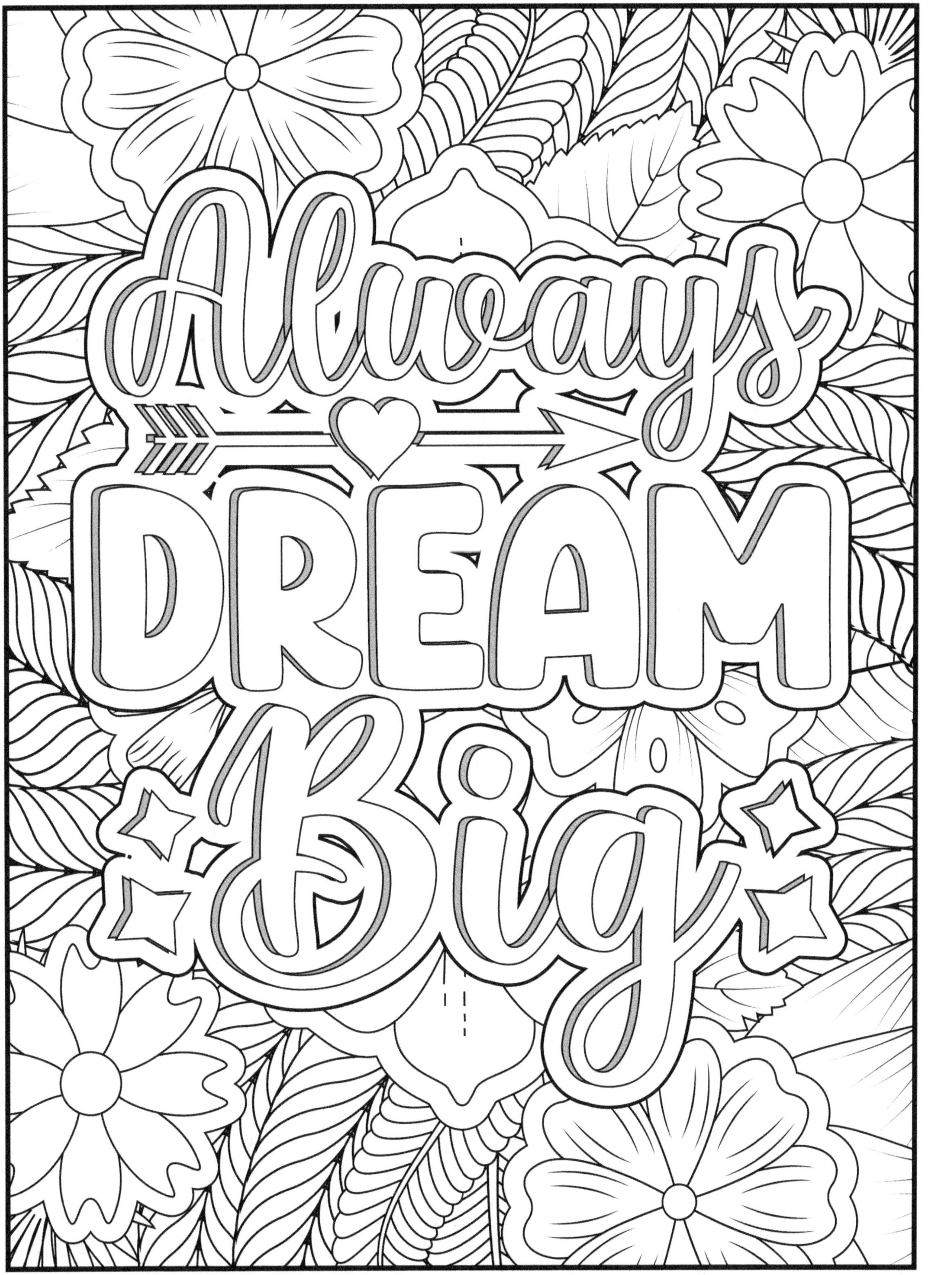
Always
DREAM
Big

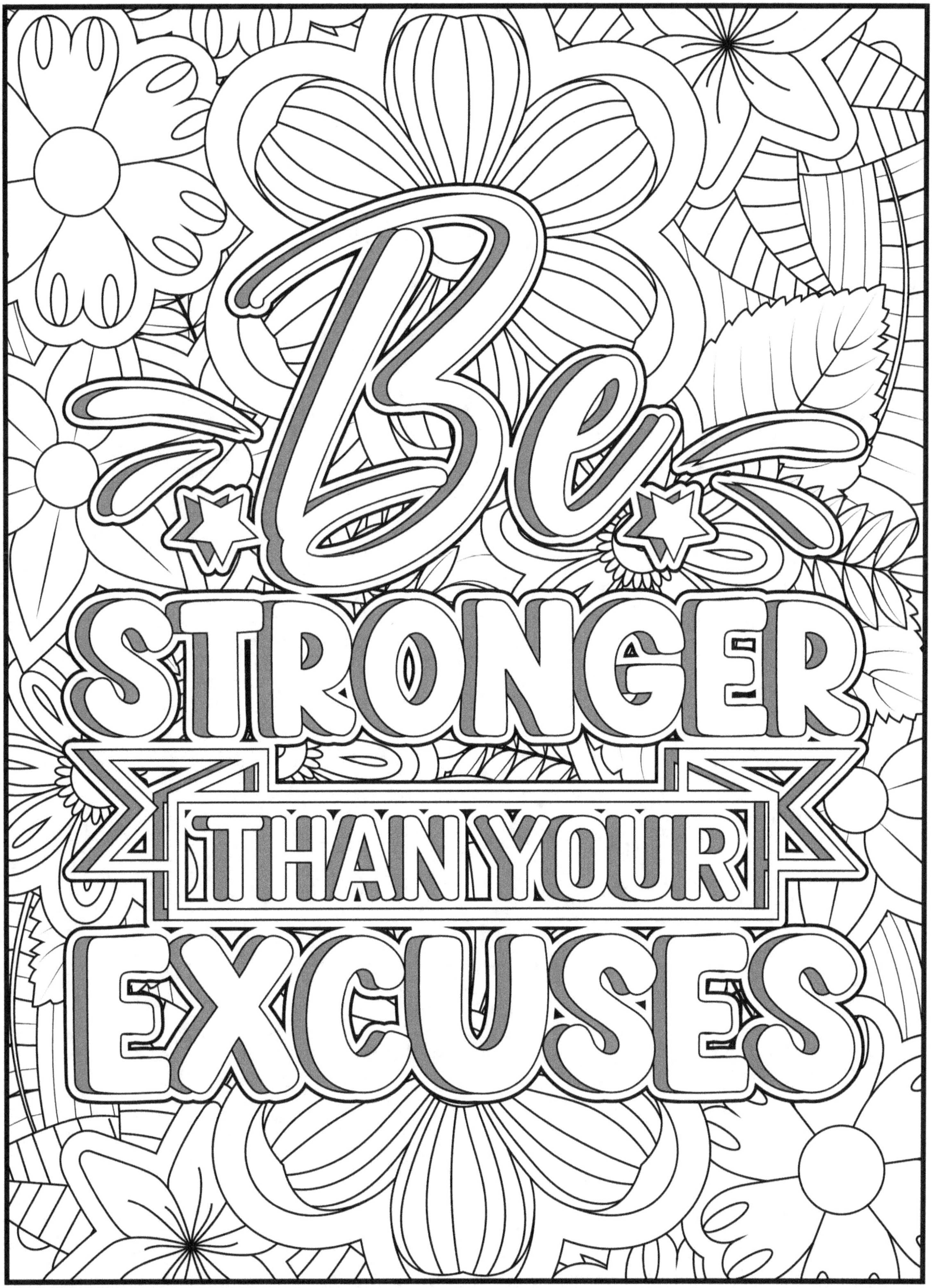
Be
STRONGER
THAN YOUR
EXCUSES

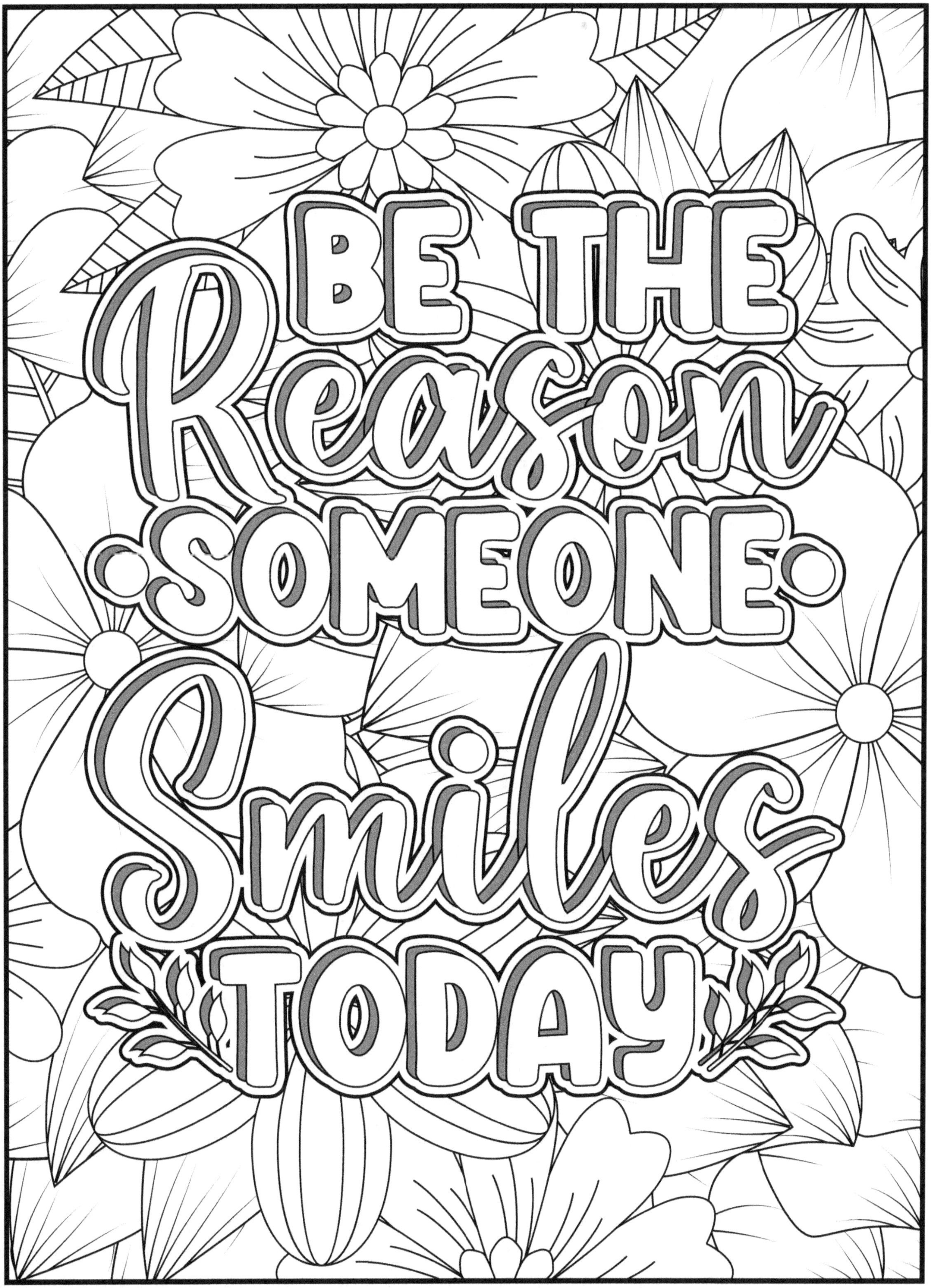
BE THE
Reason
SOMEONE
Smiles
TODAY

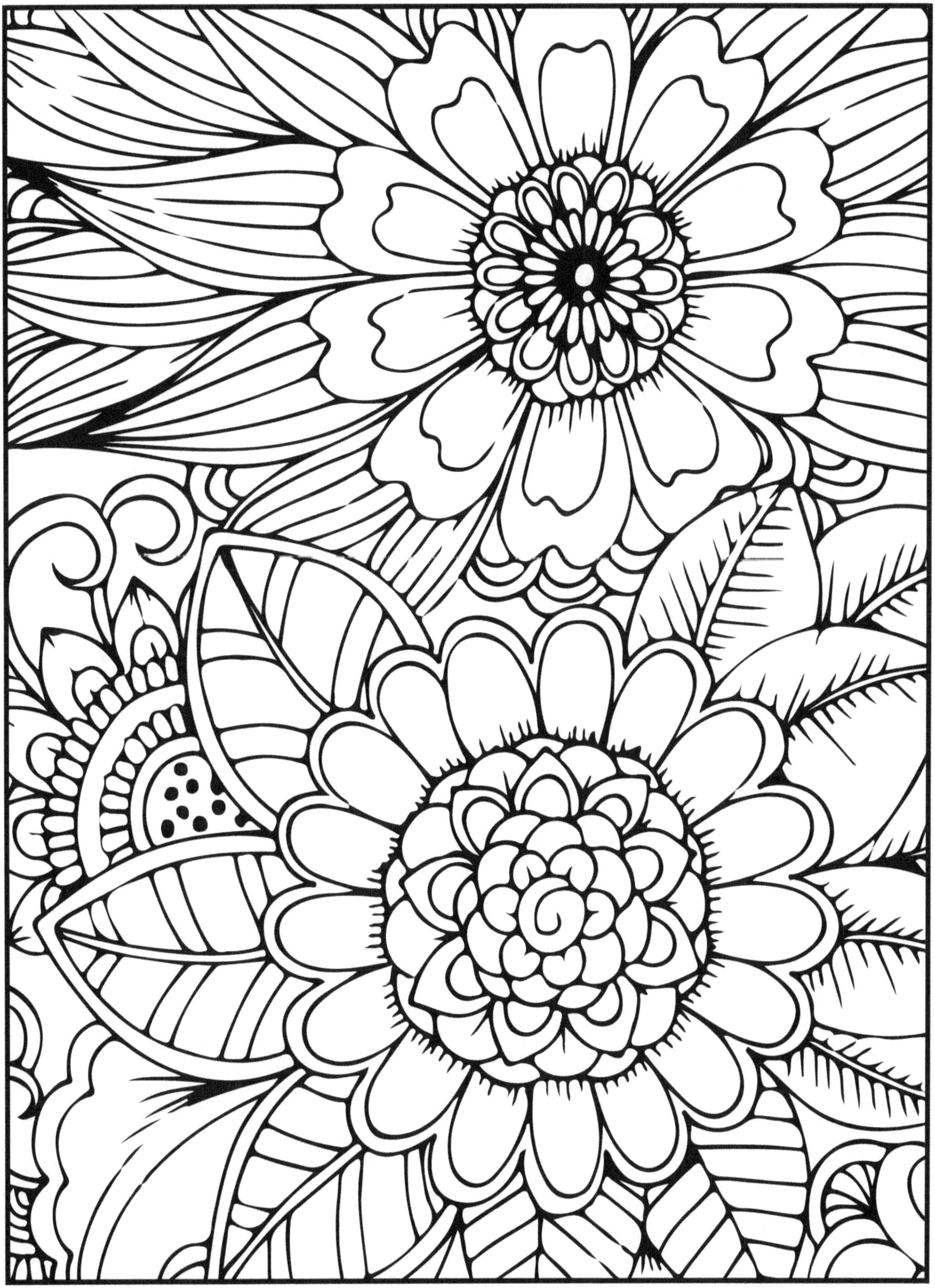

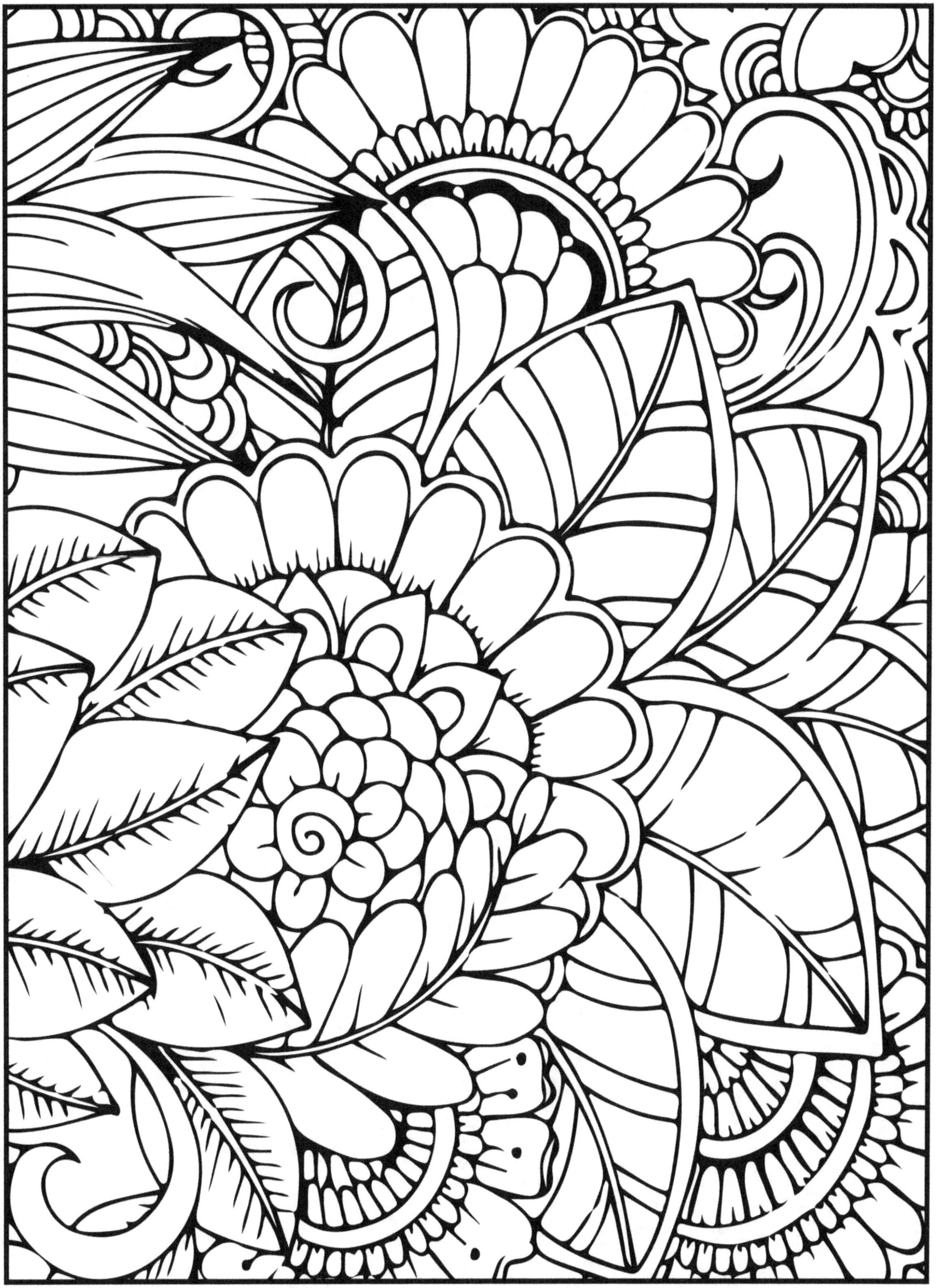

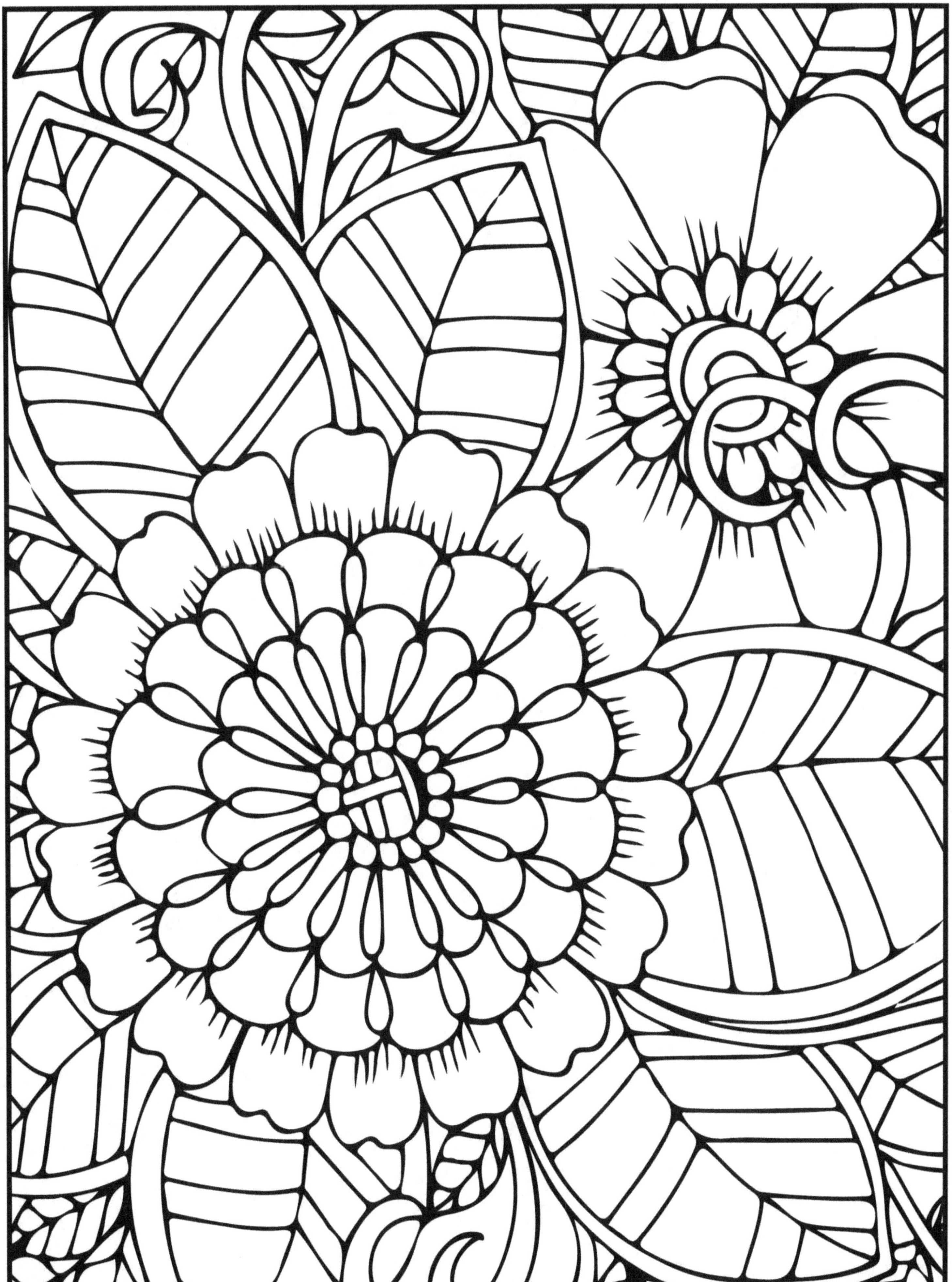

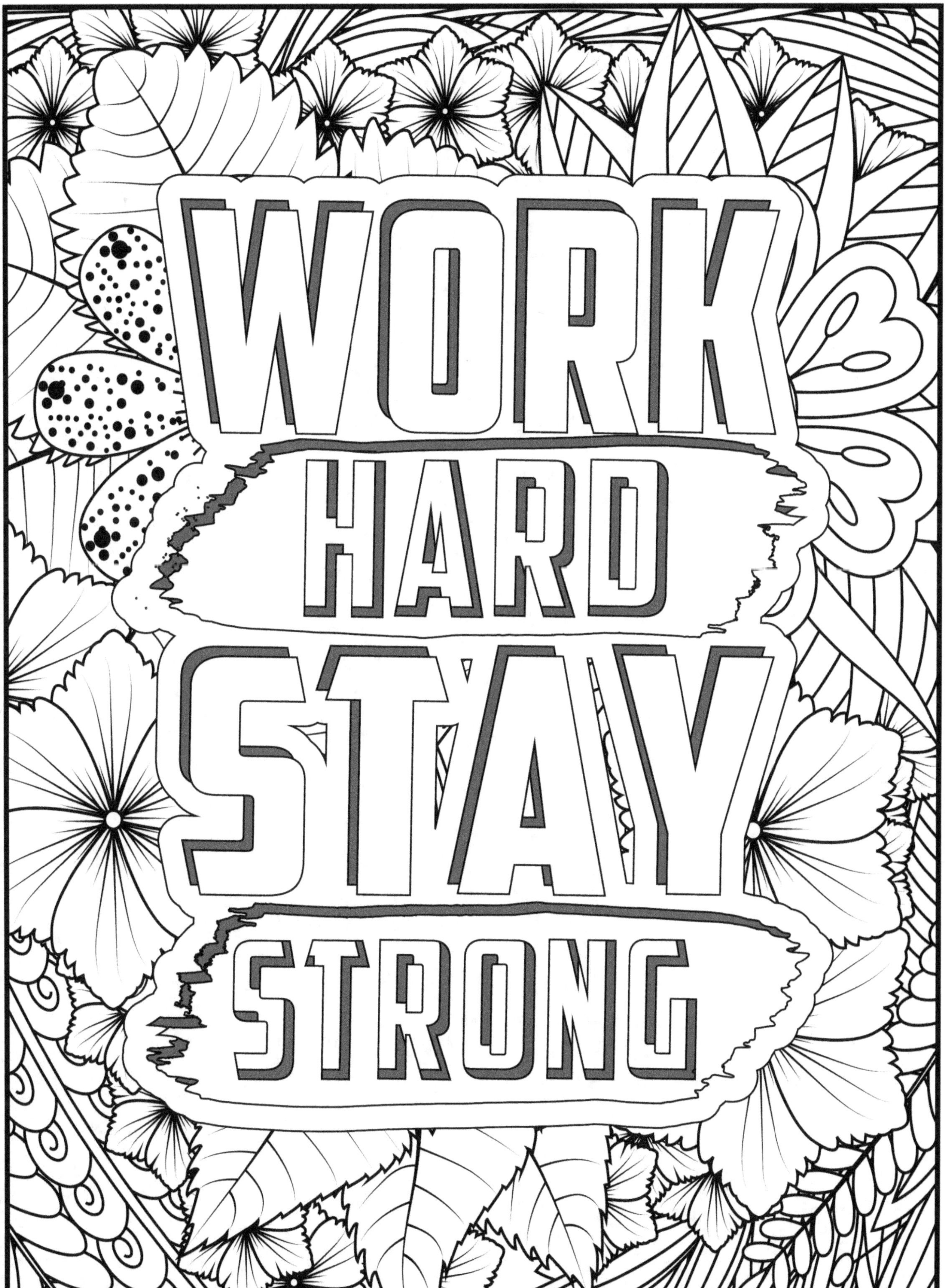
WORK
HARD
STAY
STRONG

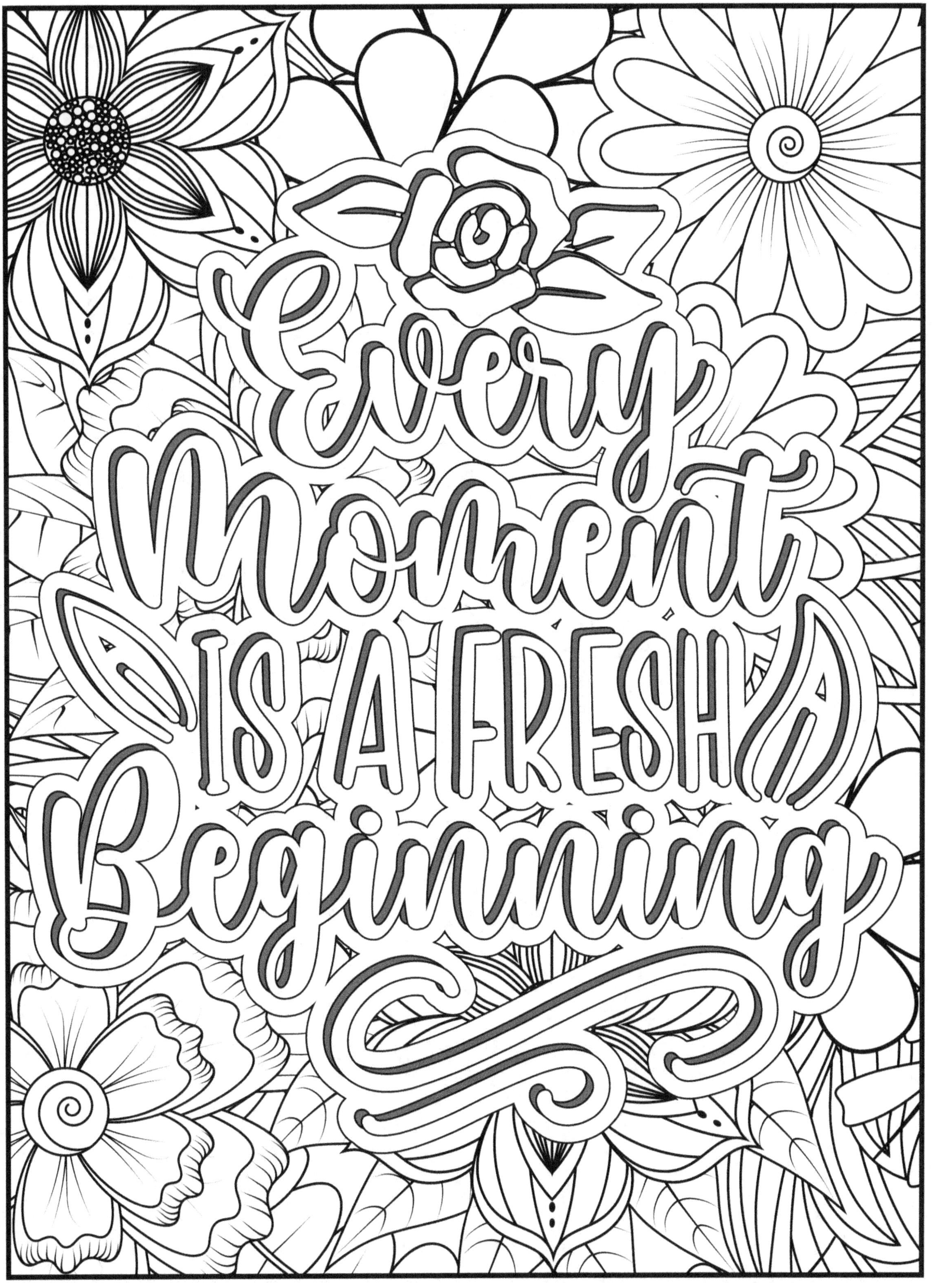
Every
Moment
IS A FRESH
Beginning

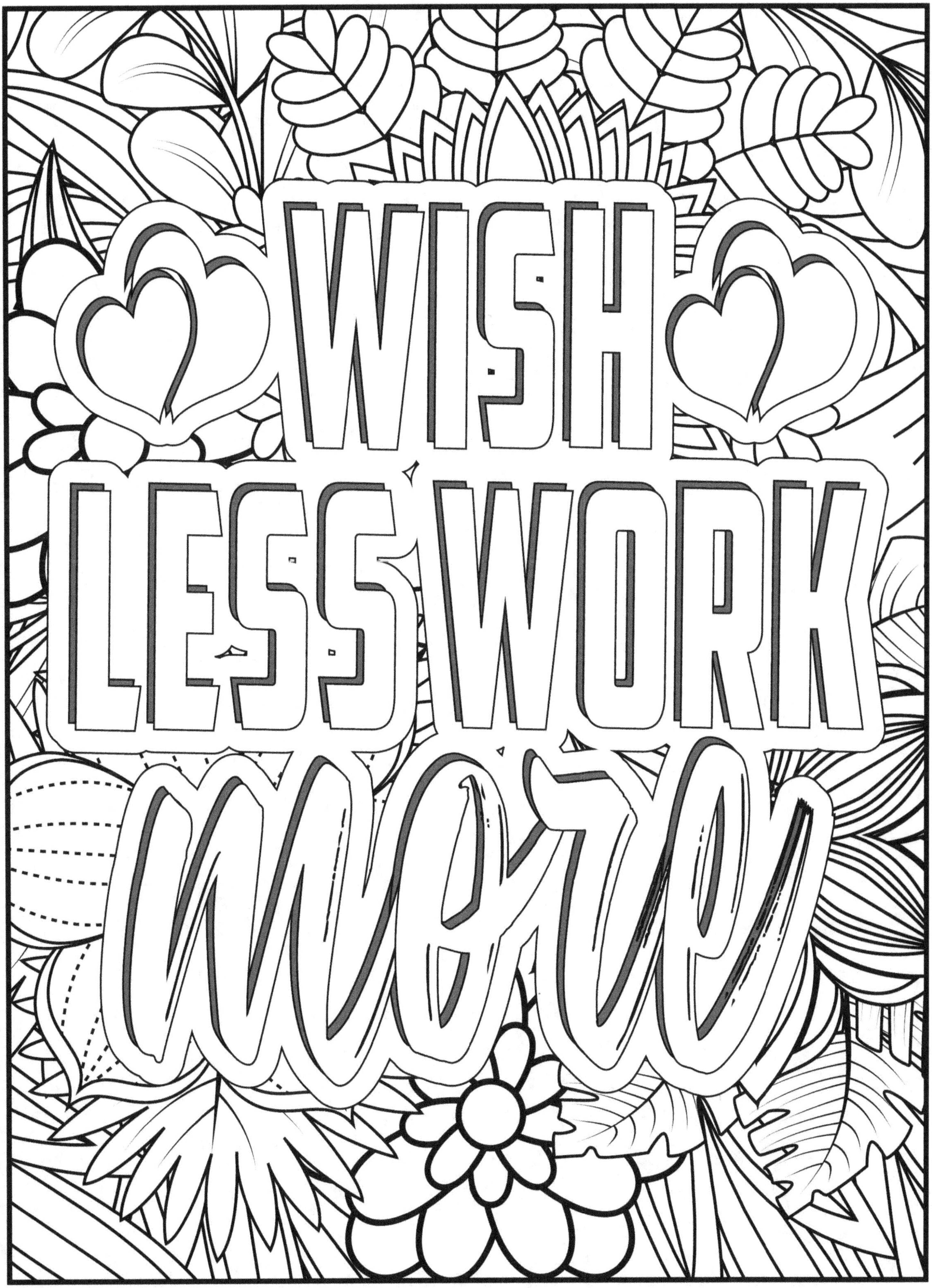
WISH
LESS WORK
more

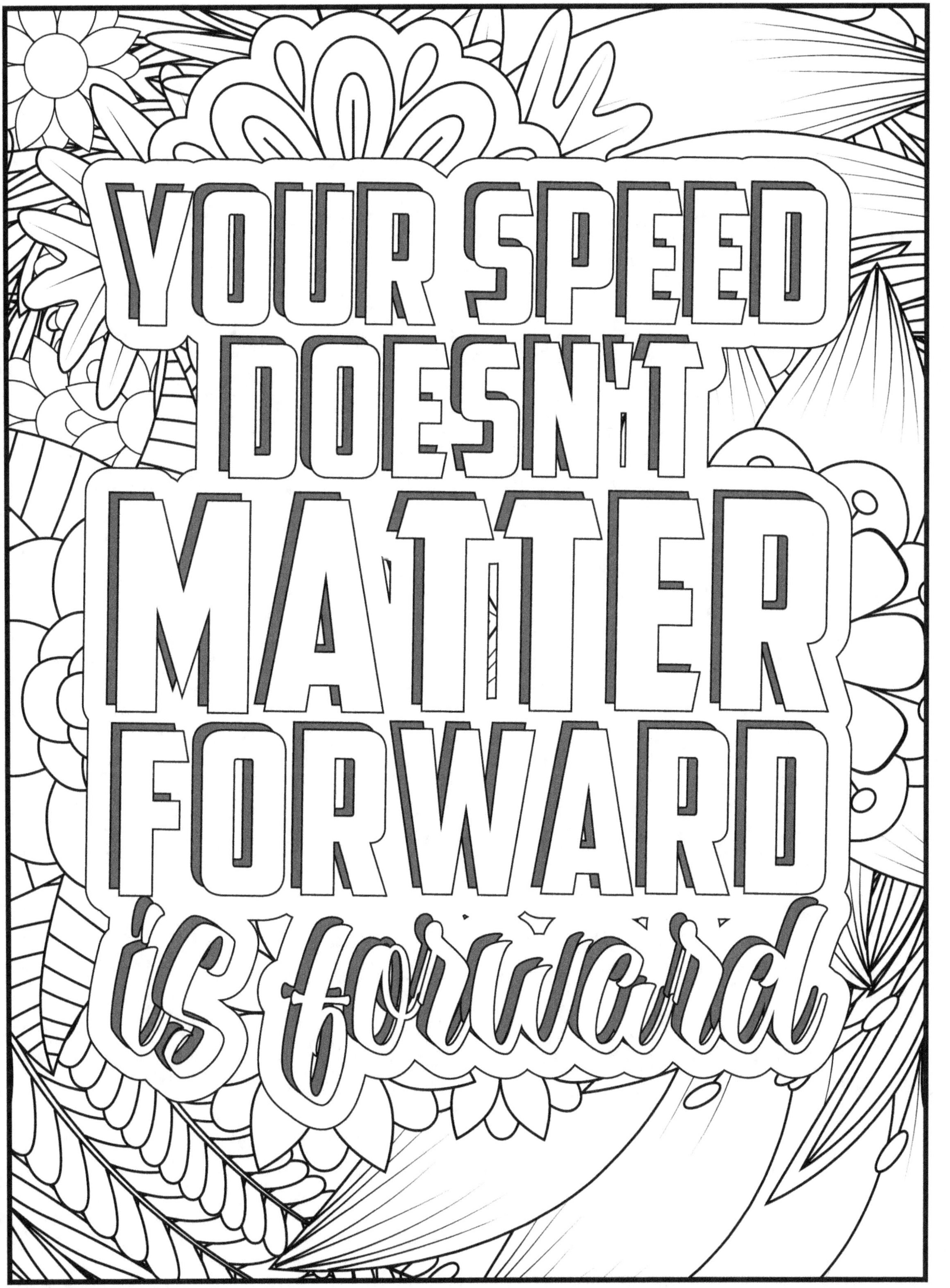
YOUR SPEED DOESN'T MATTER FORWARD is forward

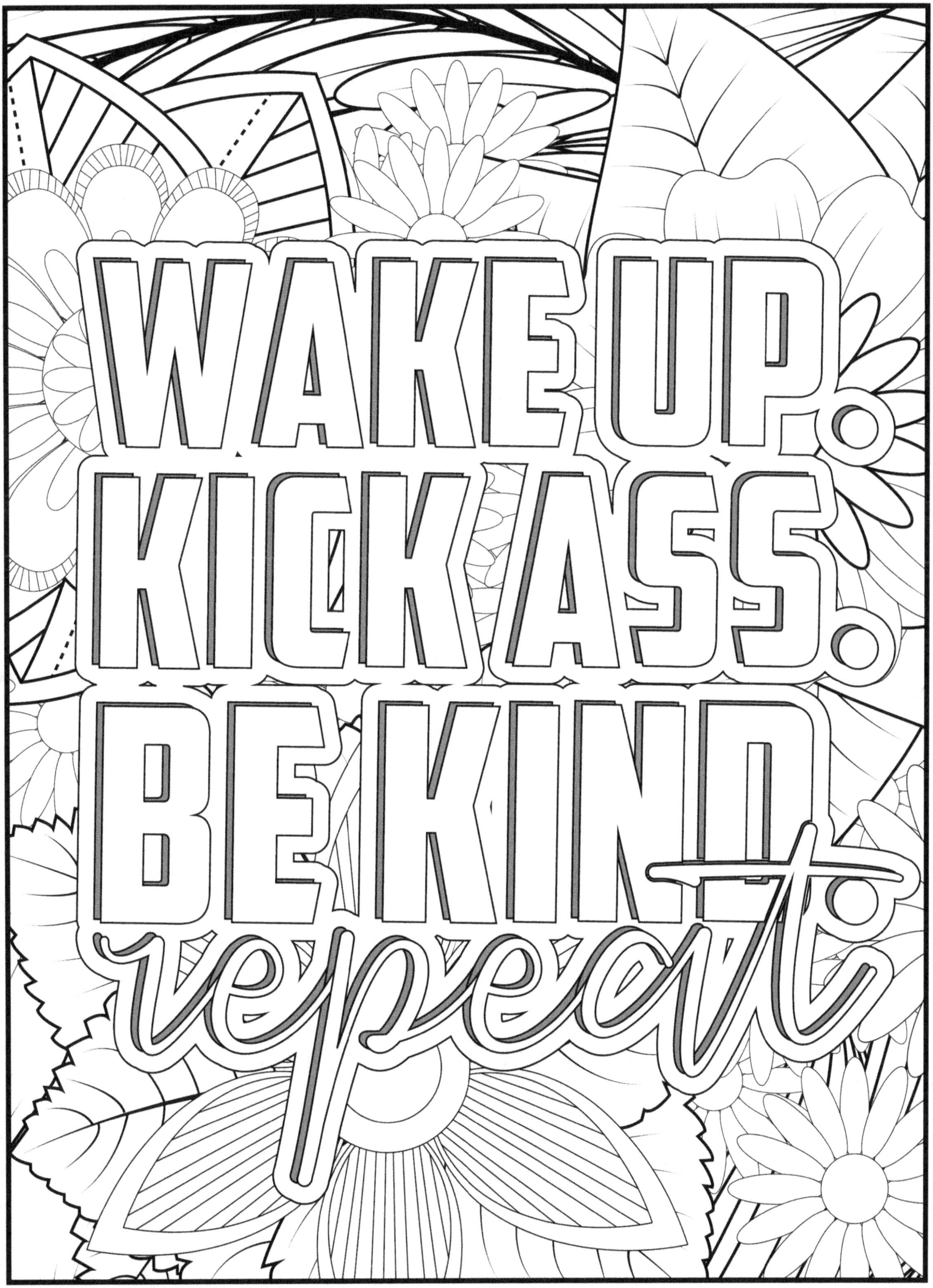
WAKE UP.
KICK ASS.
BE KIND.
repeat

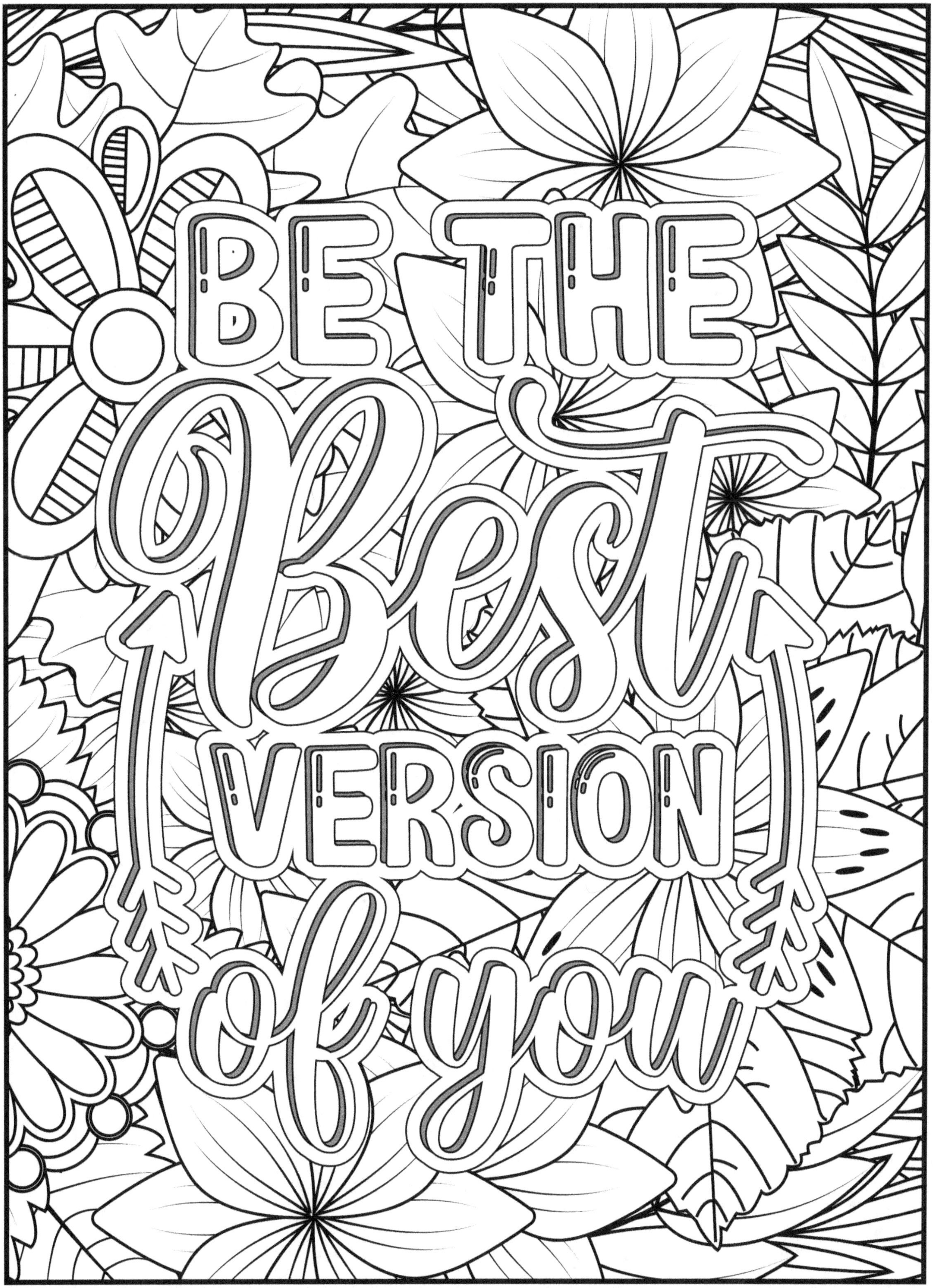
BE THE
Best
VERSION
of you

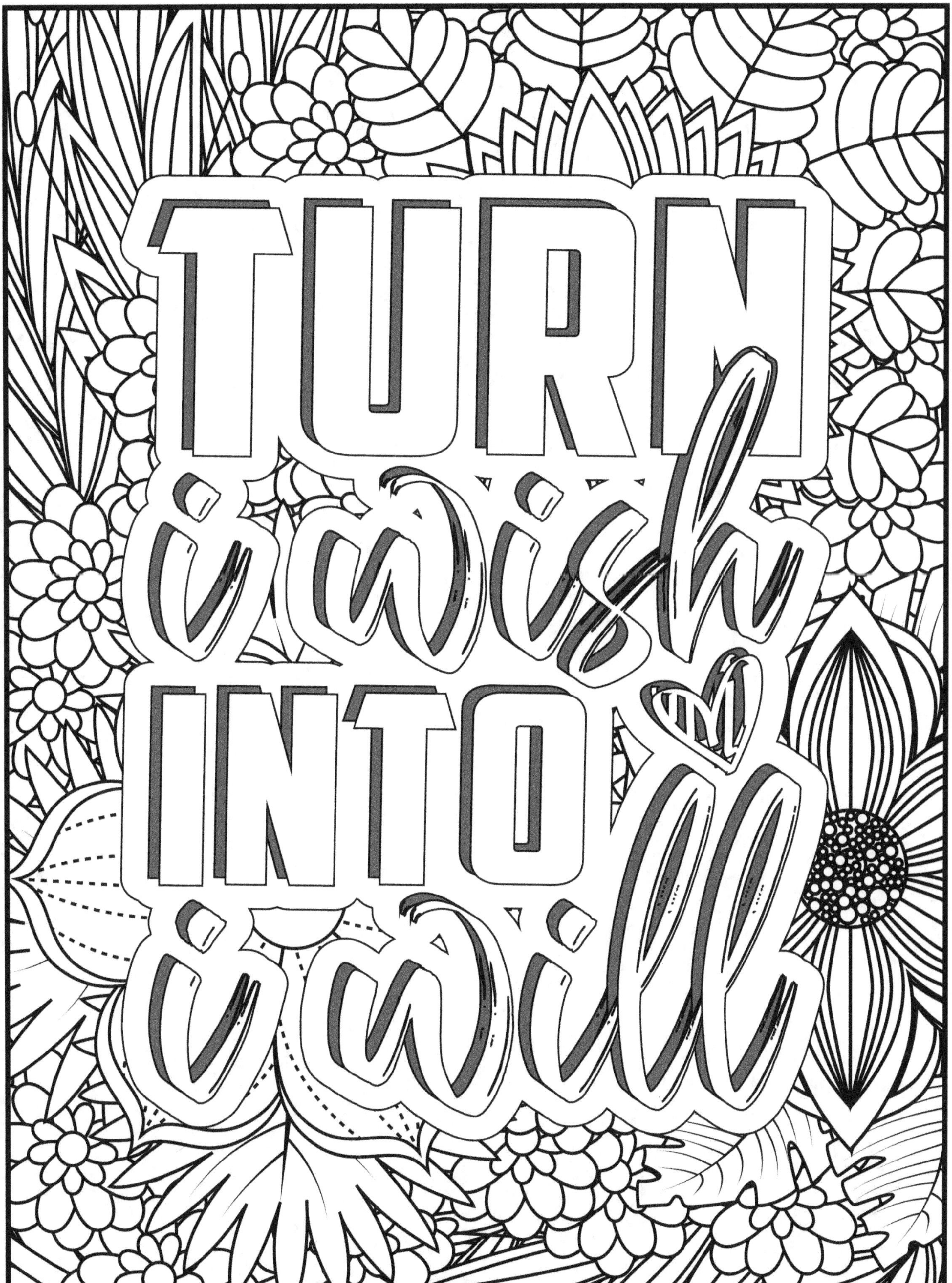
TURN
i wish
INTO
i will

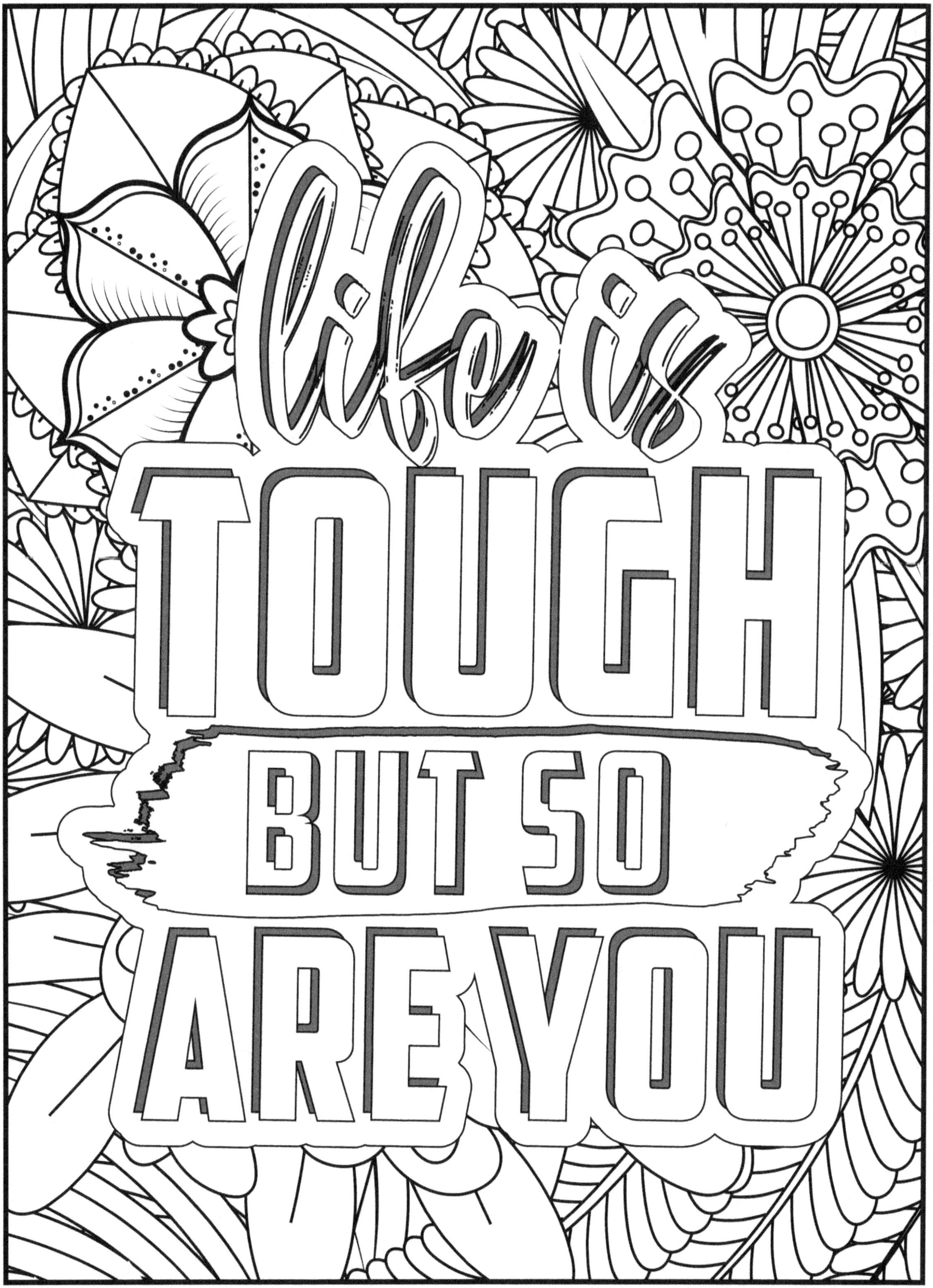
life is
TOUGH
BUT SO
ARE YOU

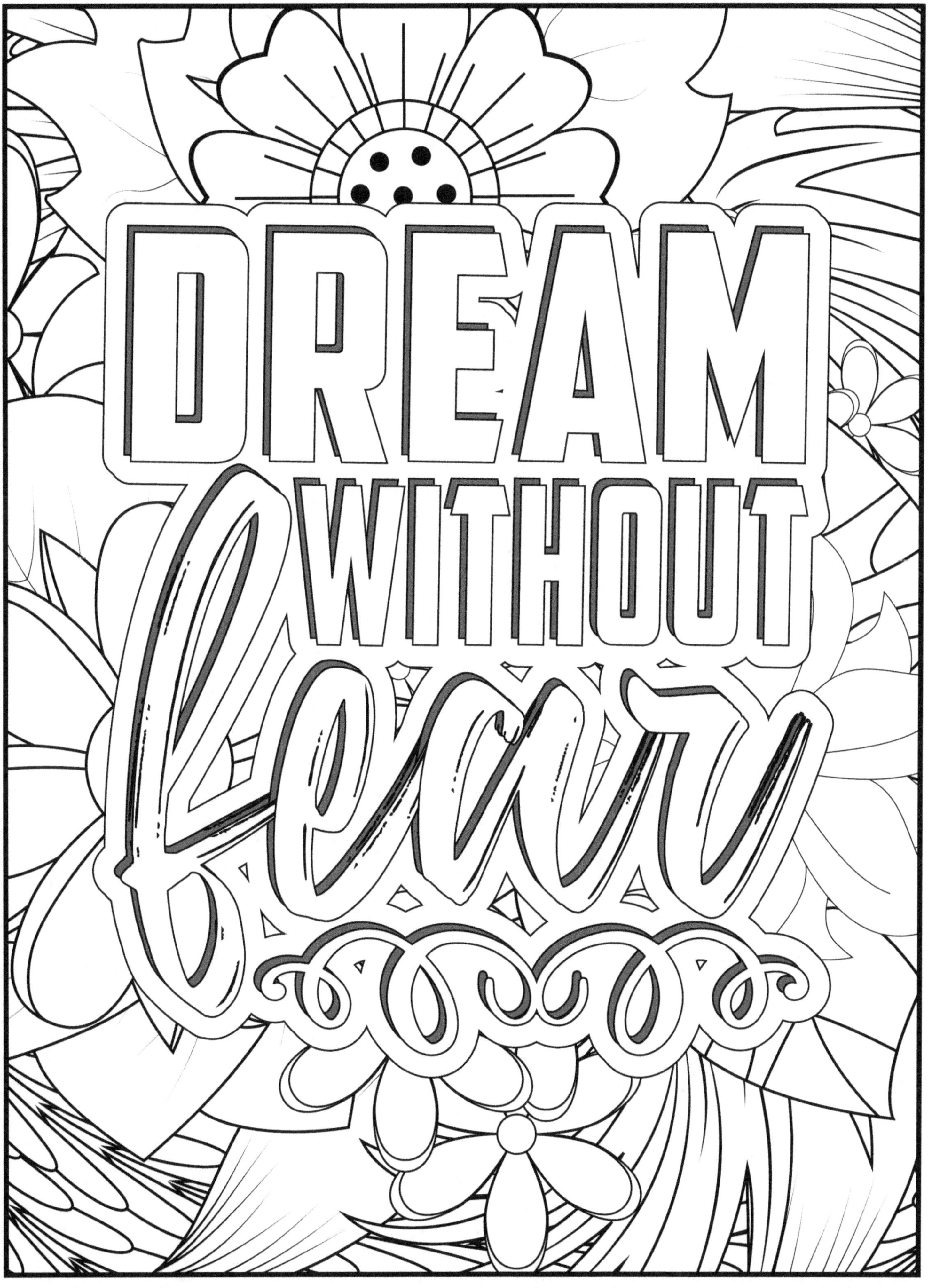
DREAM
WITHOUT
fear

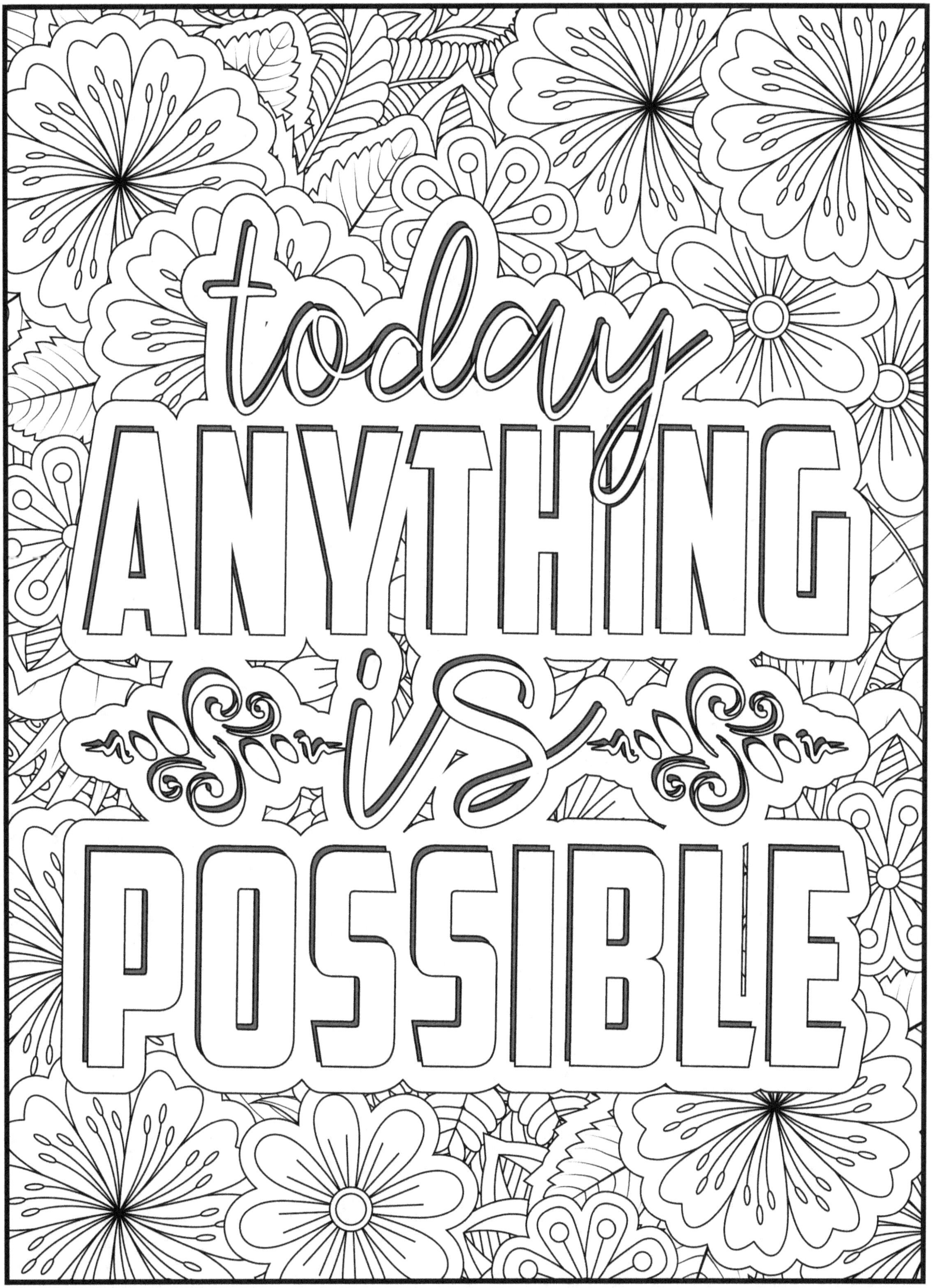
today
ANYTHING
is
POSSIBLE

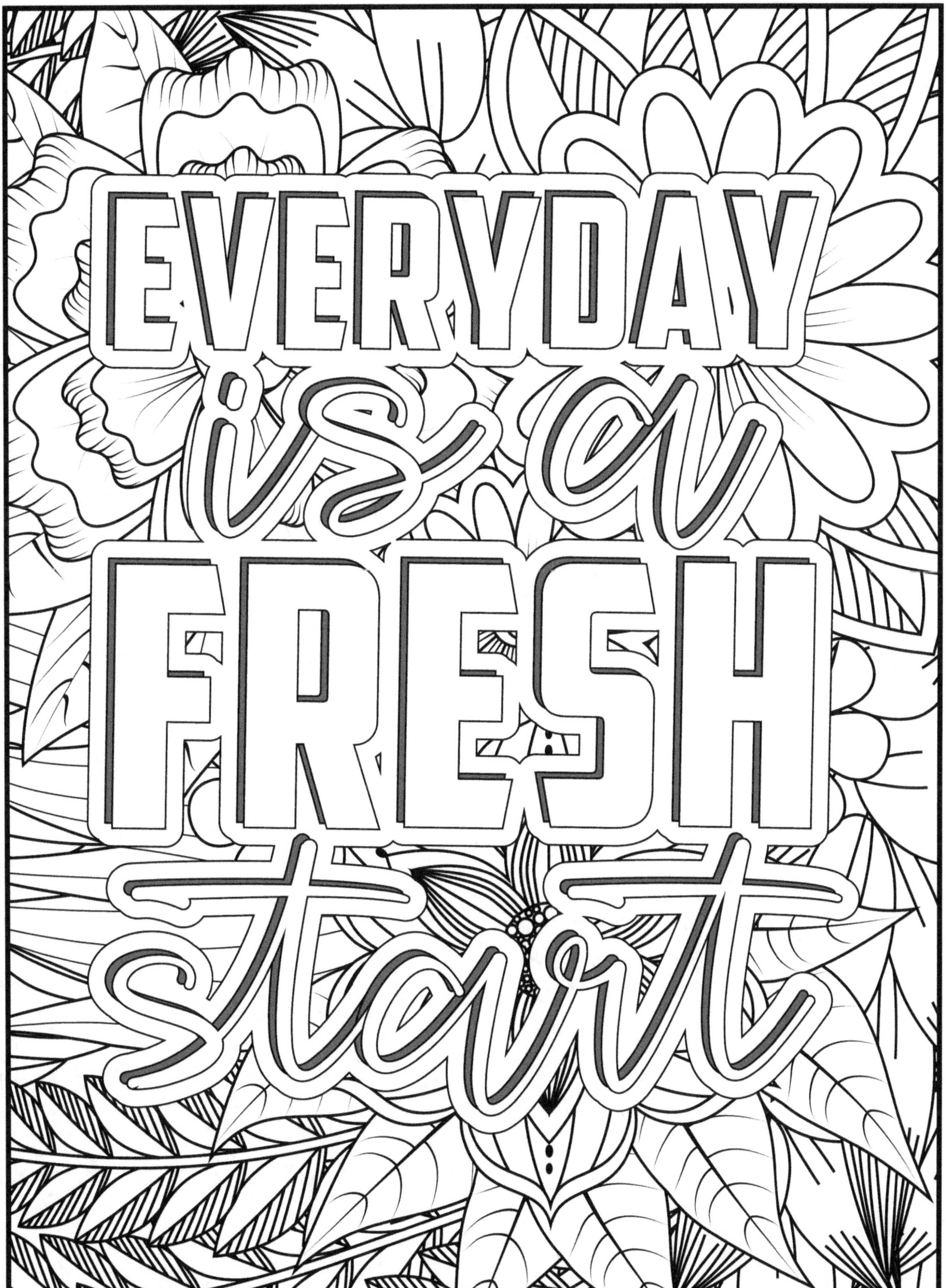
EVERYDAY
is a
FRESH
start

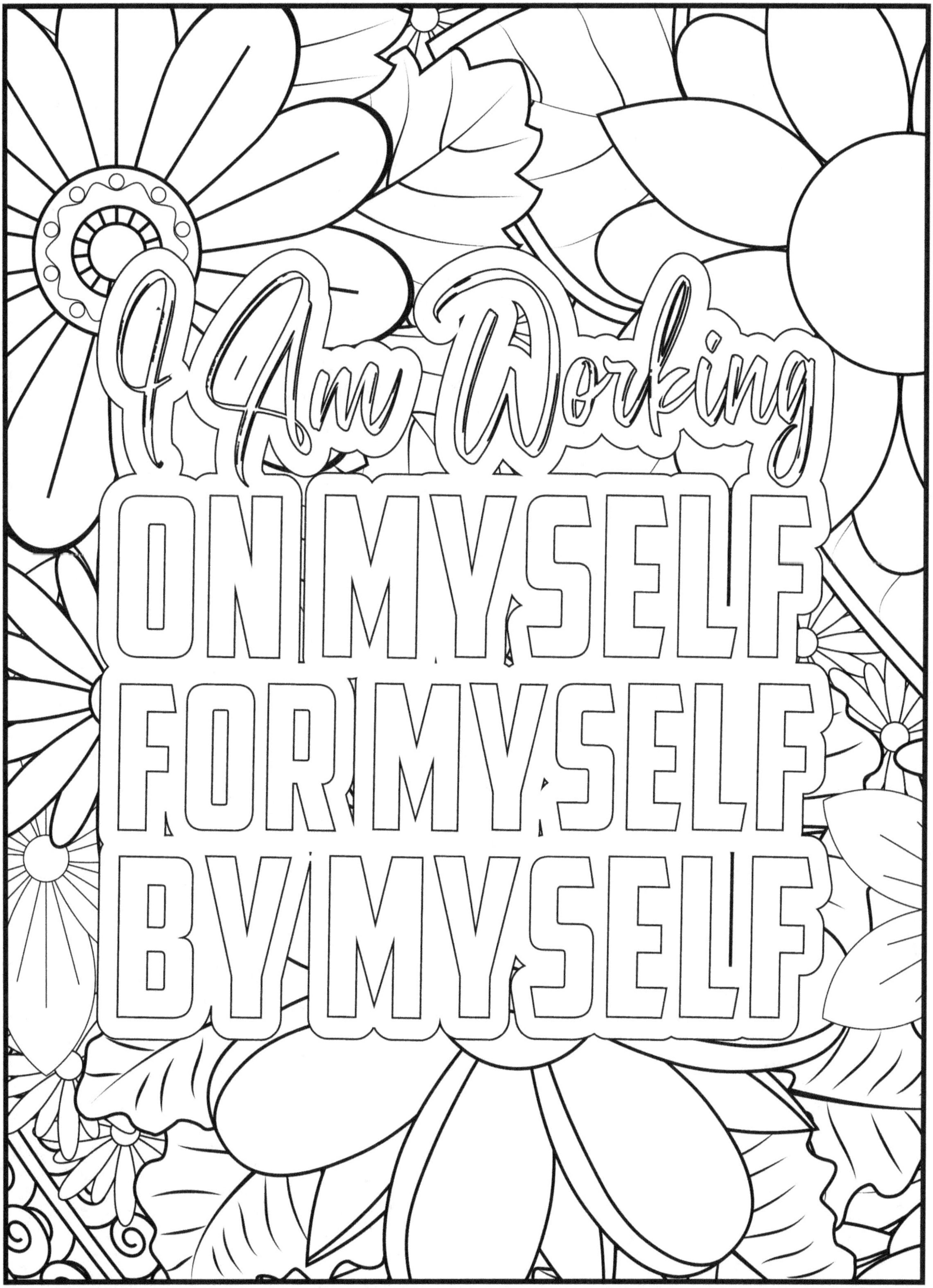
I Am Working
ON MYSELF
FOR MYSELF
BY MYSELF

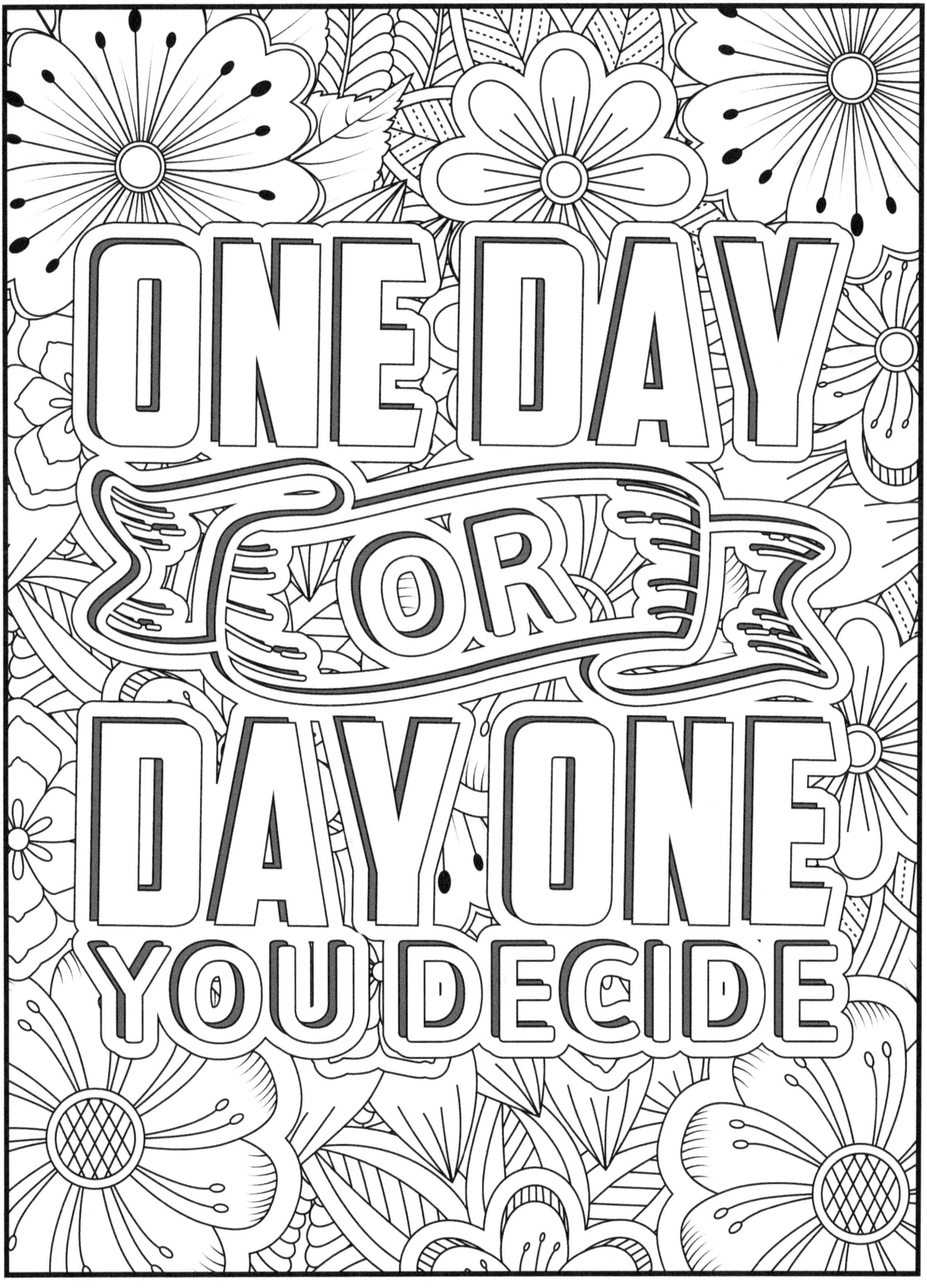
ONE DAY
OR
DAY ONE
YOU DECIDE

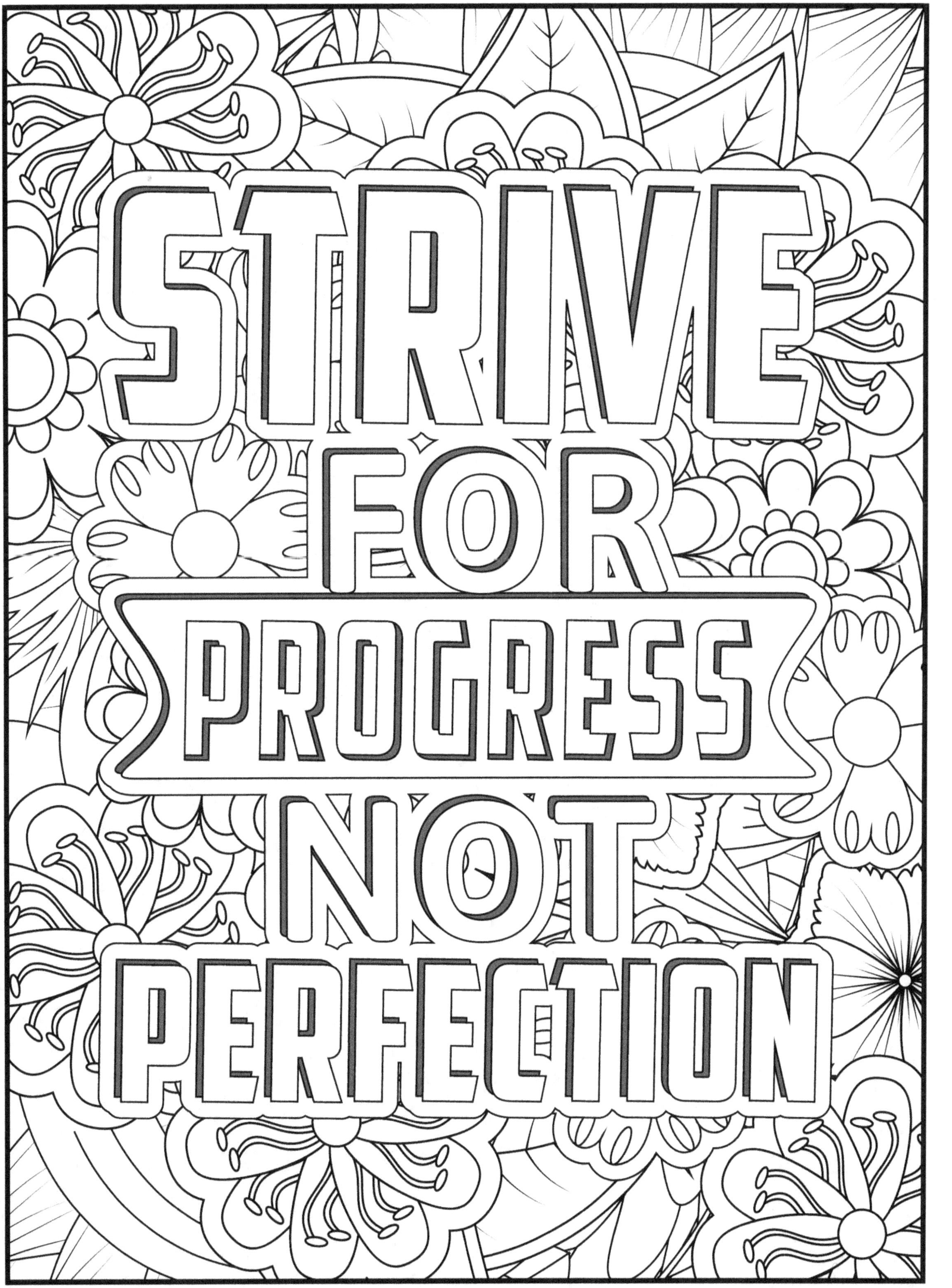
STRIVE
FOR
PROGRESS
NOT
PERFECTION

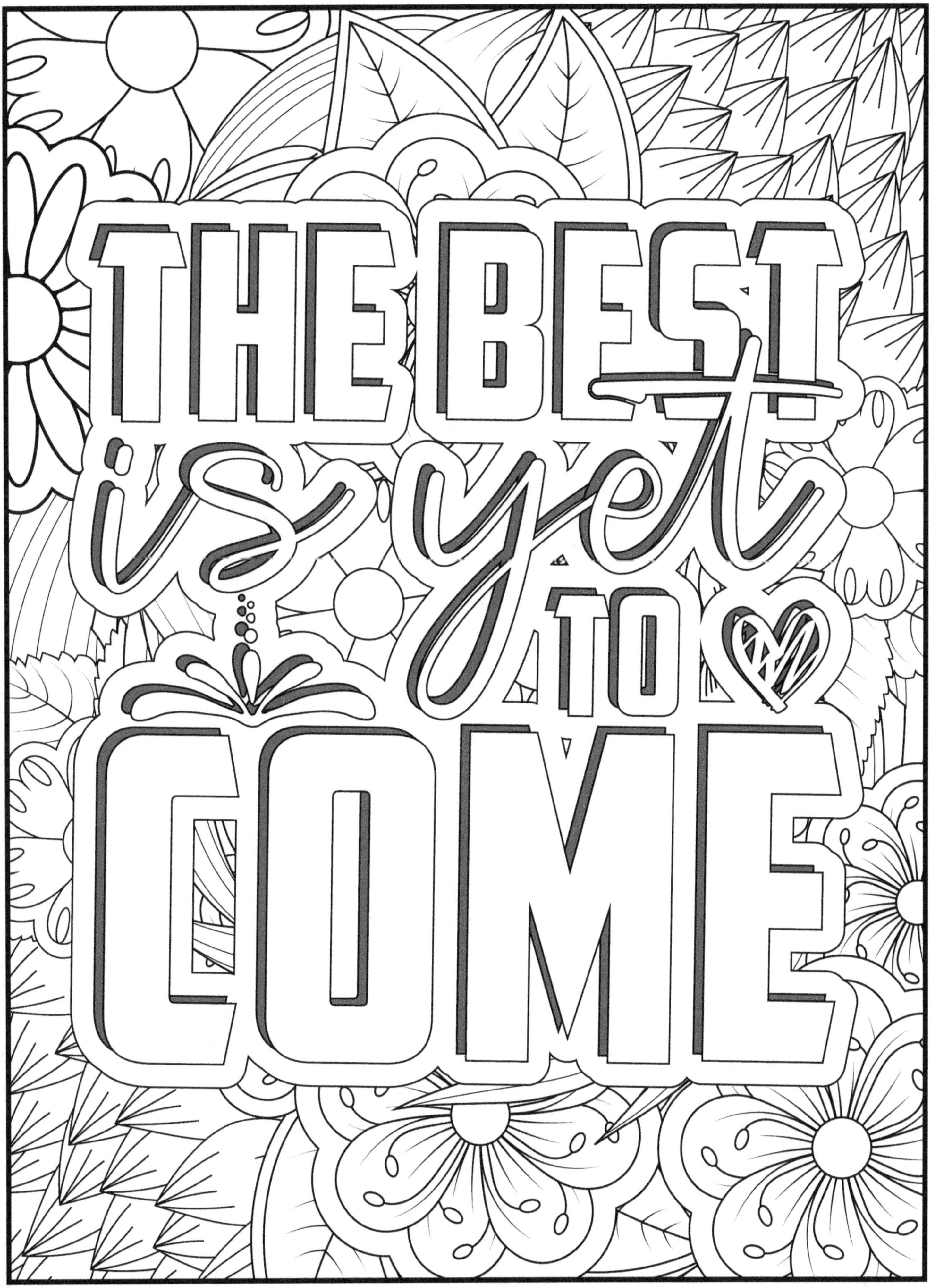
THE BEST
is yet
TO
COME

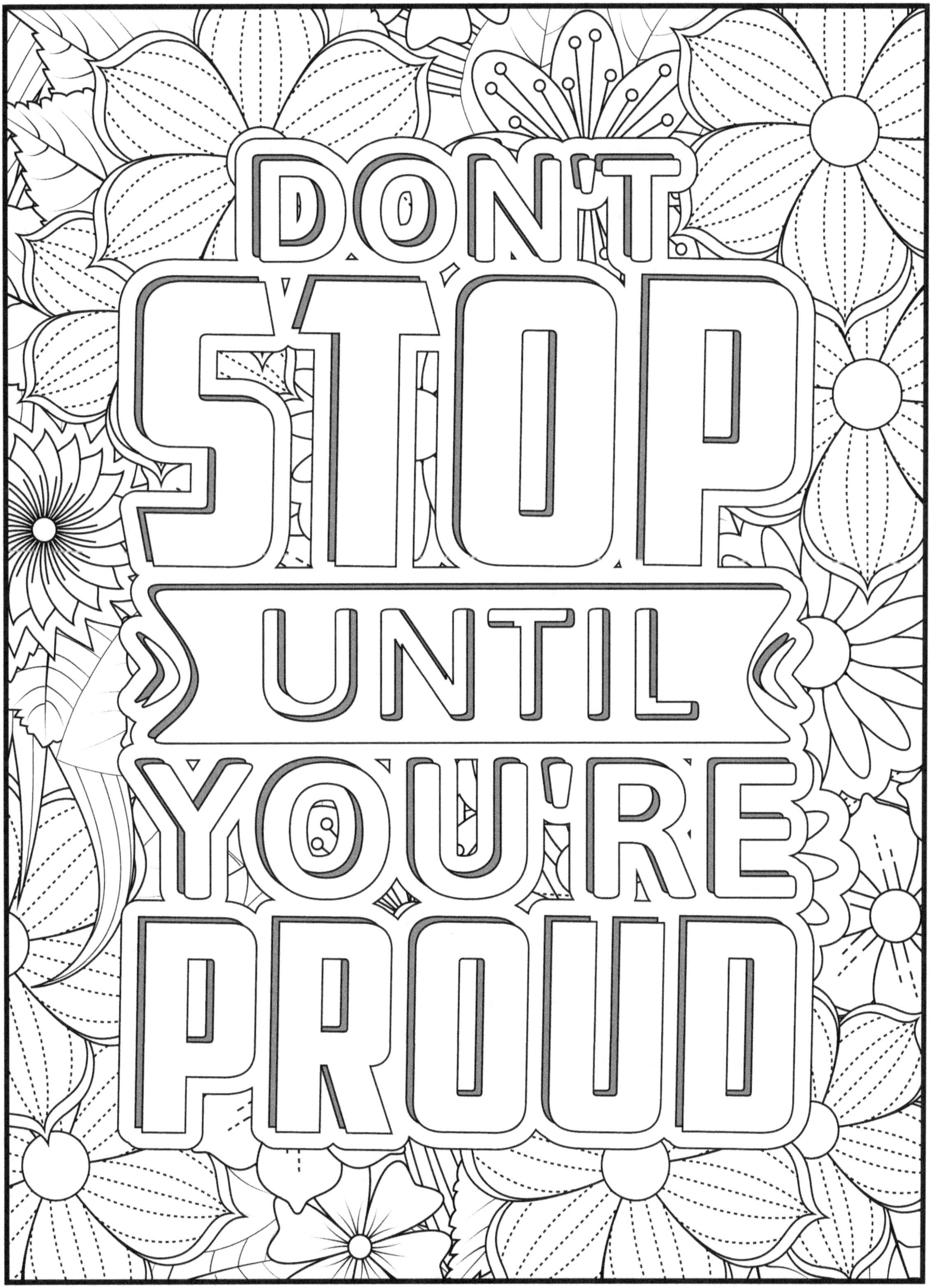
DON'T
STOP
UNTIL
YOU'RE
PROUD

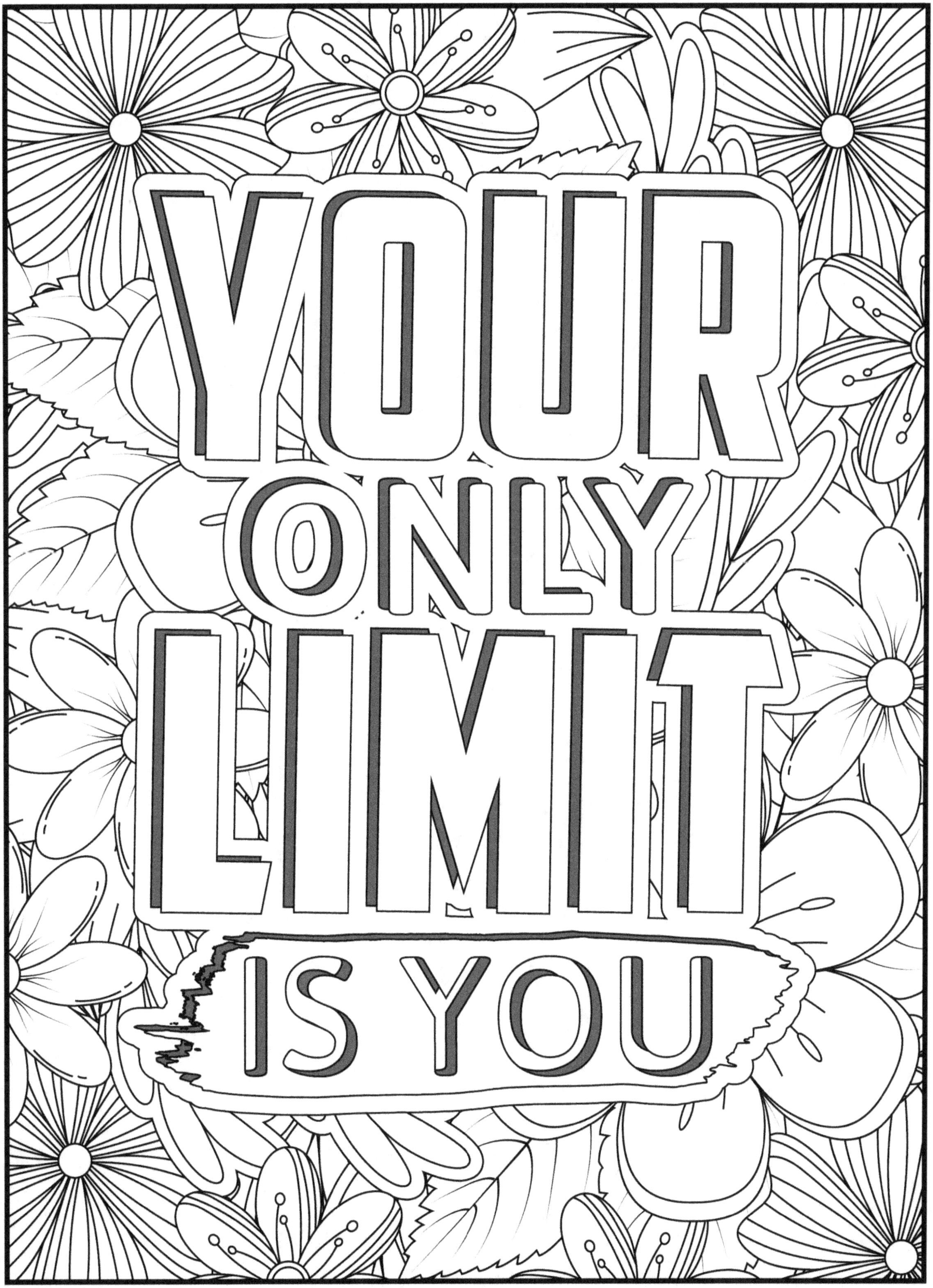
YOUR ONLY LIMIT
IS YOU

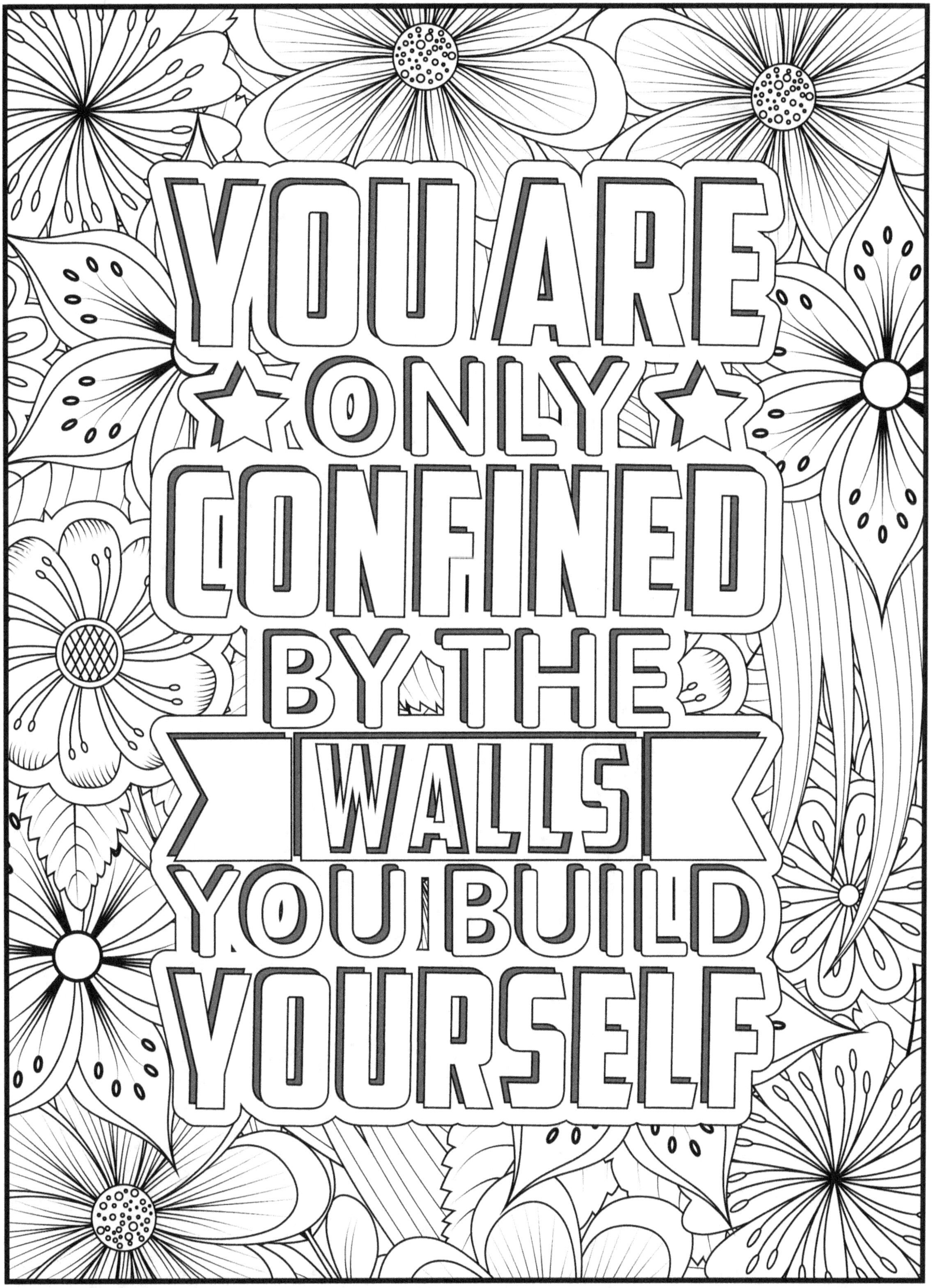
YOU ARE
ONLY
CONFINED
BY THE
WALLS
YOU BUILD
YOURSELF

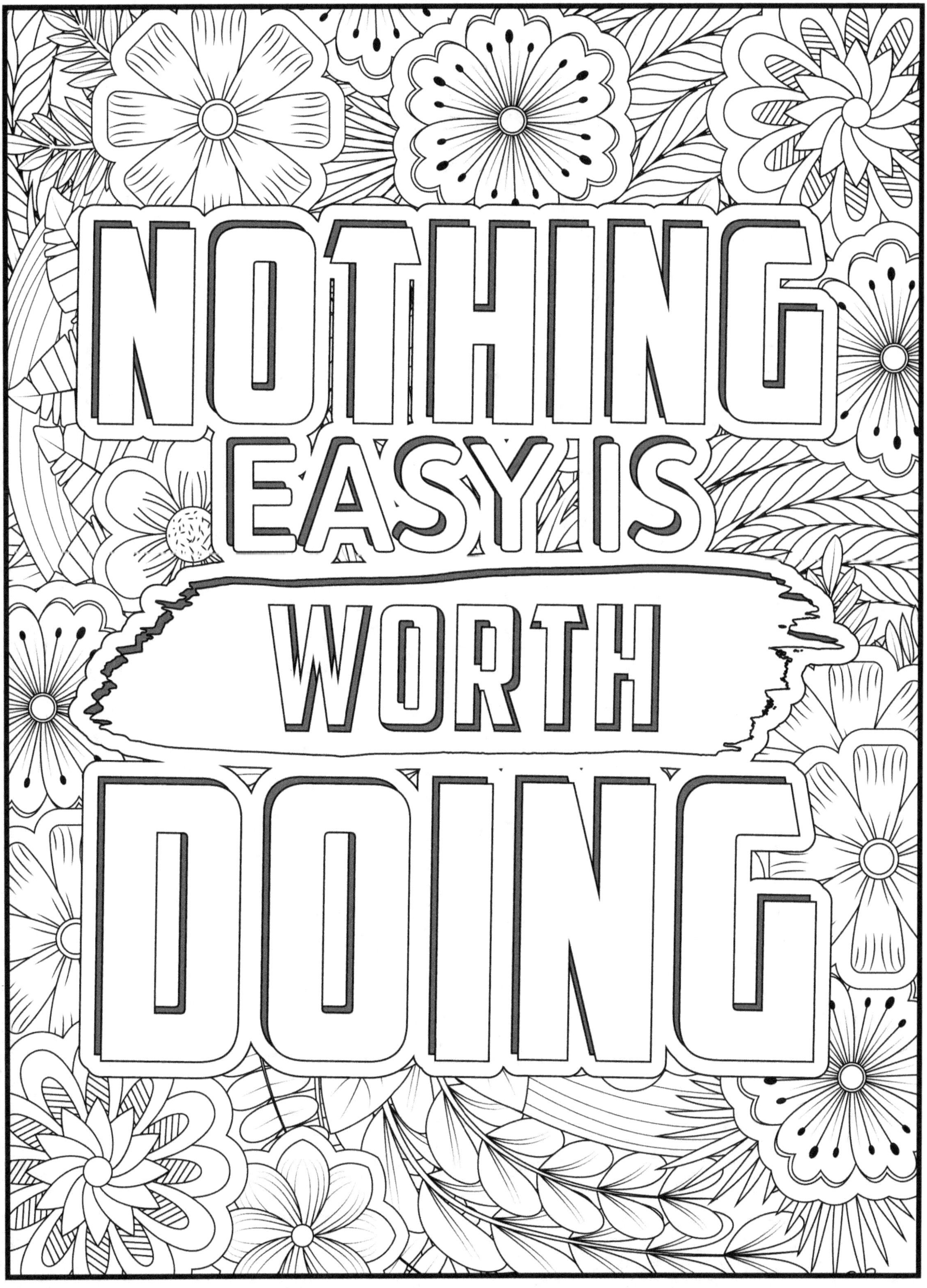
NOTHING
EASY IS
WORTH
DOING

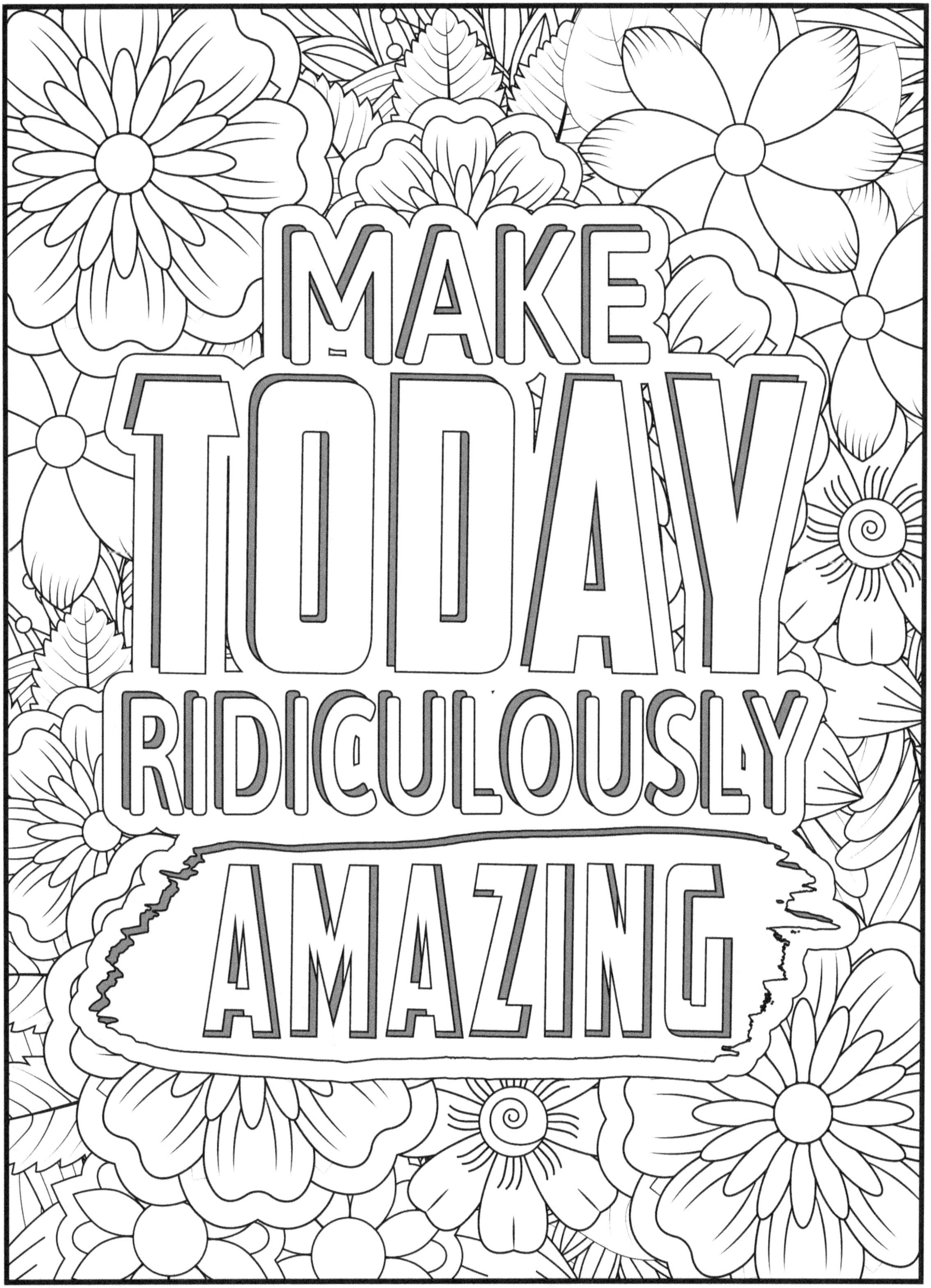
MAKE
TODAY
RIDICULOUSLY
AMAZING

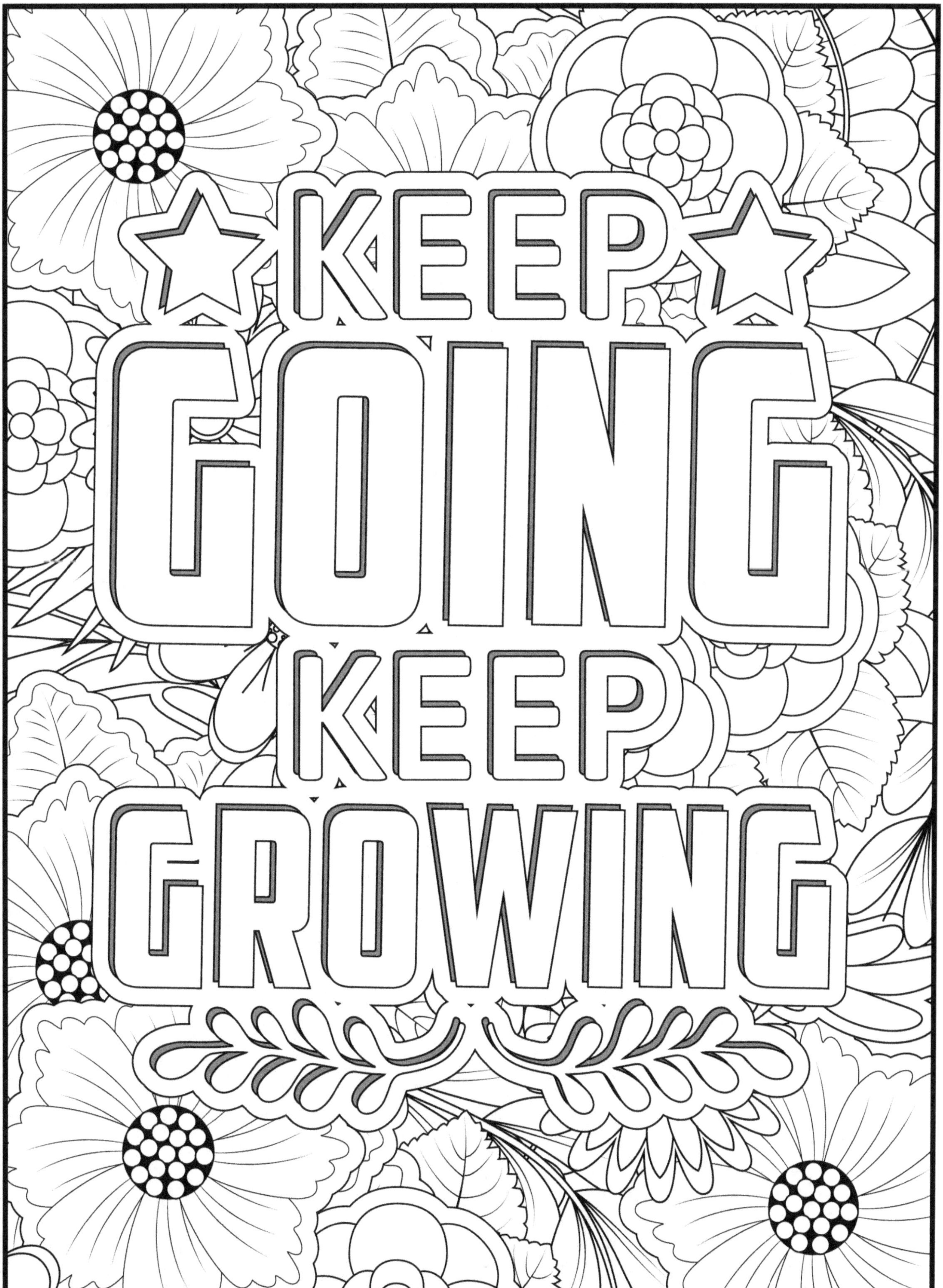
KEEP
GOING
KEEP
GROWING

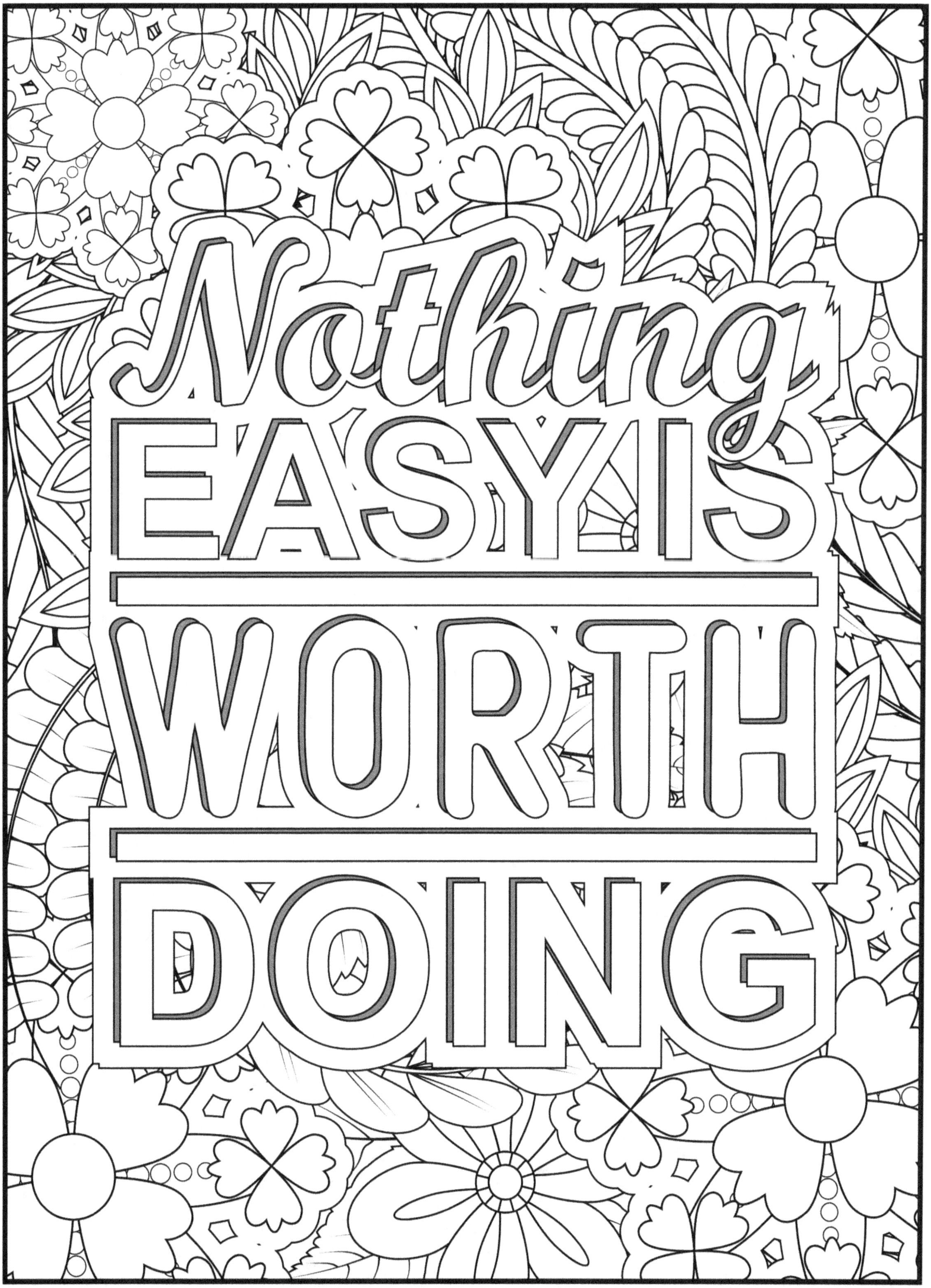
Nothing
EASY IS
WORTH
DOING

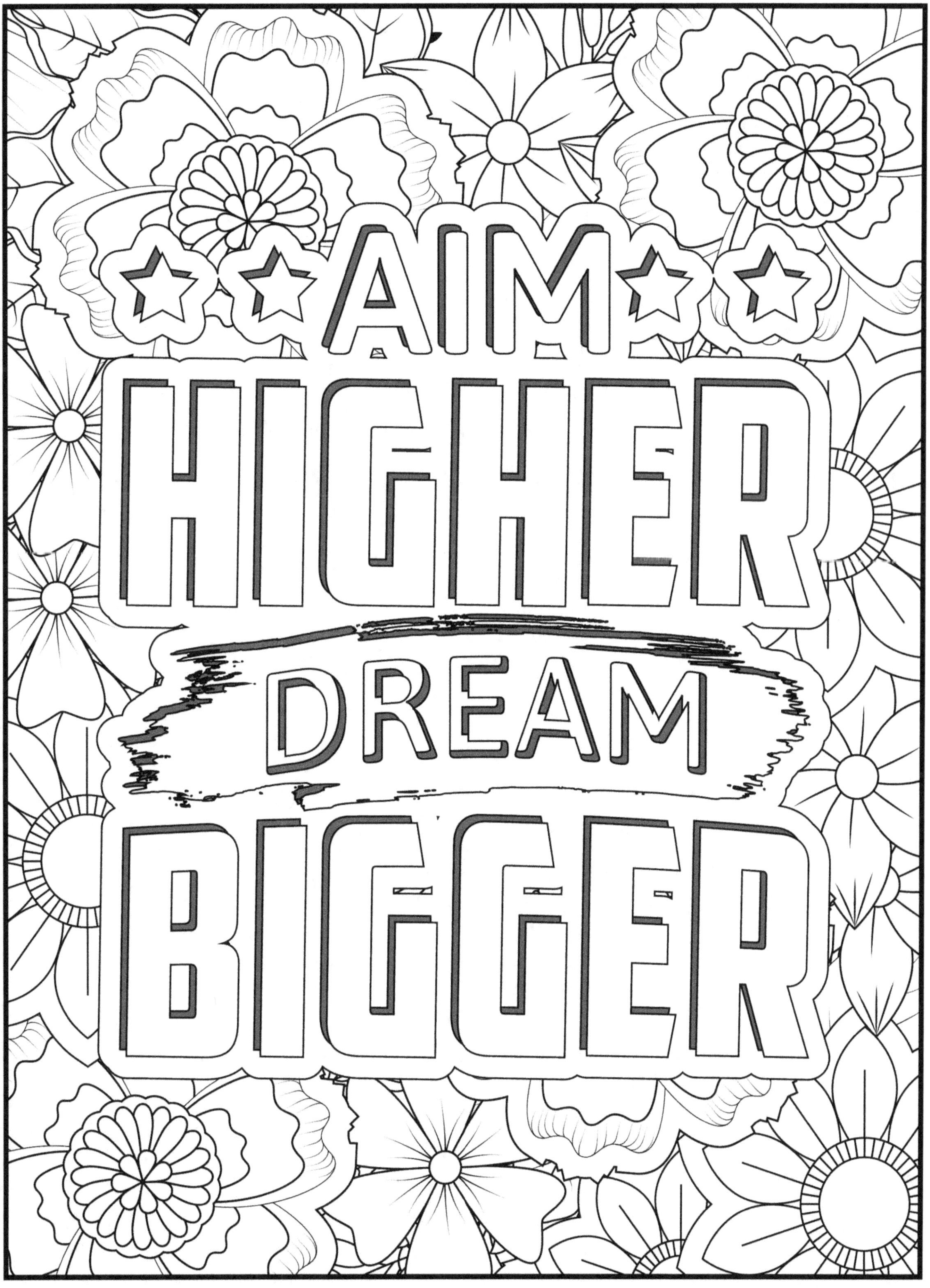
AIM
HIGHER
DREAM
BIGGER

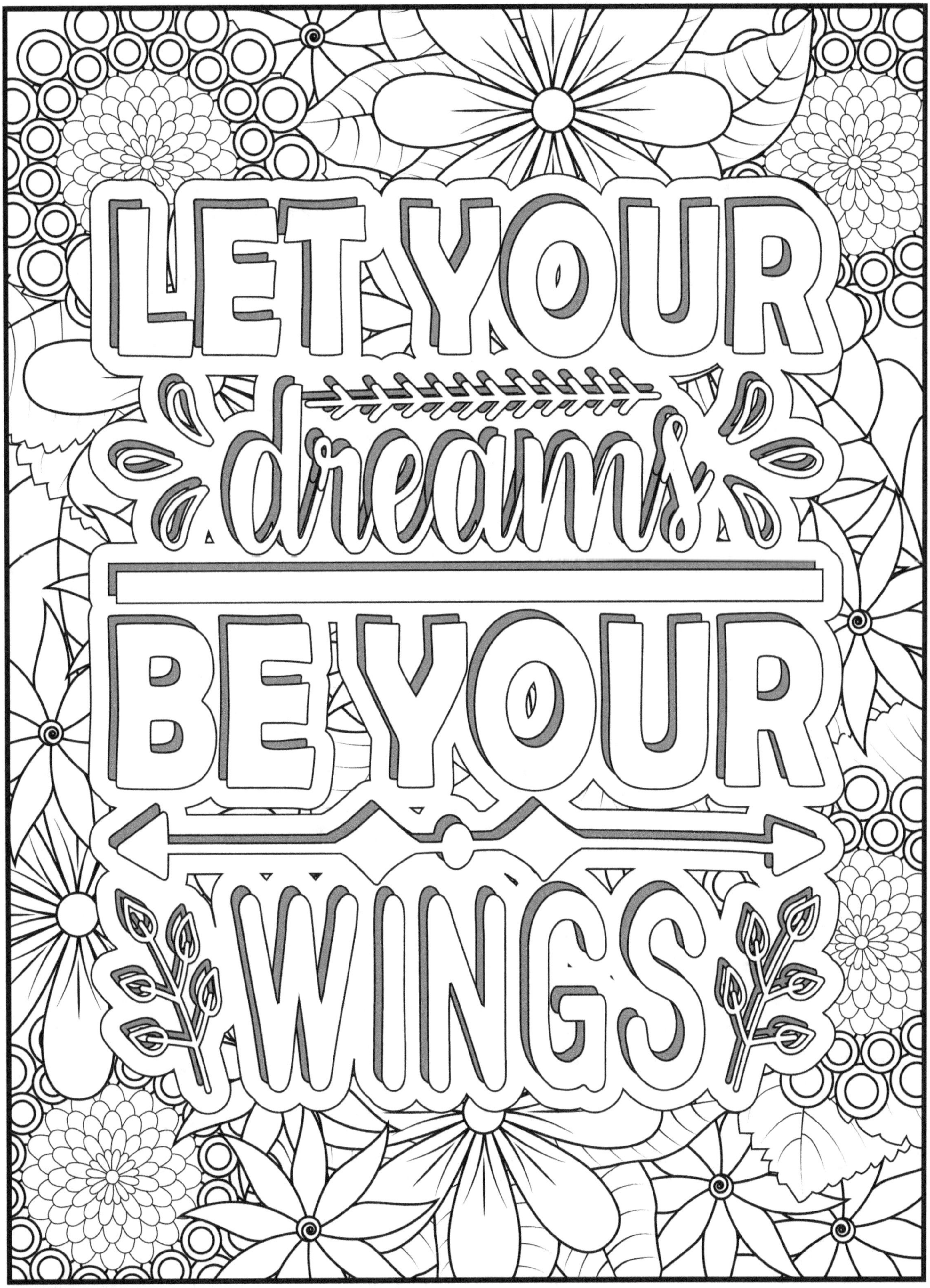
LET YOUR
dreams
BE YOUR
WINGS

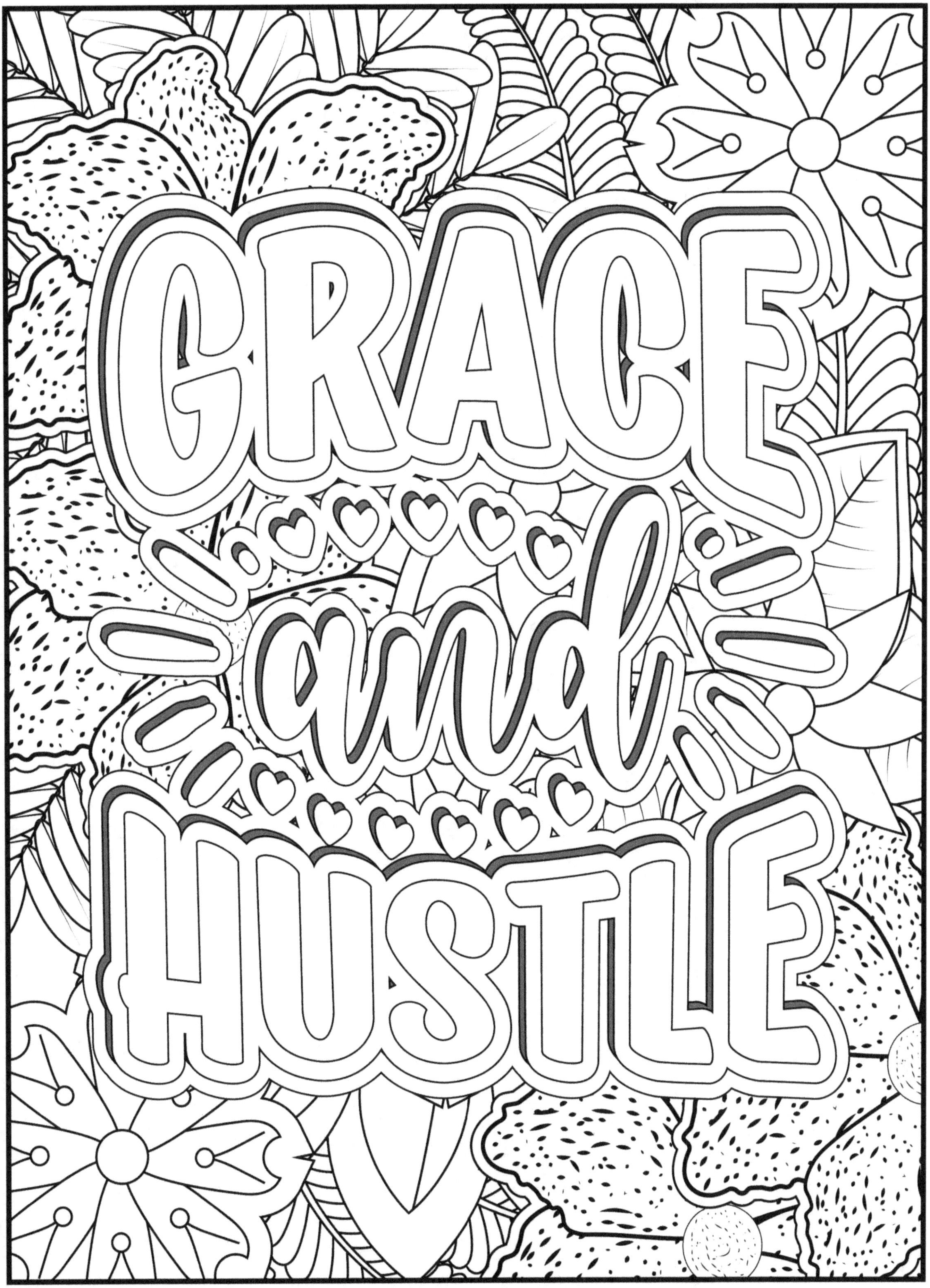
GRACE
and
HUSTLE

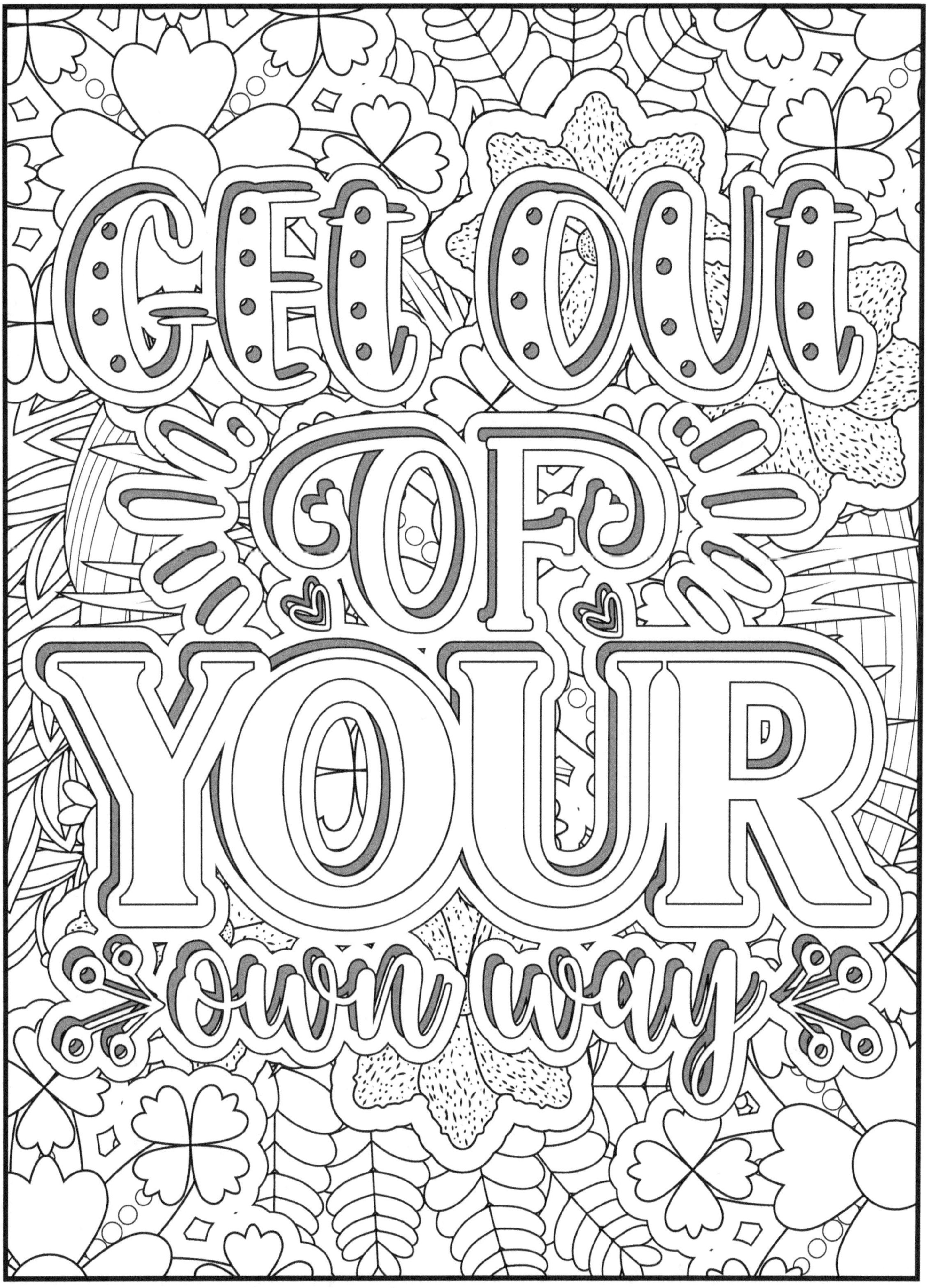
GET OUT
OF
YOUR
own way

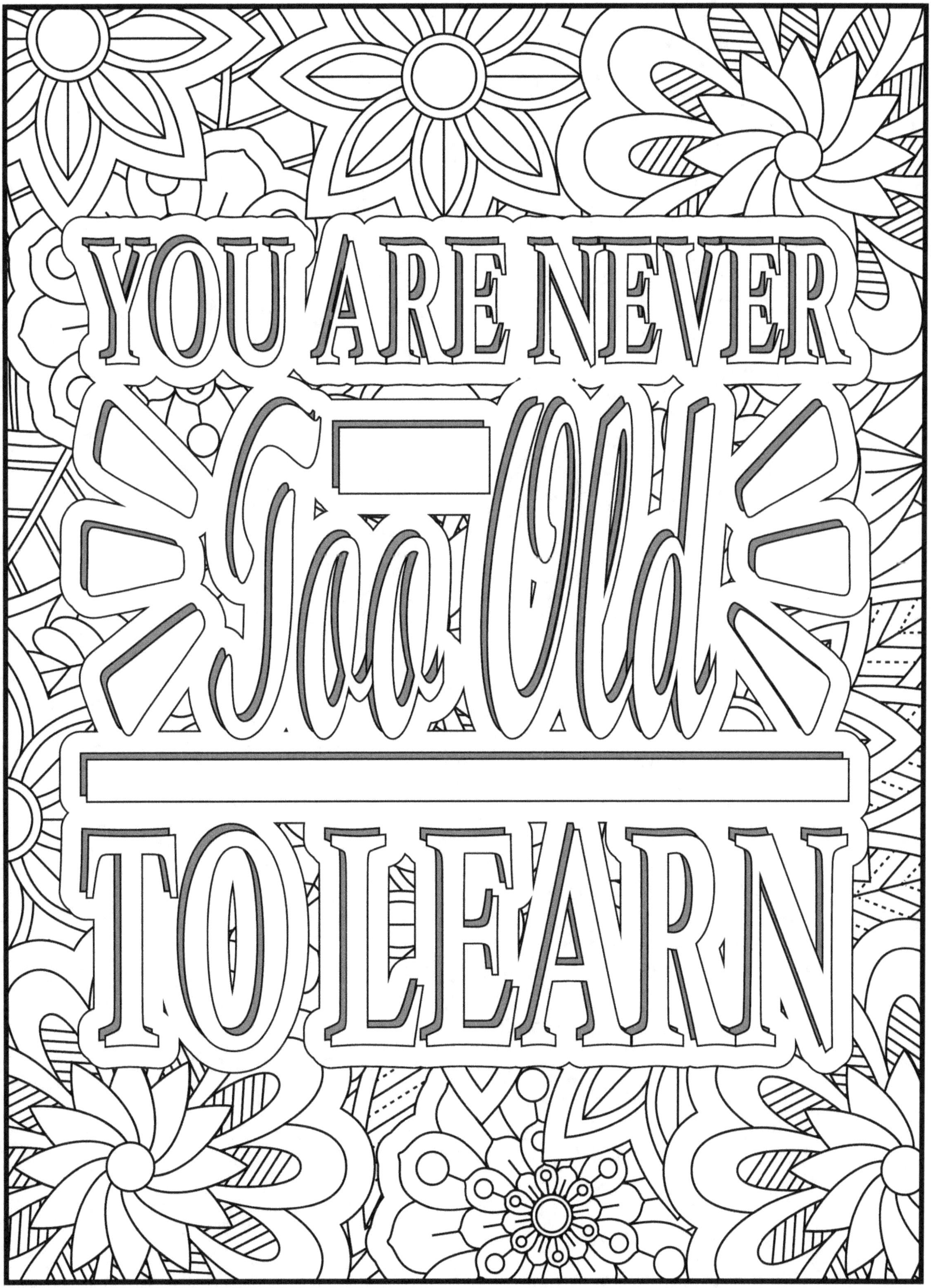
YOU ARE NEVER
Too Old
TO LEARN

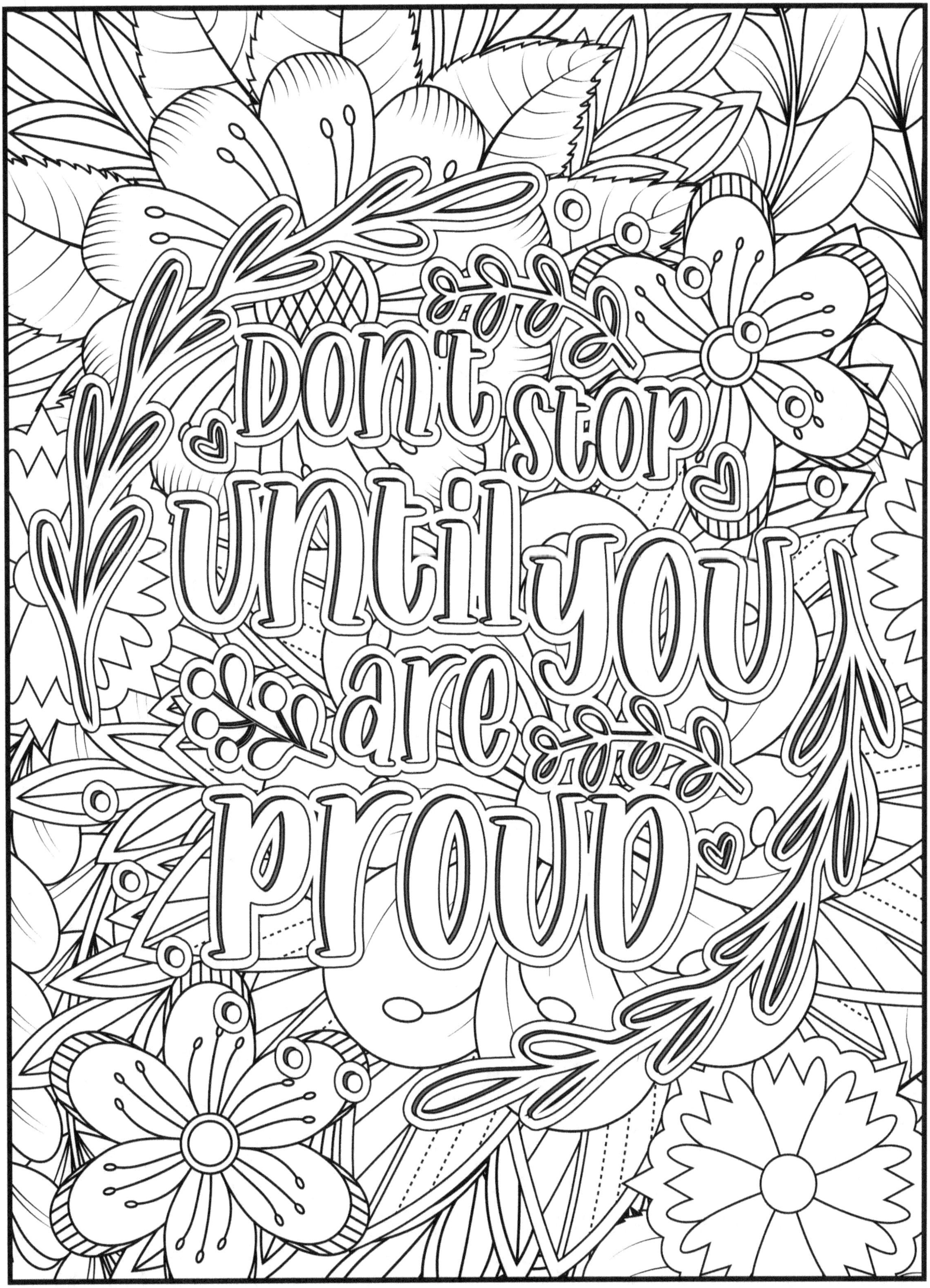
Don't stop
until you
are
proud

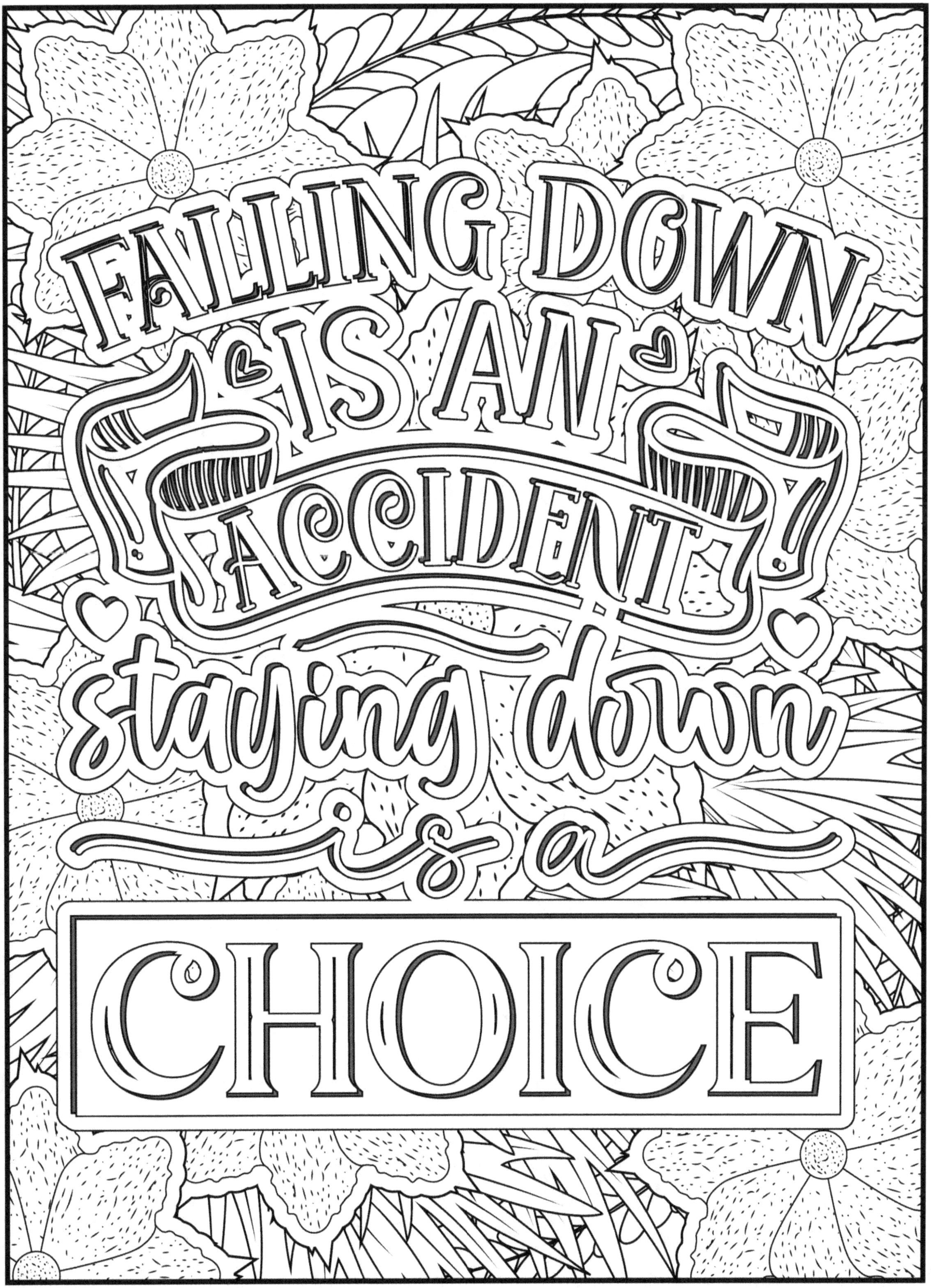
FALLING DOWN
IS AN
ACCIDENT
staying down
is a
CHOICE

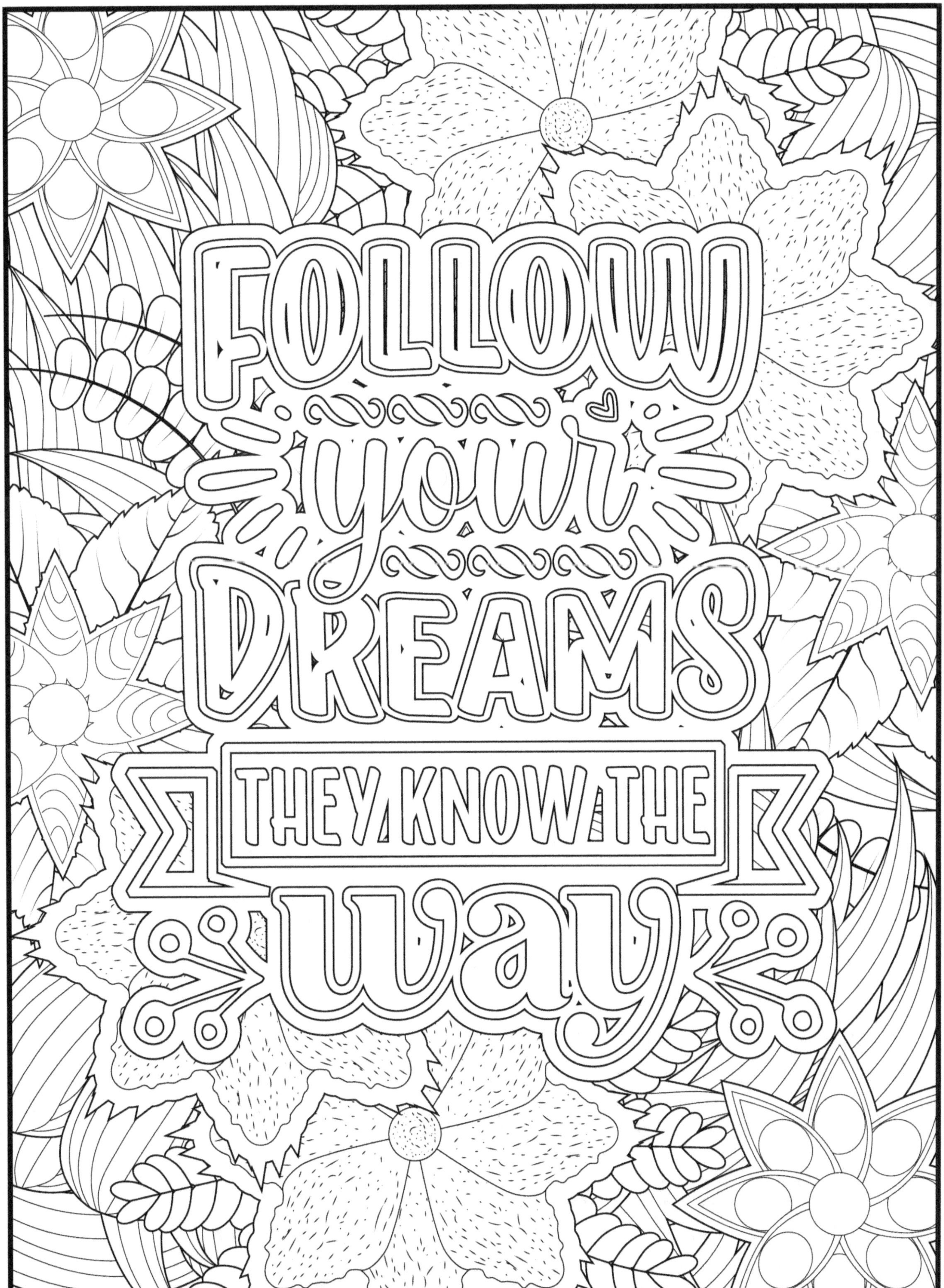
FOLLOW
your
DREAMS
THEY KNOW THE
way

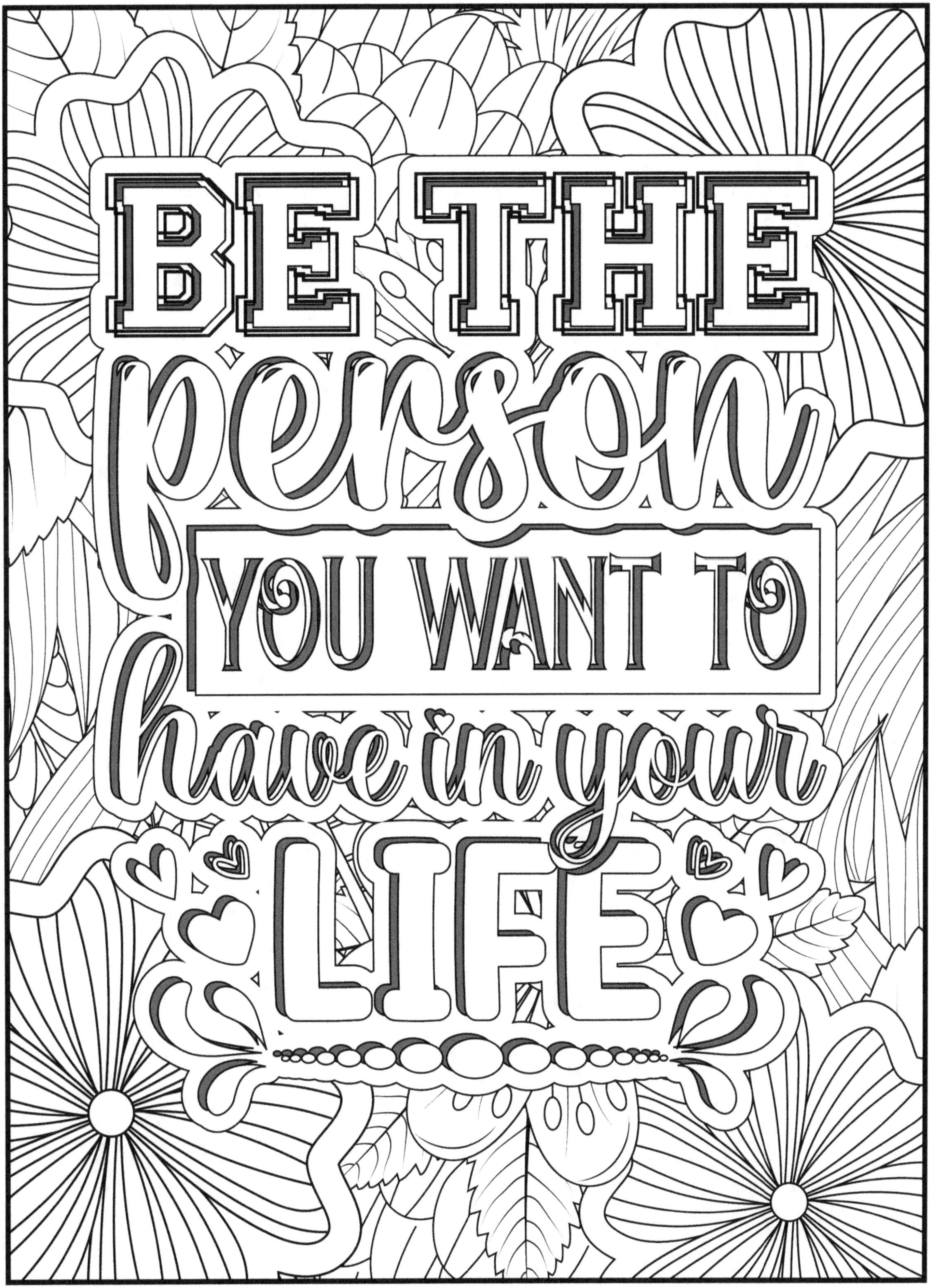
BE THE
person
YOU WANT TO
have in your
LIFE

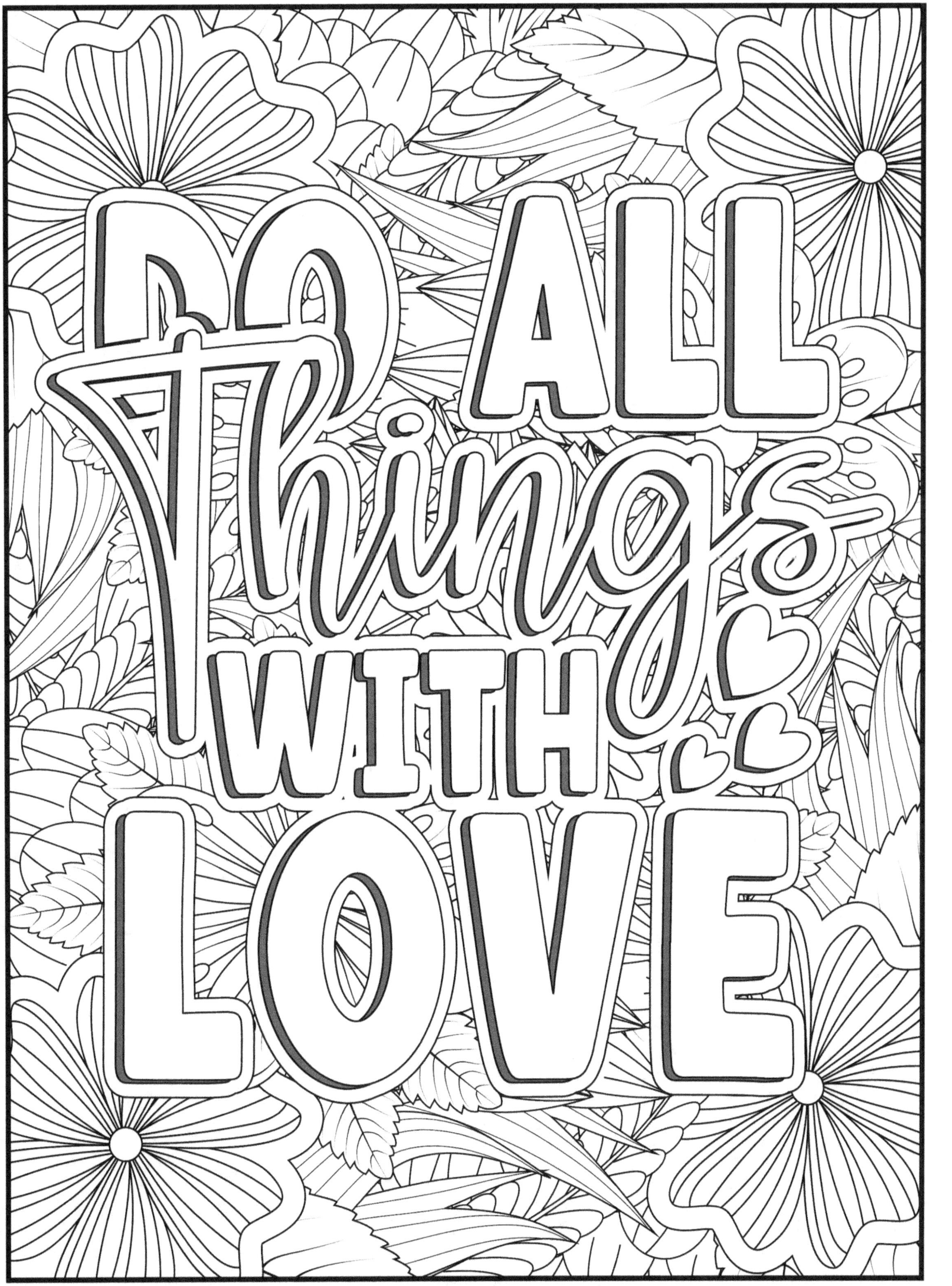
DO ALL
Things
WITH
LOVE

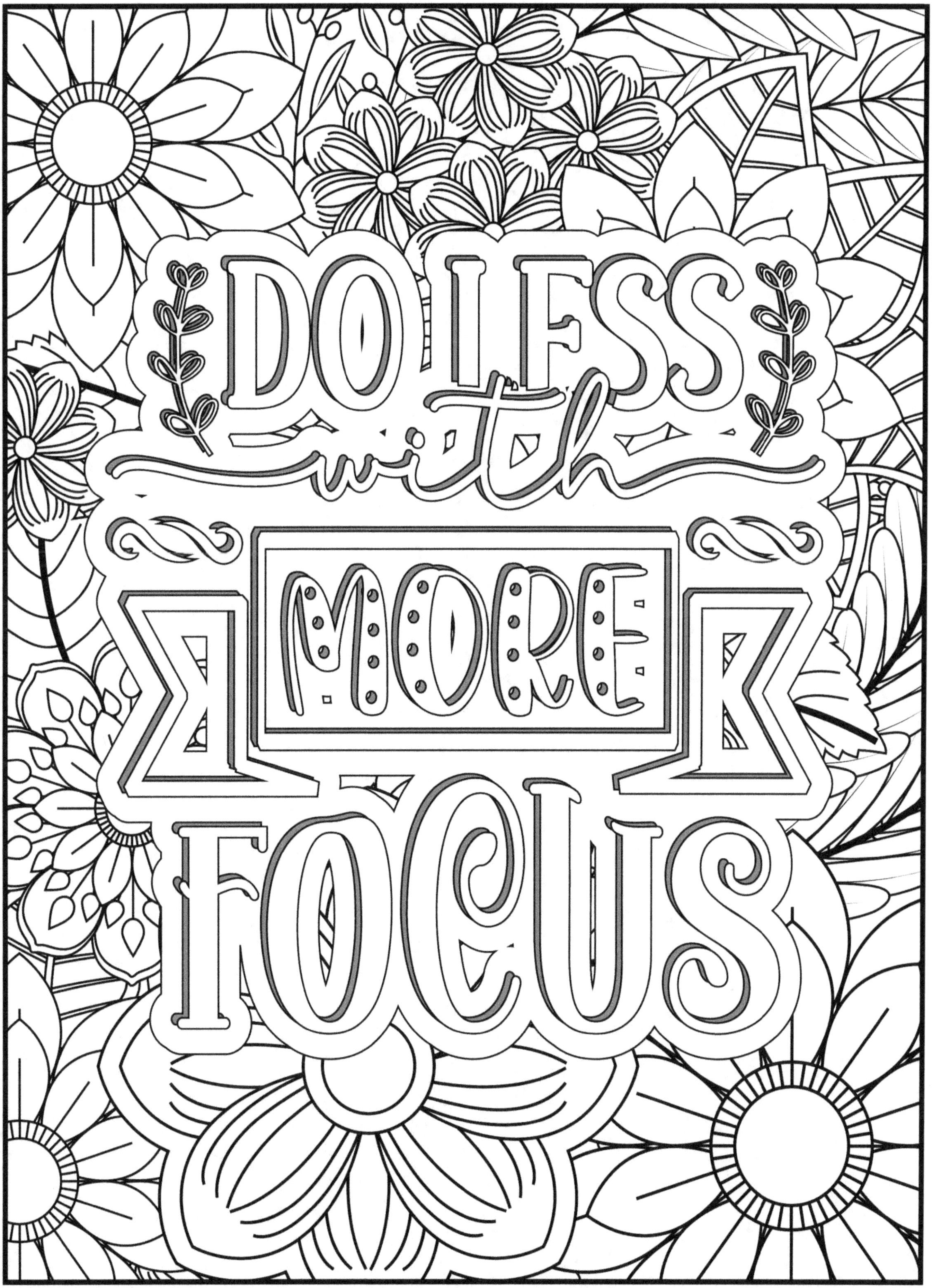
DO LESS
with
MORE
FOCUS

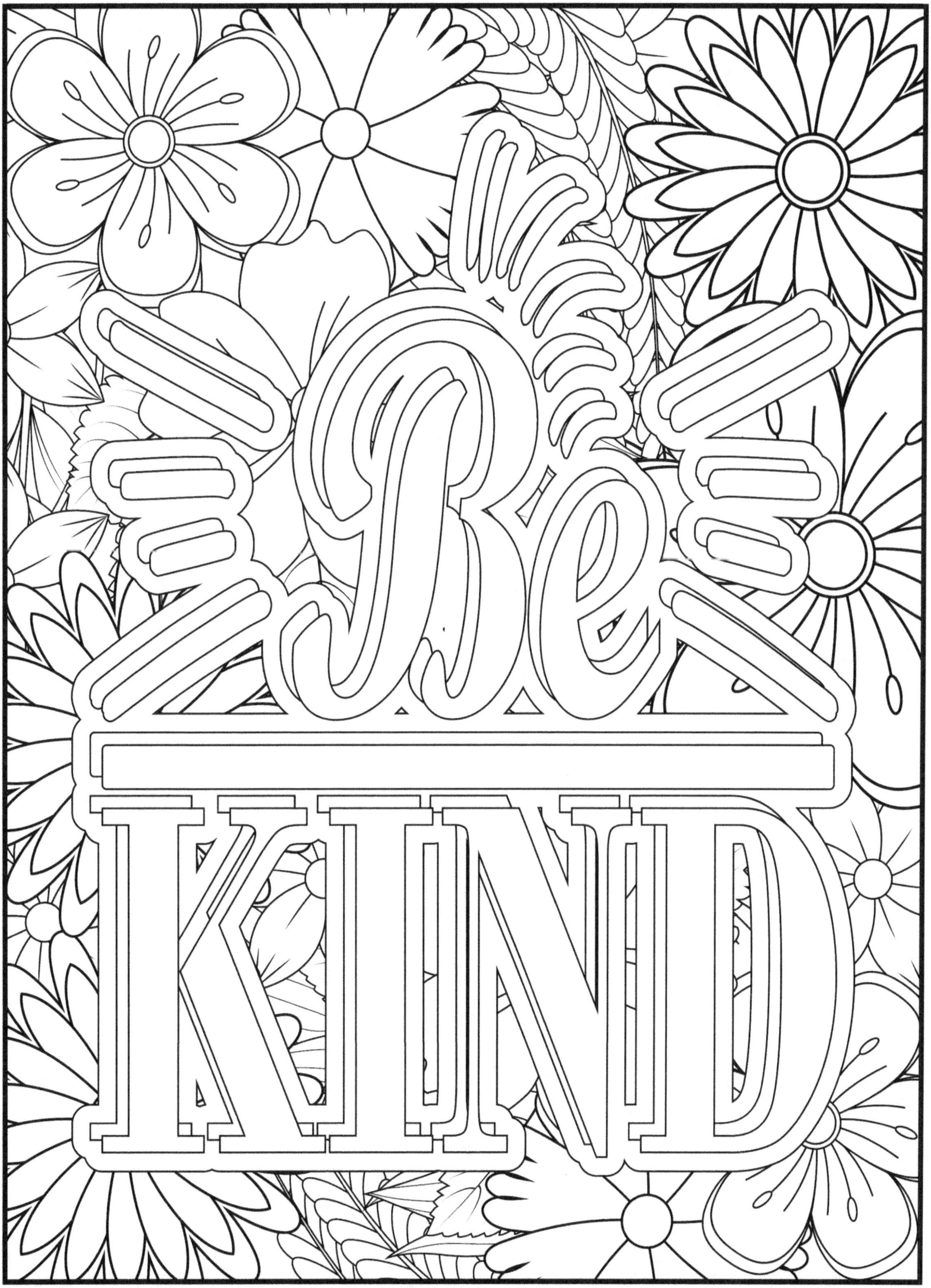
Be
KIND

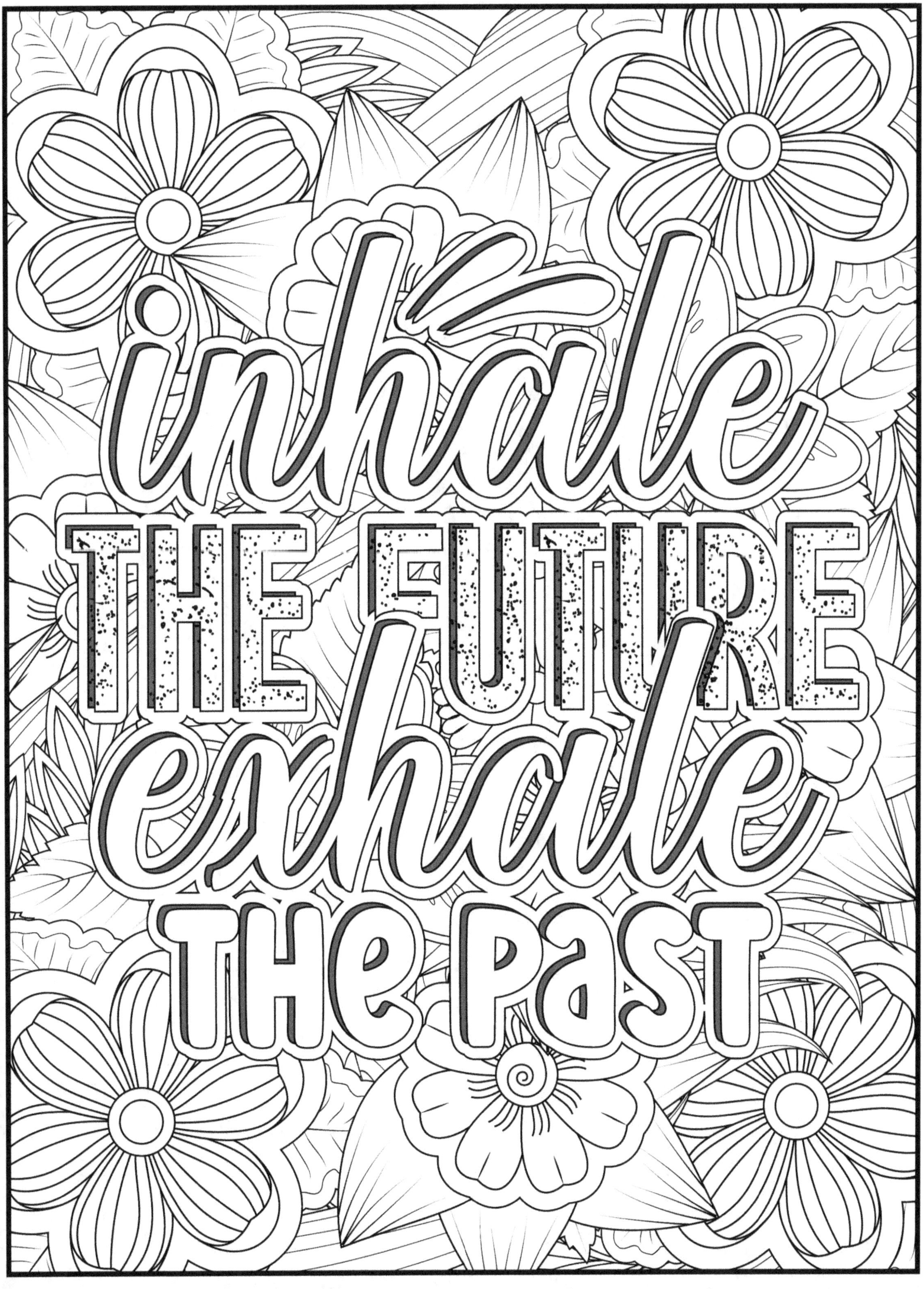
inhale
THE FUTURE
exhale
THE PAST

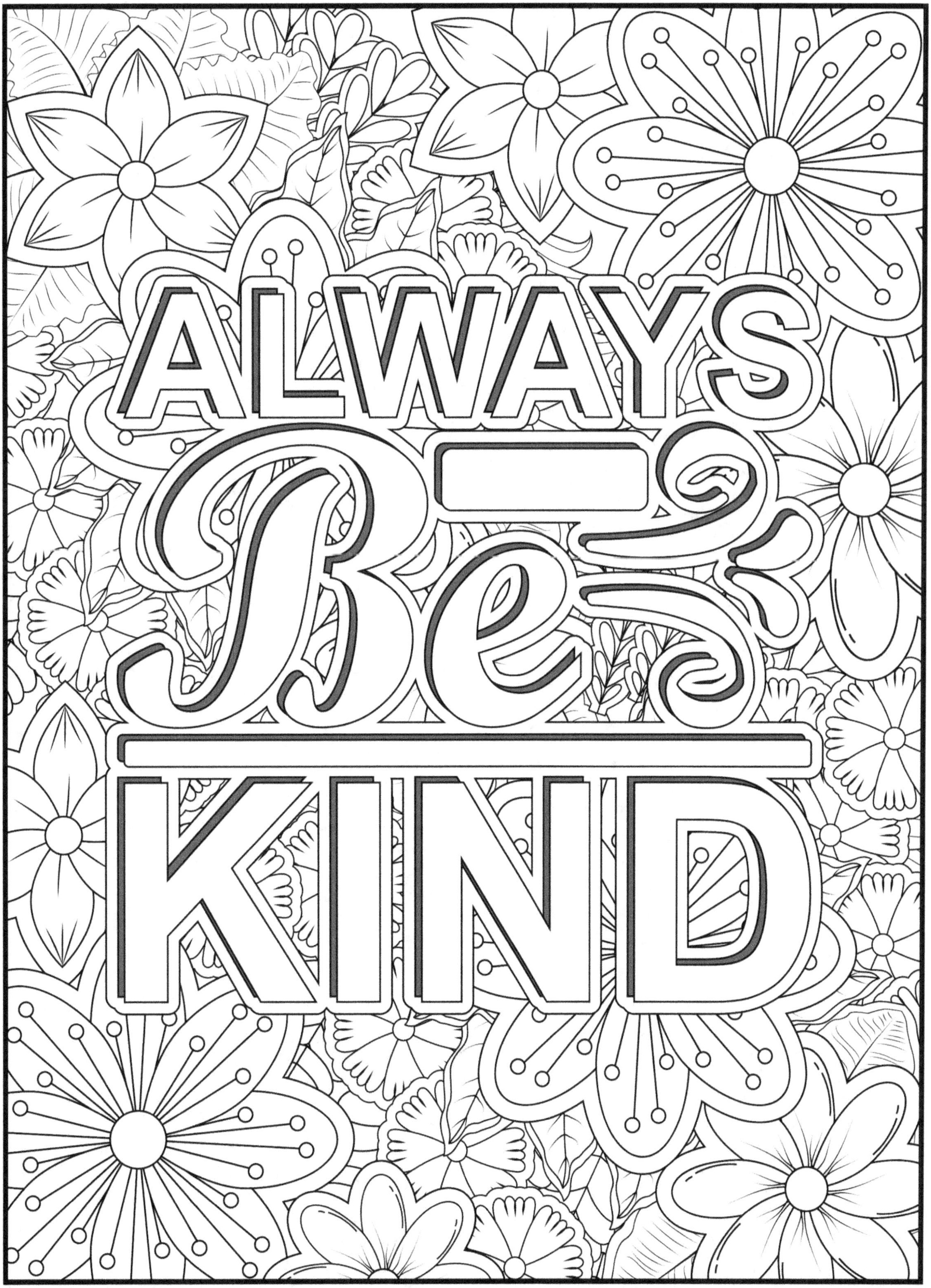
ALWAYS
Be
KIND

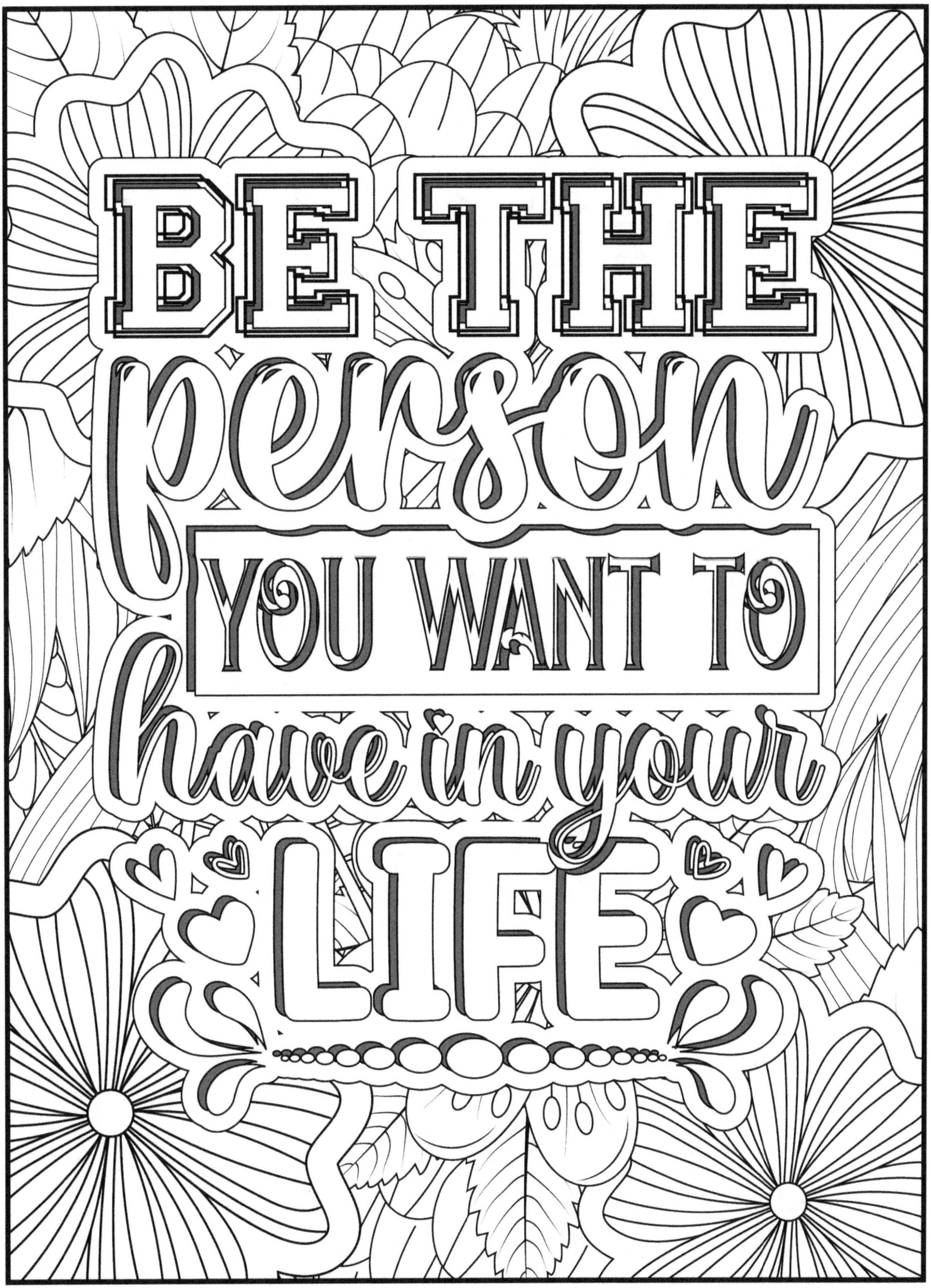
BE THE
person
YOU WANT TO
have in your
LIFE

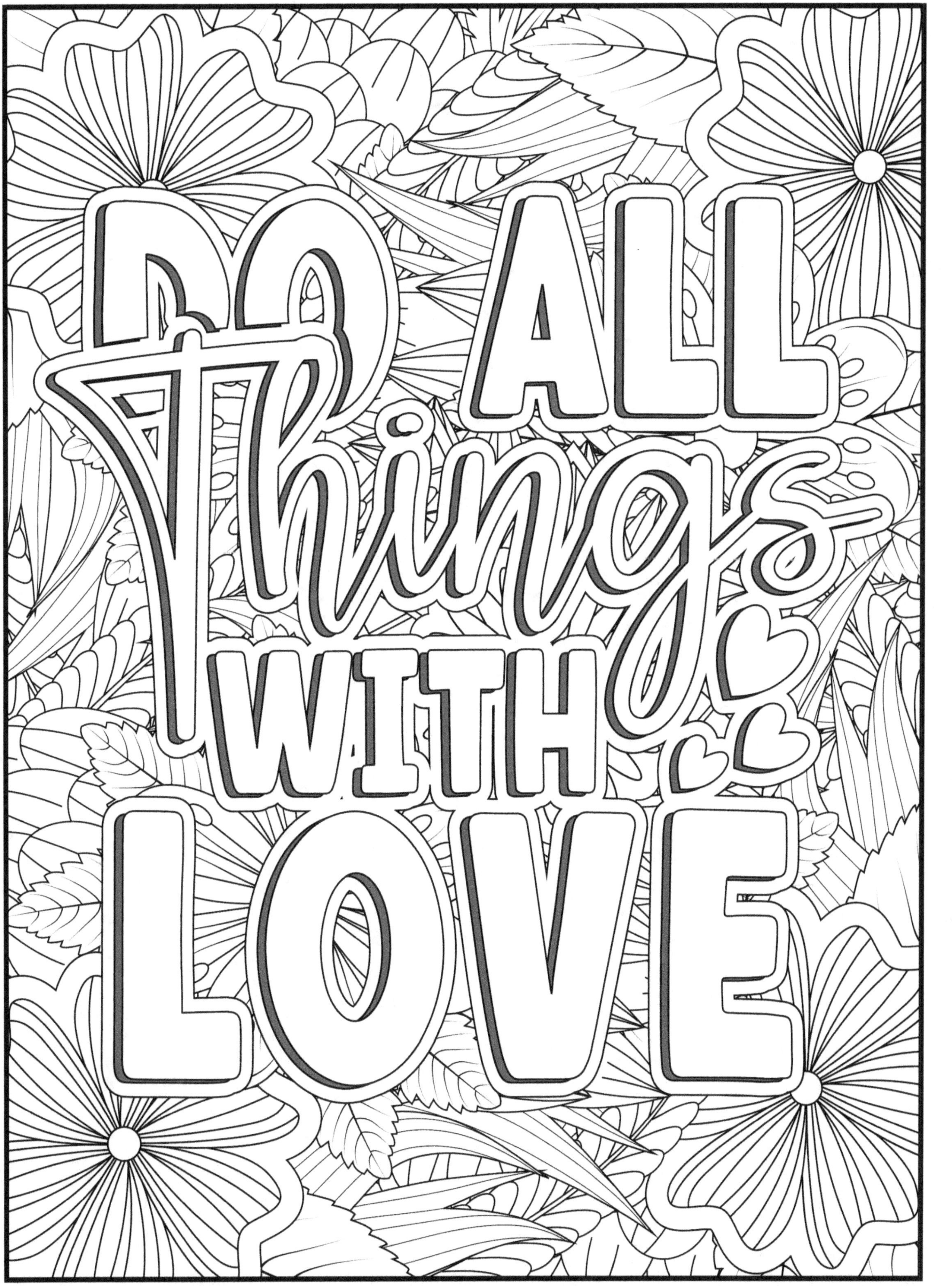
DO ALL
Things
WITH
LOVE

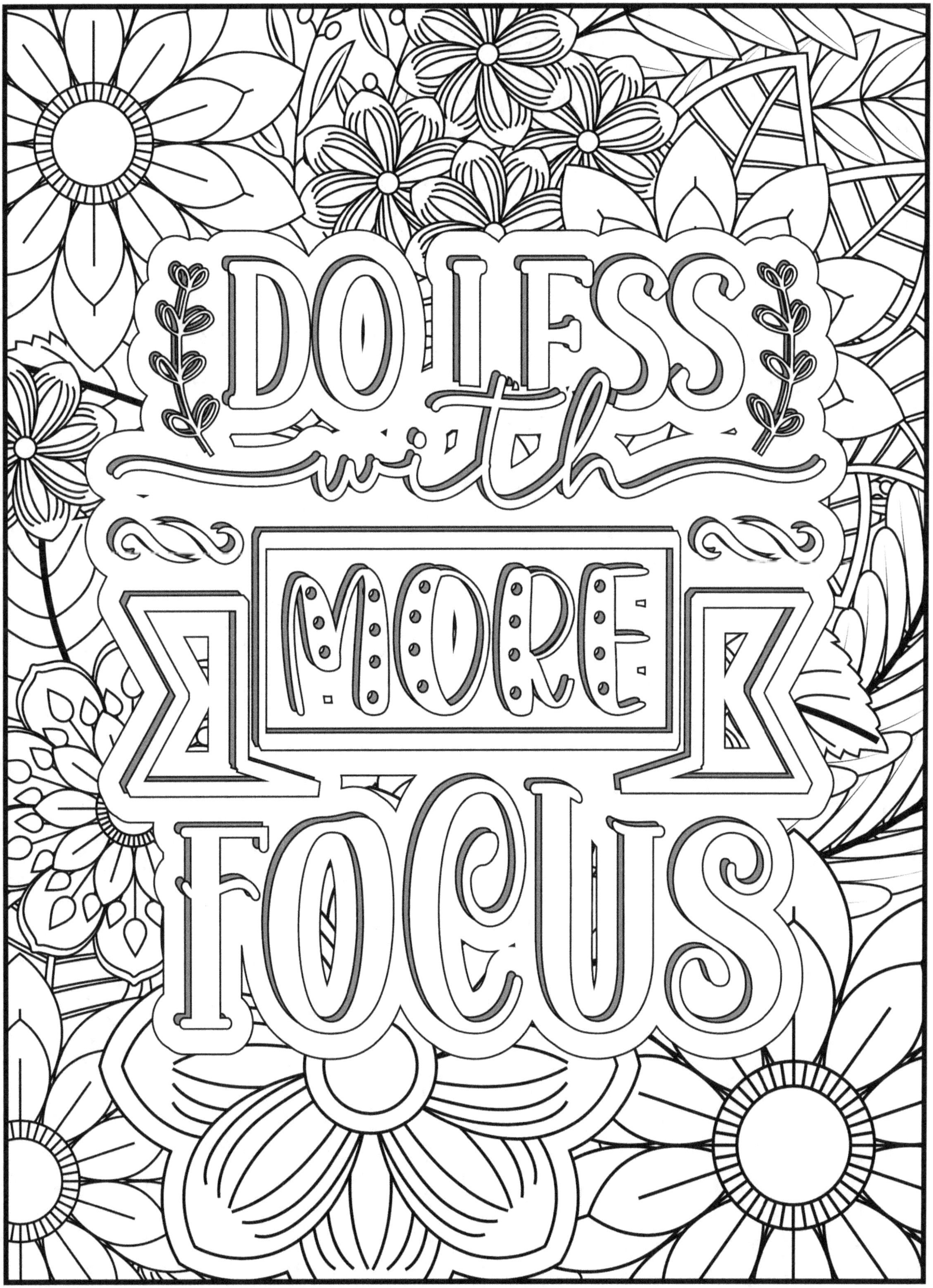
DO LESS
with
MORE
FOCUS

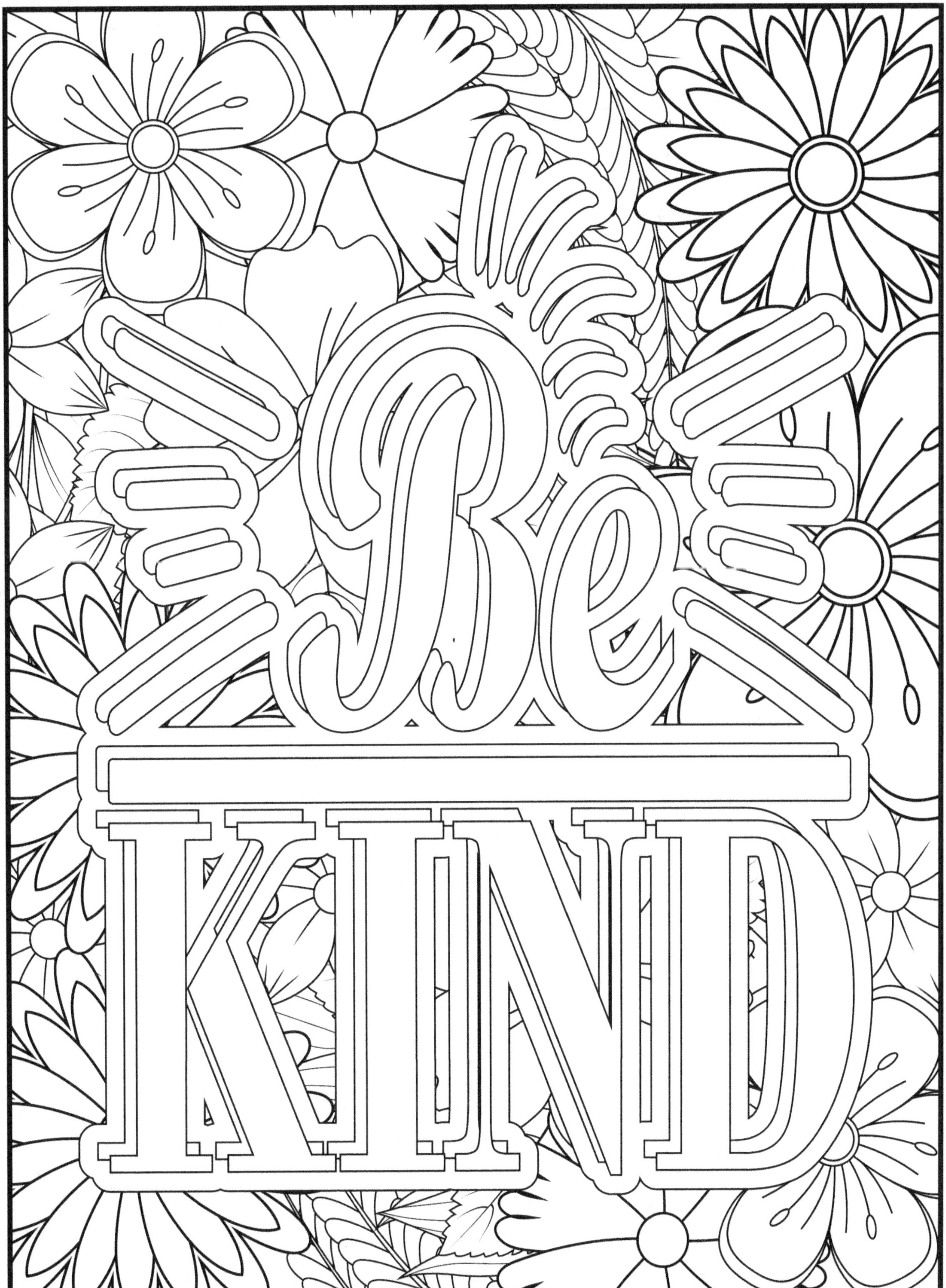
Be
KIND

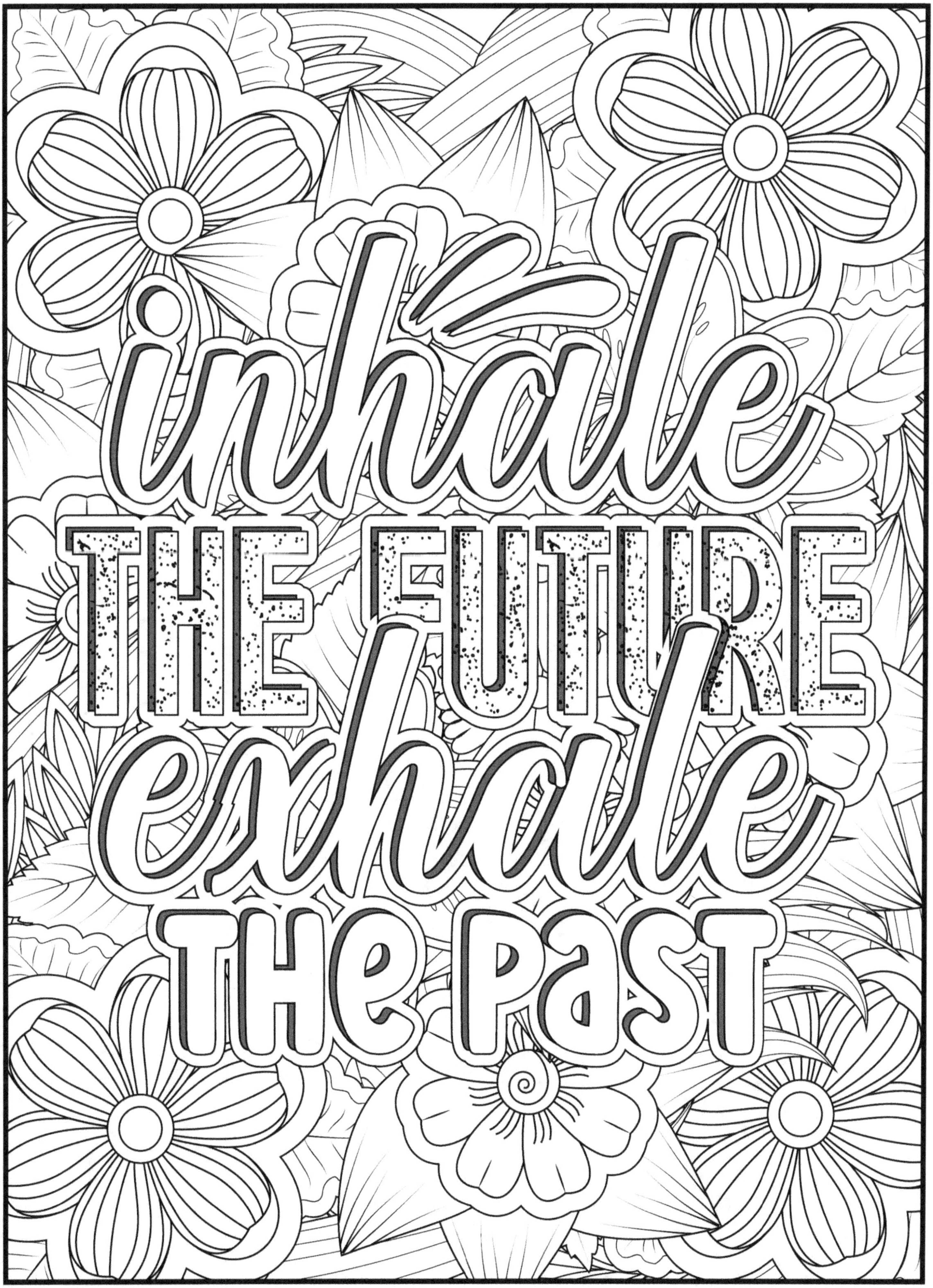
inhale
THE FUTURE
exhale
THE PAST

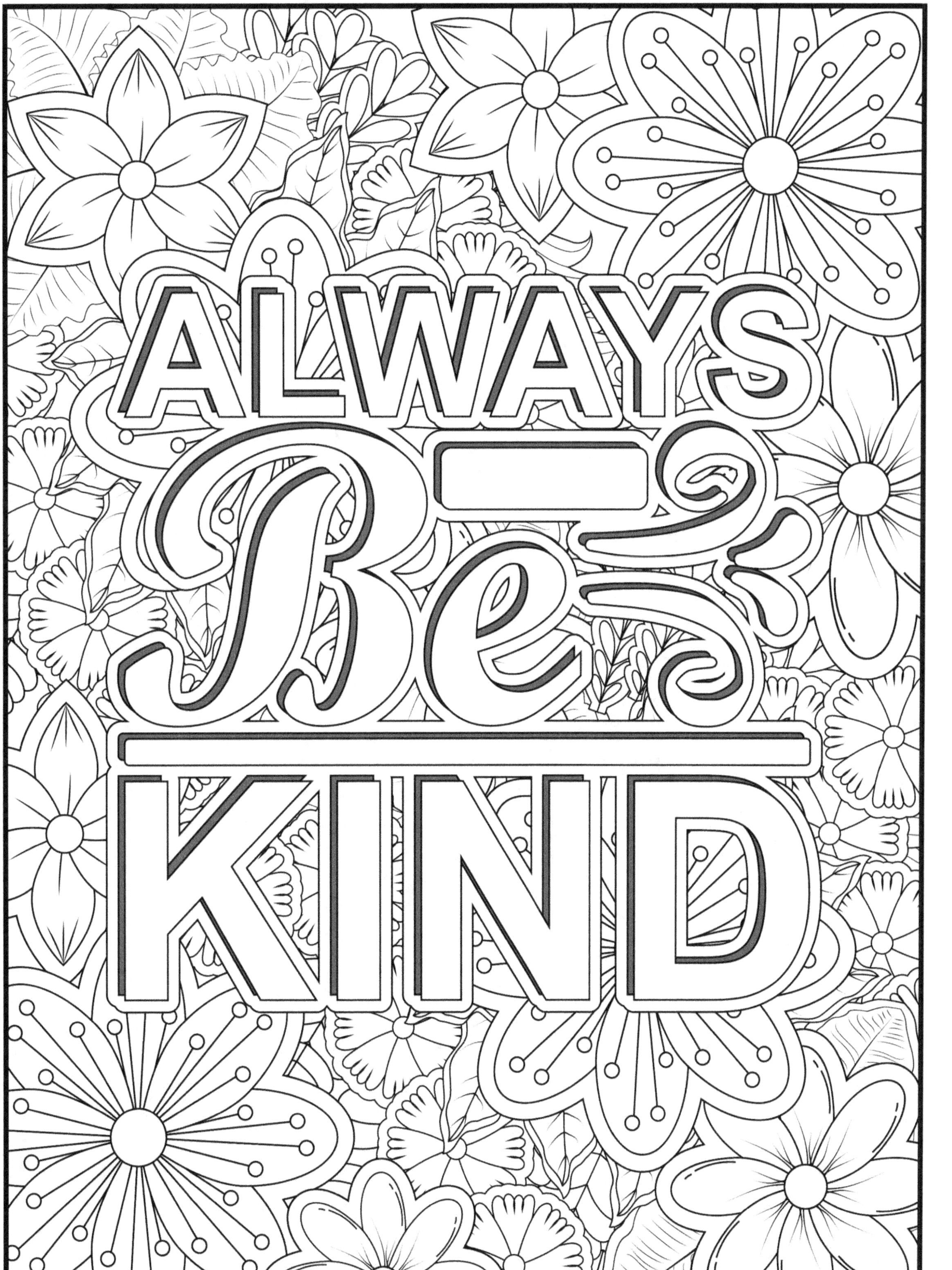
ALWAYS
Be
KIND

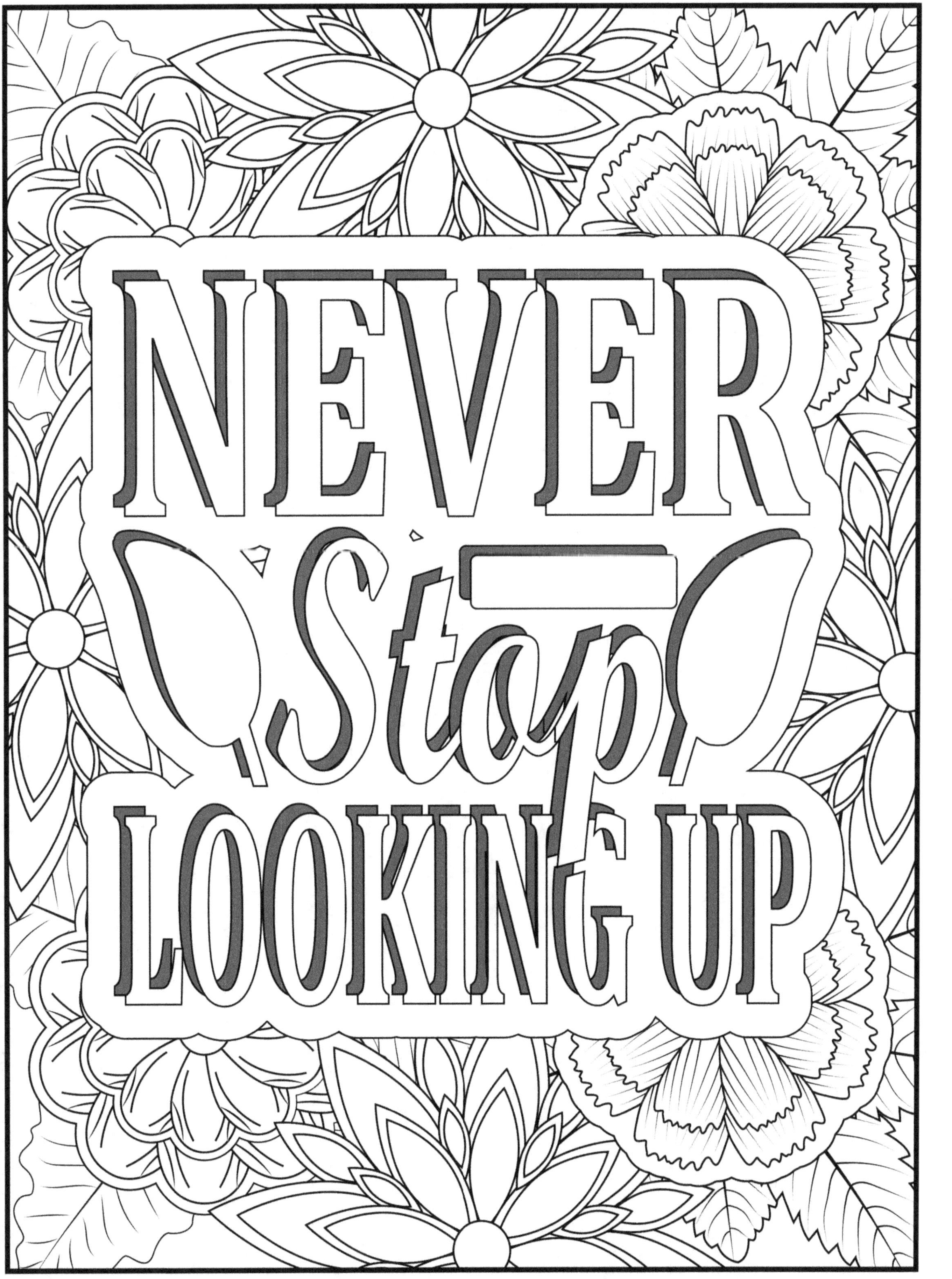
NEVER
Stop
LOOKING UP

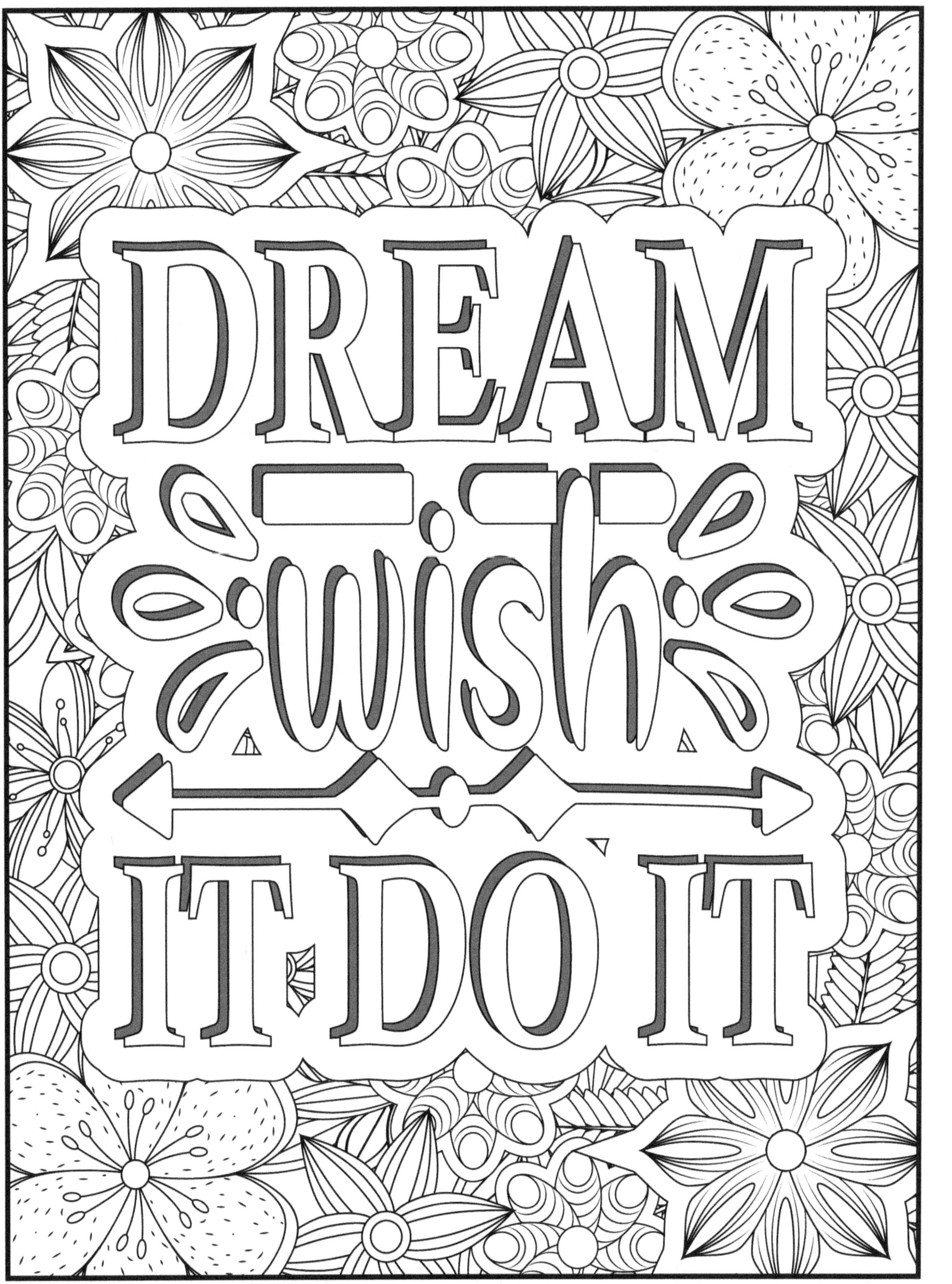
DREAM
wish
IT DO IT

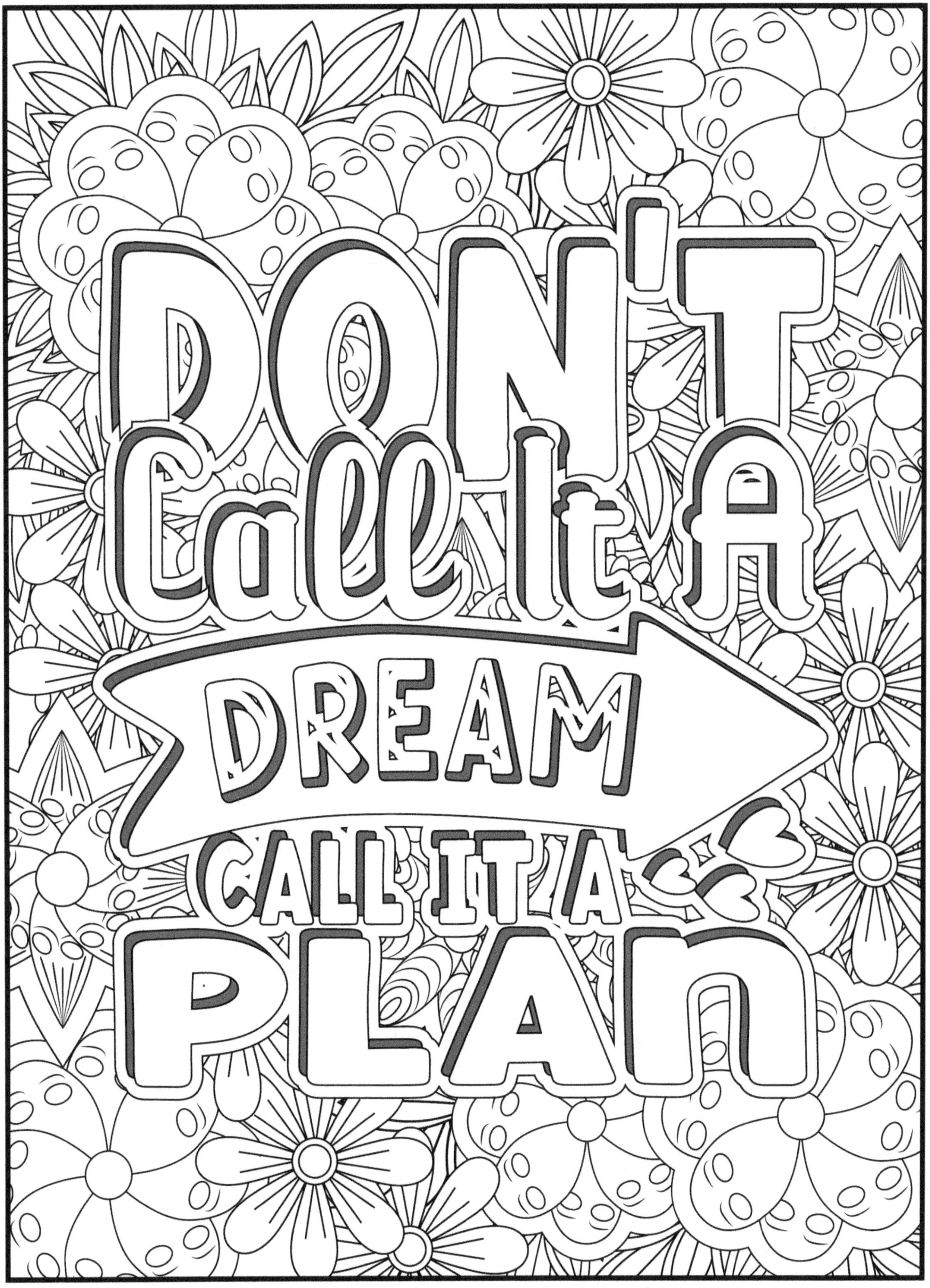
DON'T
Call It A
DREAM
CALL IT A
PLAN

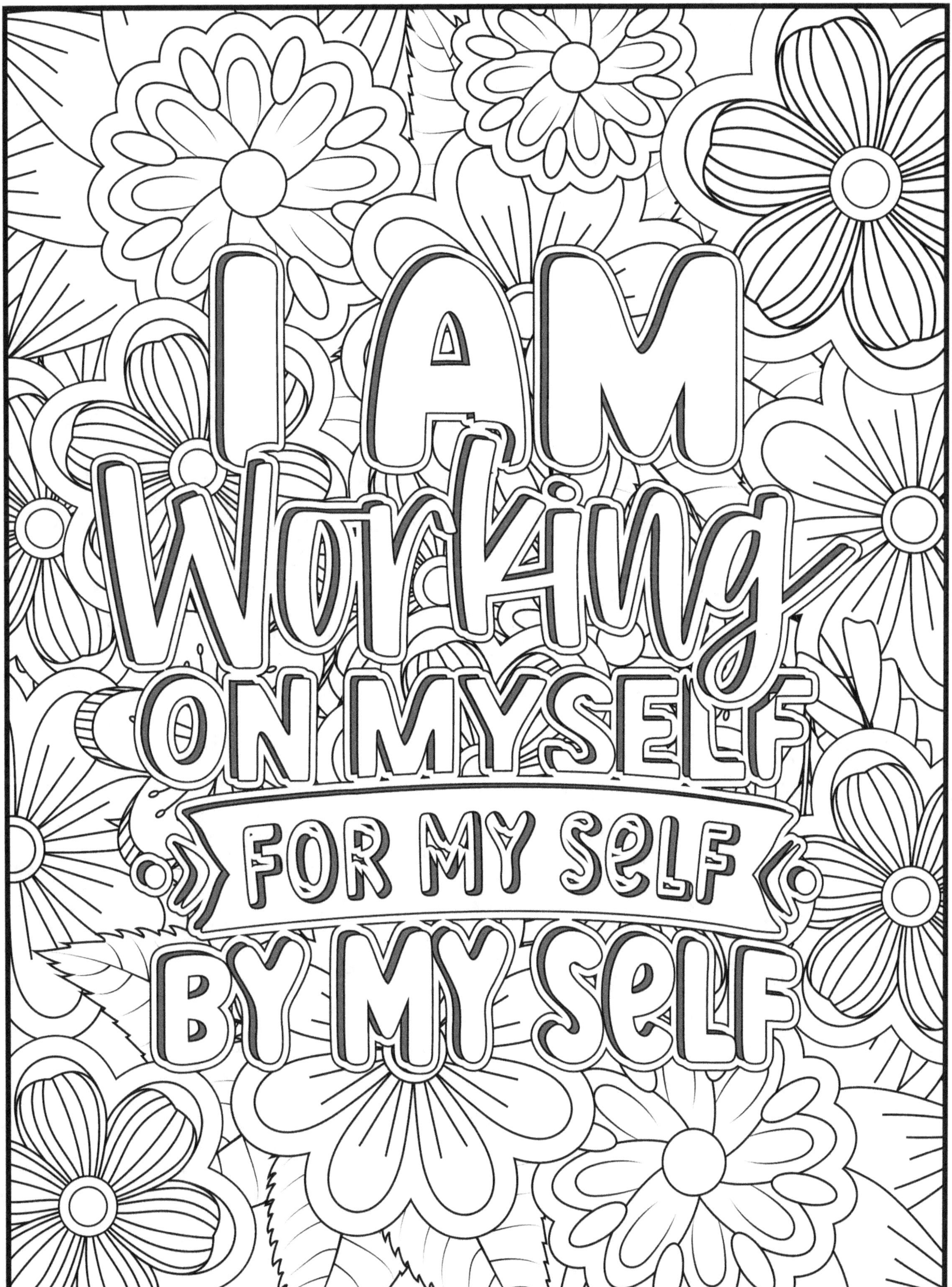
I AM
Working
ON MYSELF
FOR MY SELF
BY MY SELF

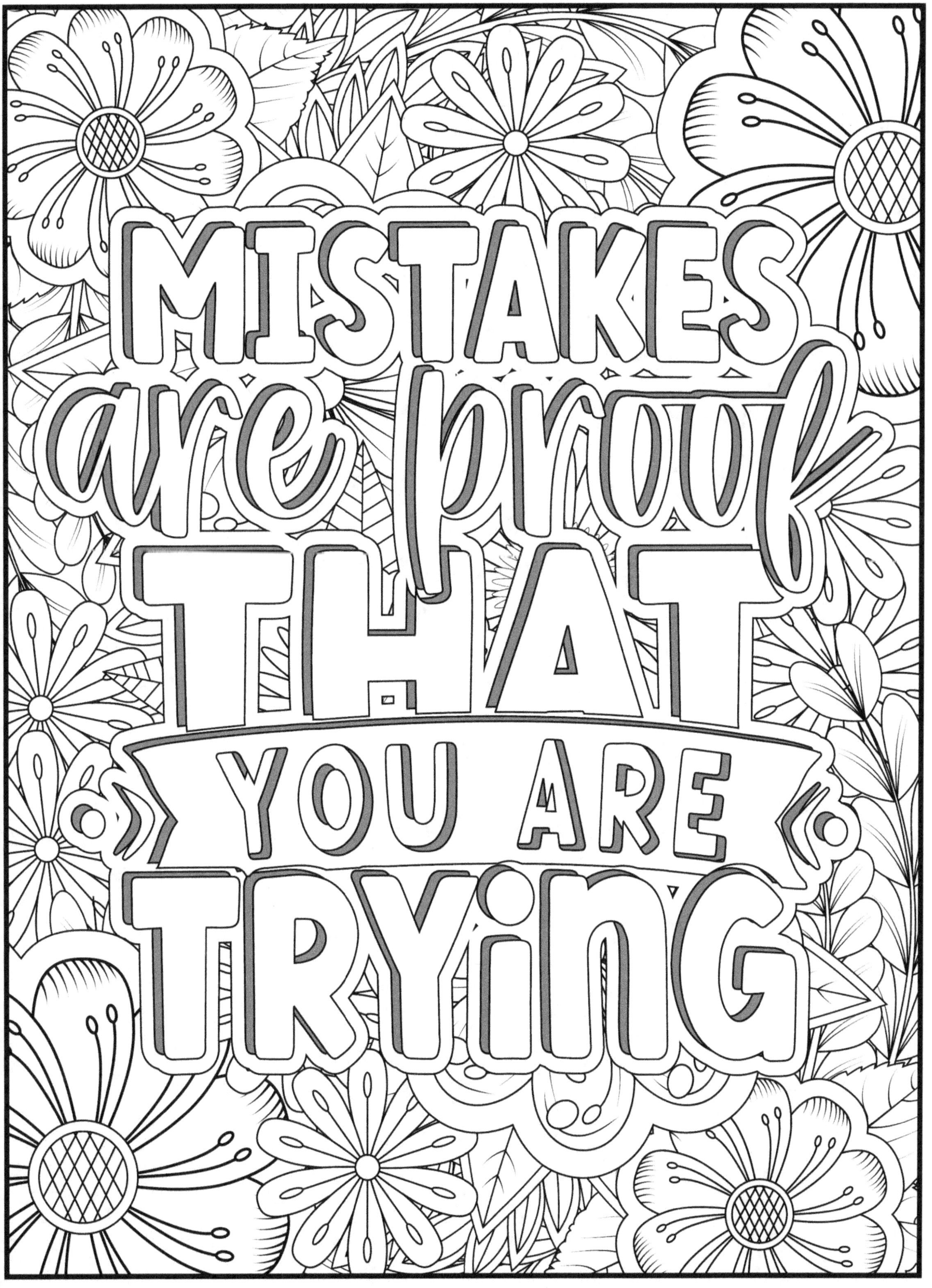
MISTAKES
are proof
THAT
YOU ARE
TRYinG

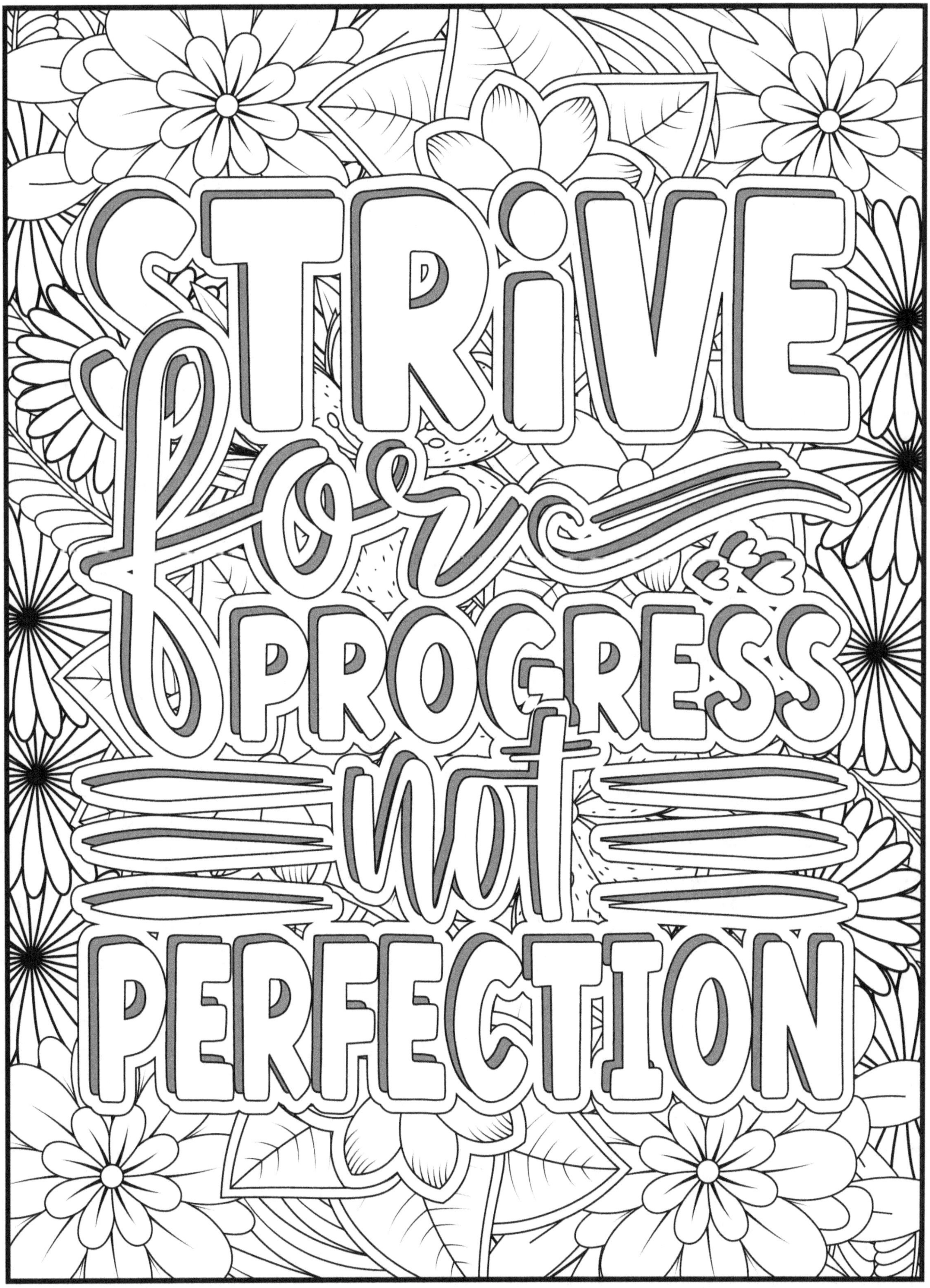
STRIVE
for
PROGRESS
not
PERFECTION

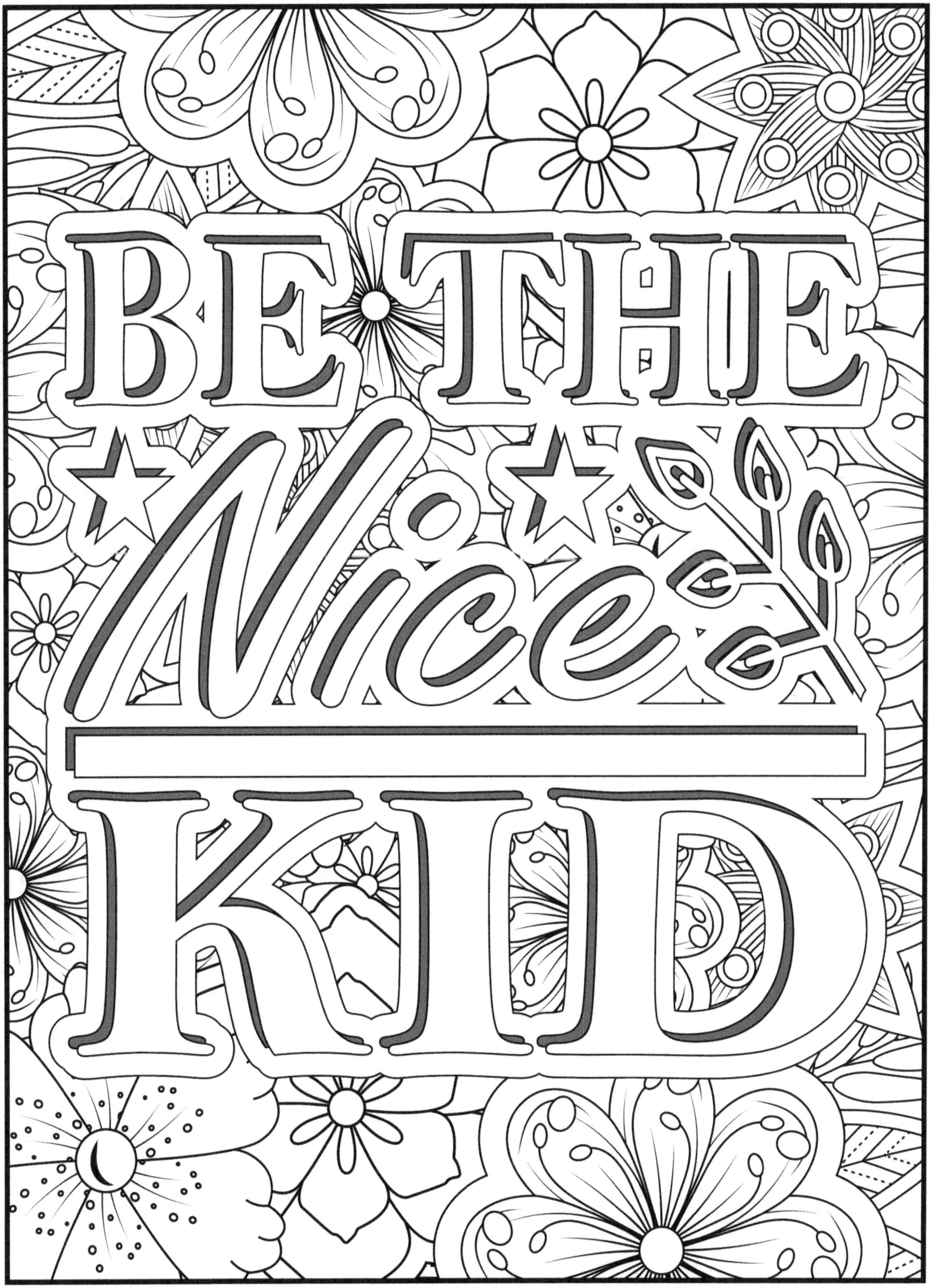
BE THE
Nice
KID

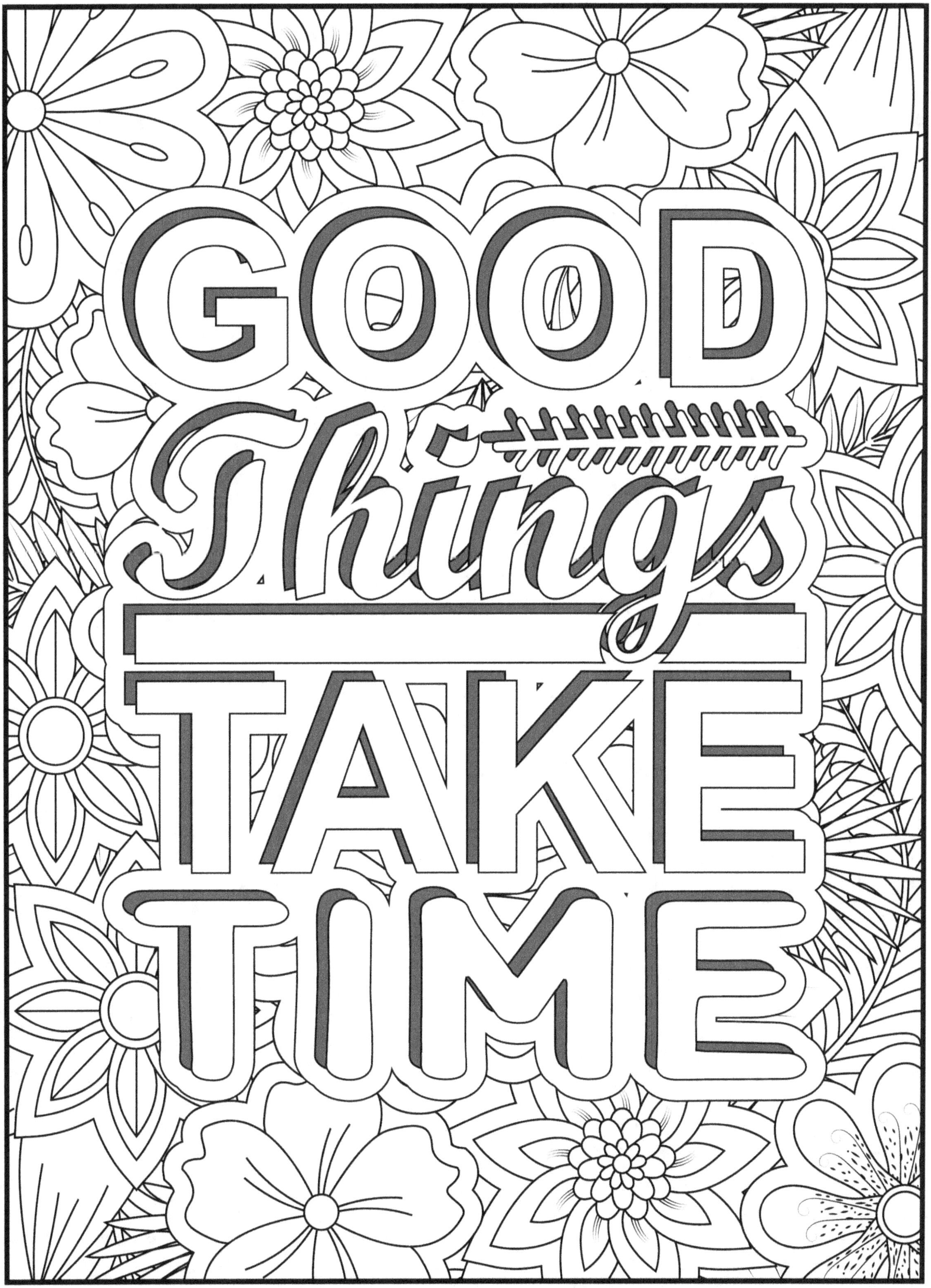
GOOD
Things
TAKE
TIME

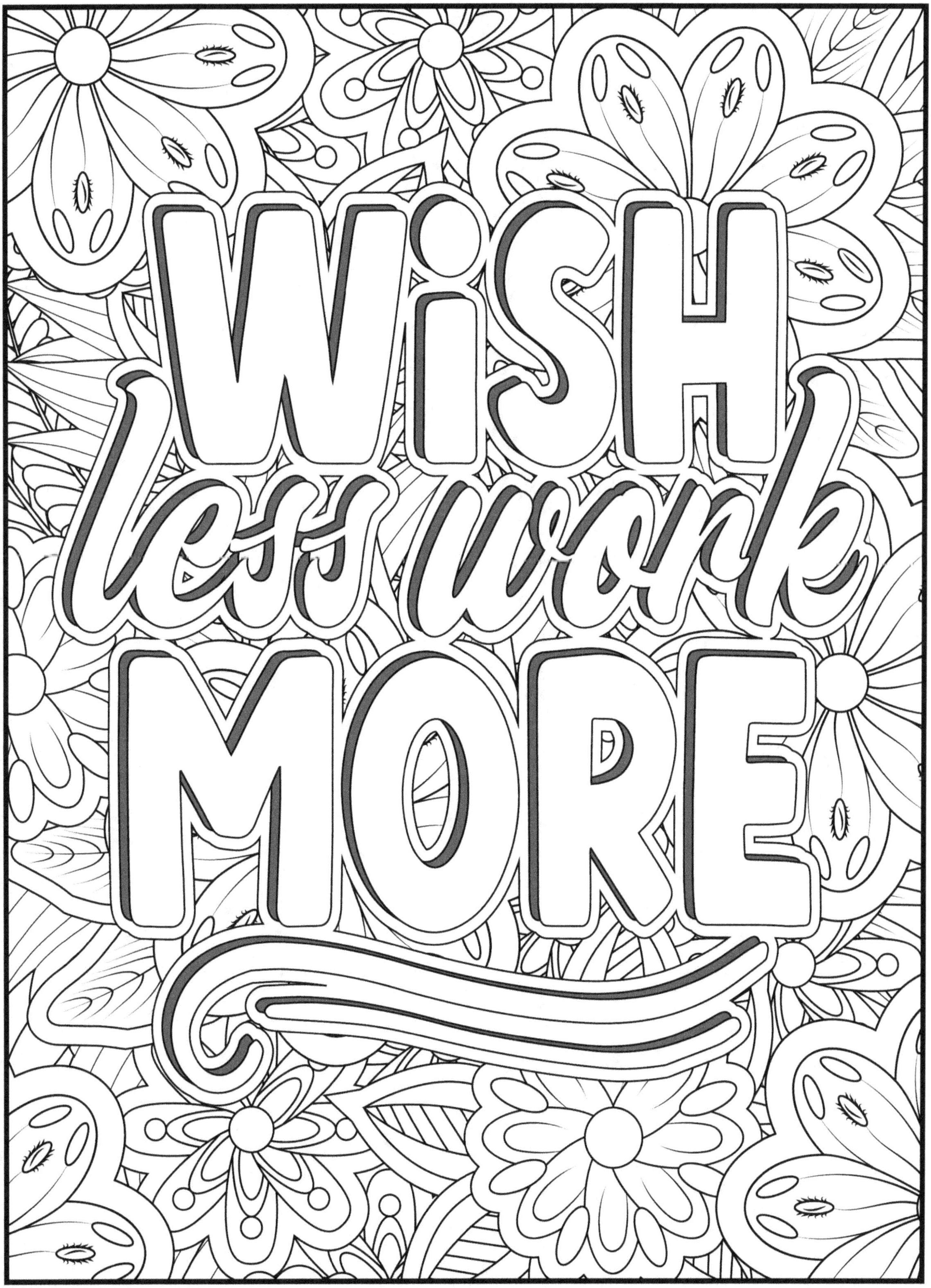
WiSH
less work
MORE

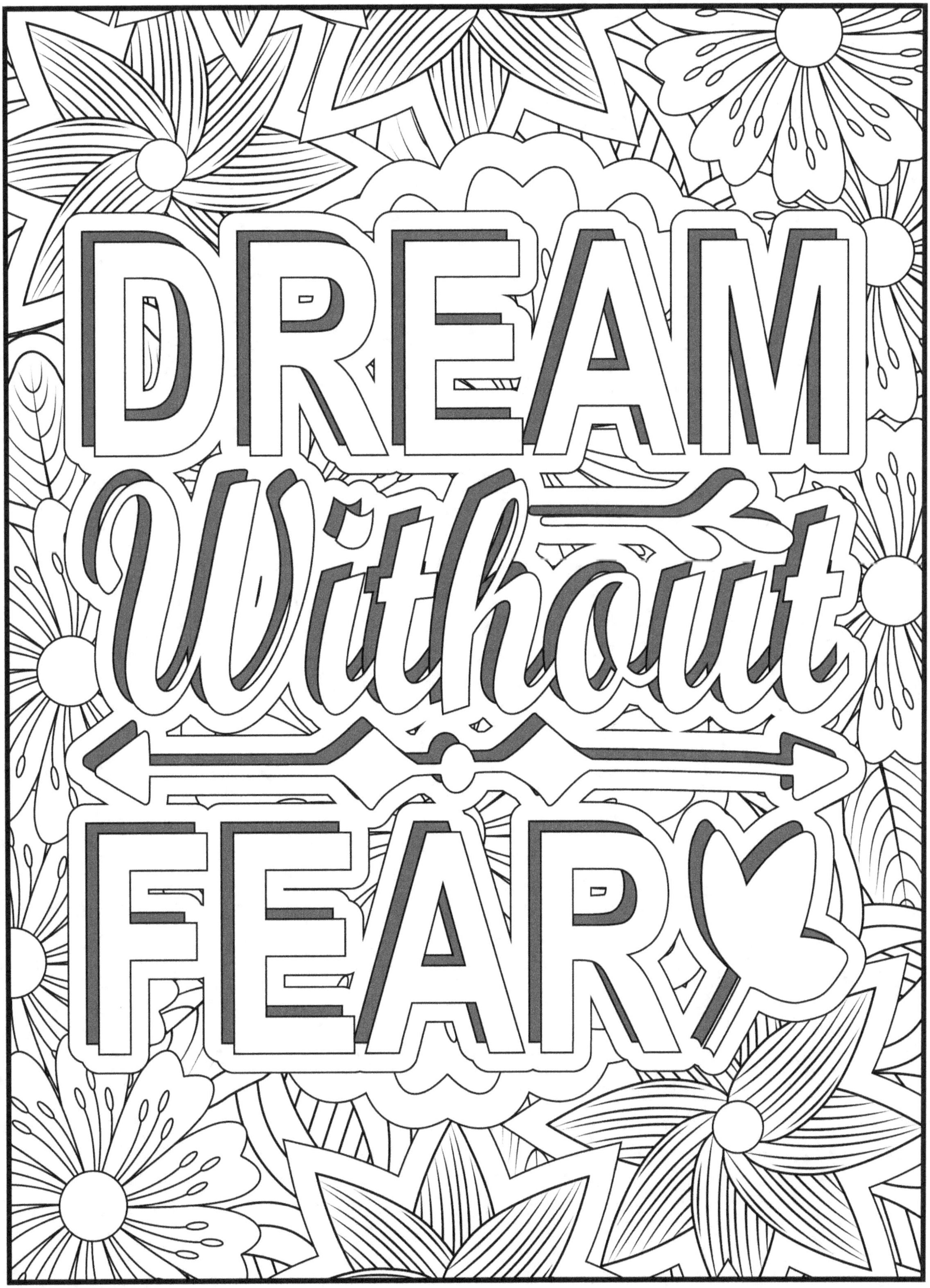
DREAM
Without
FEAR

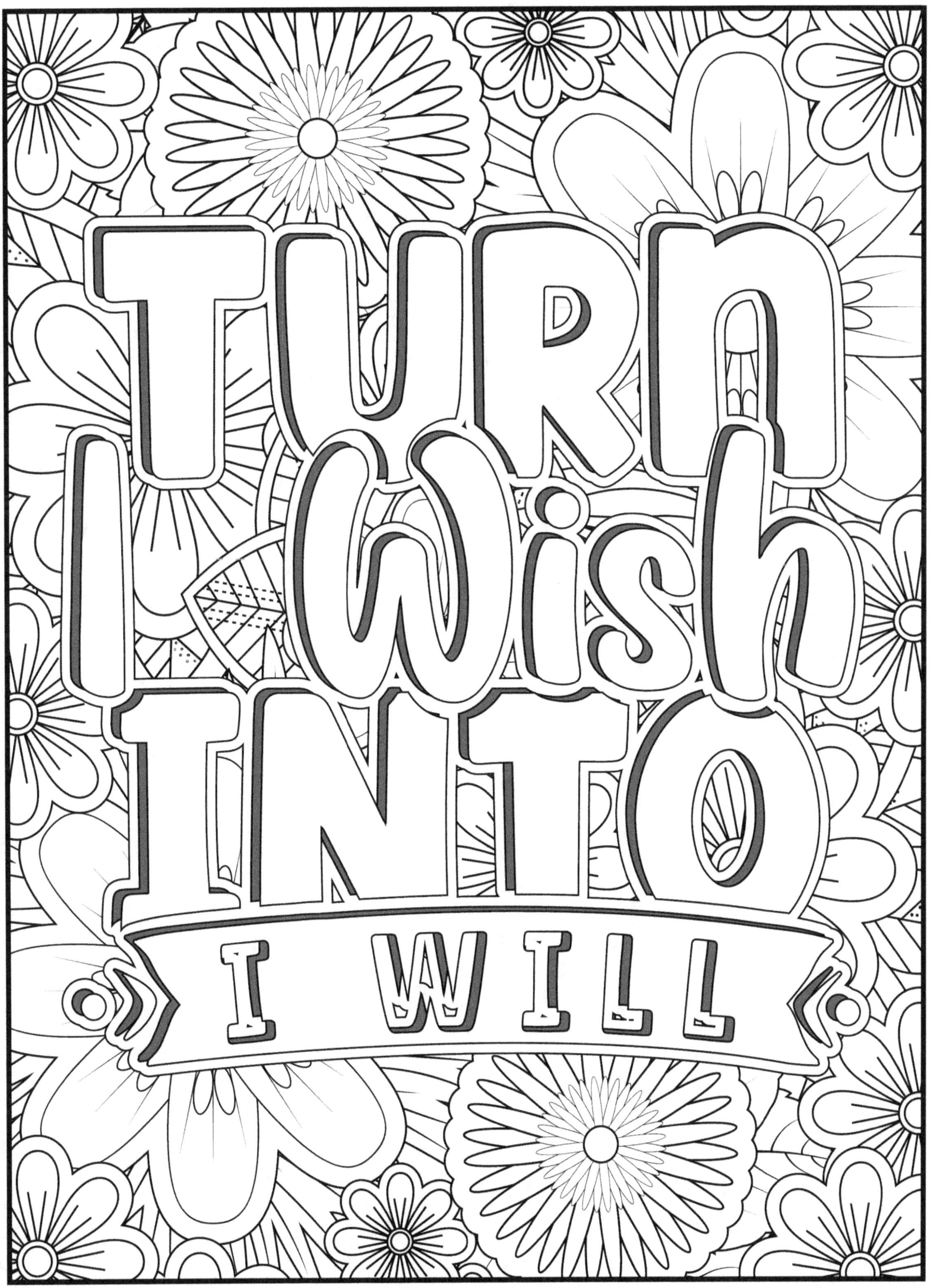
Turn
Wish
INTO
I WILL

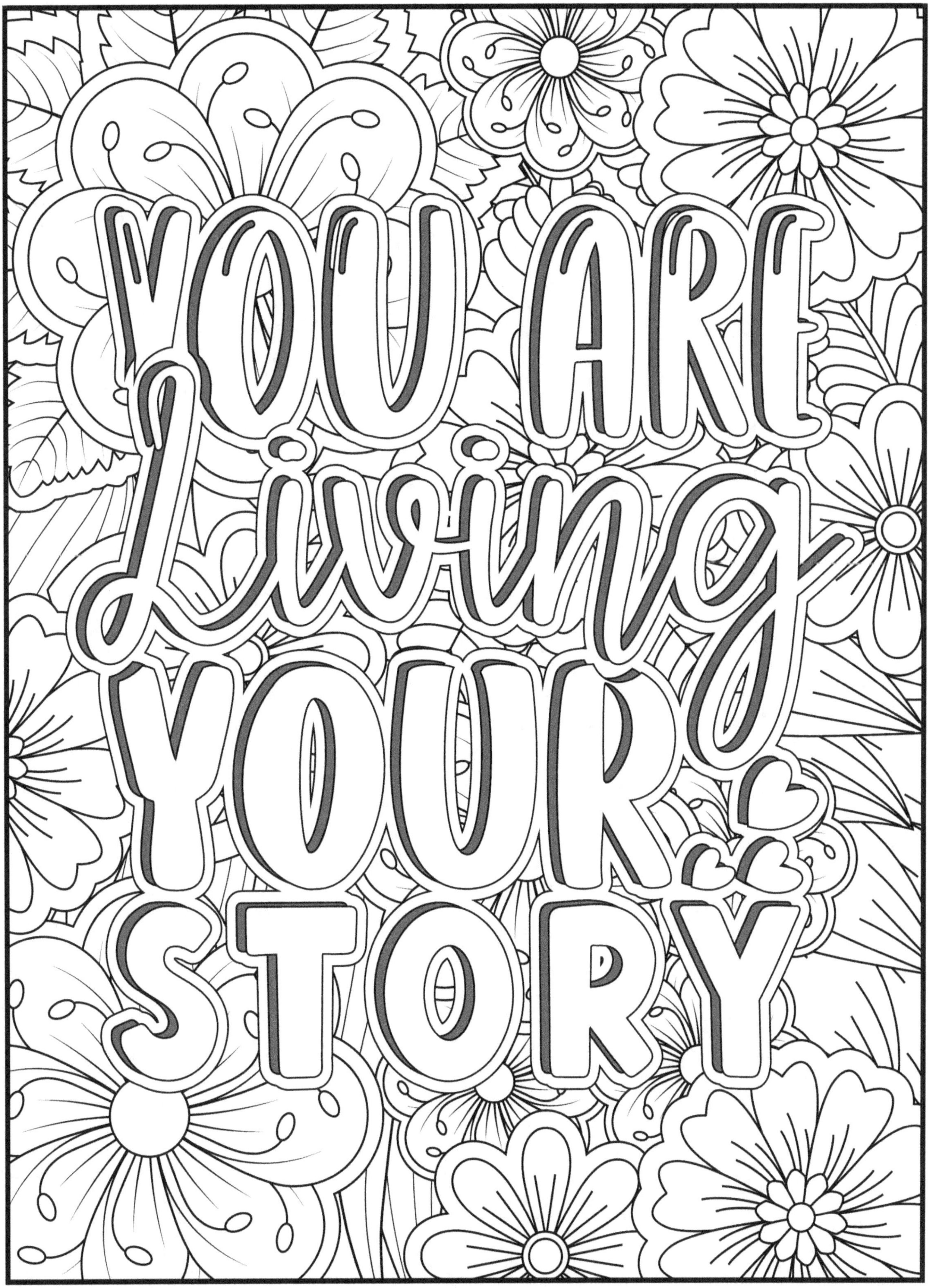
YOU ARE
living
YOUR
STORY

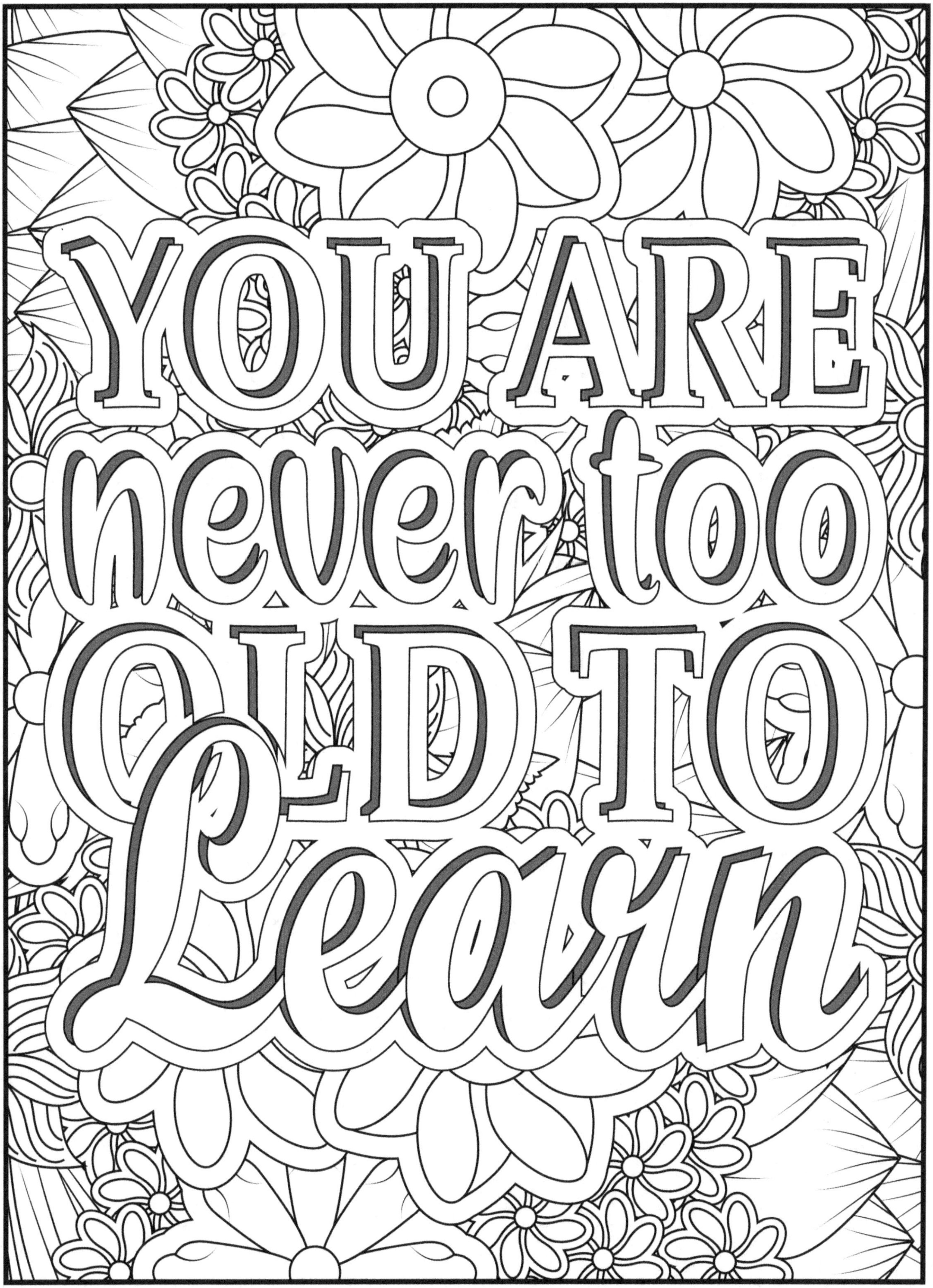
YOU ARE
never too
OLD TO
Learn

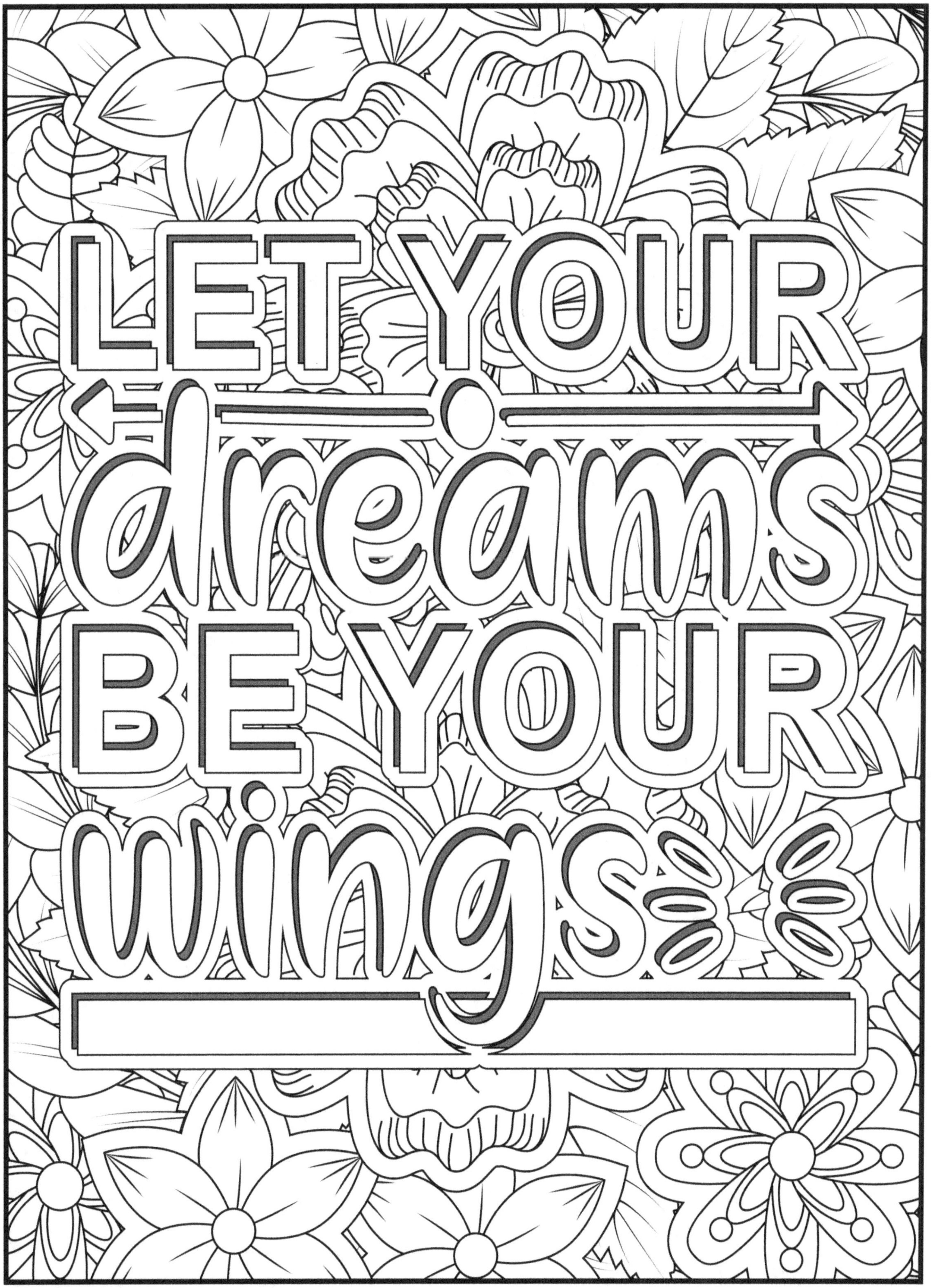
LET YOUR
dreams
BE YOUR
wings

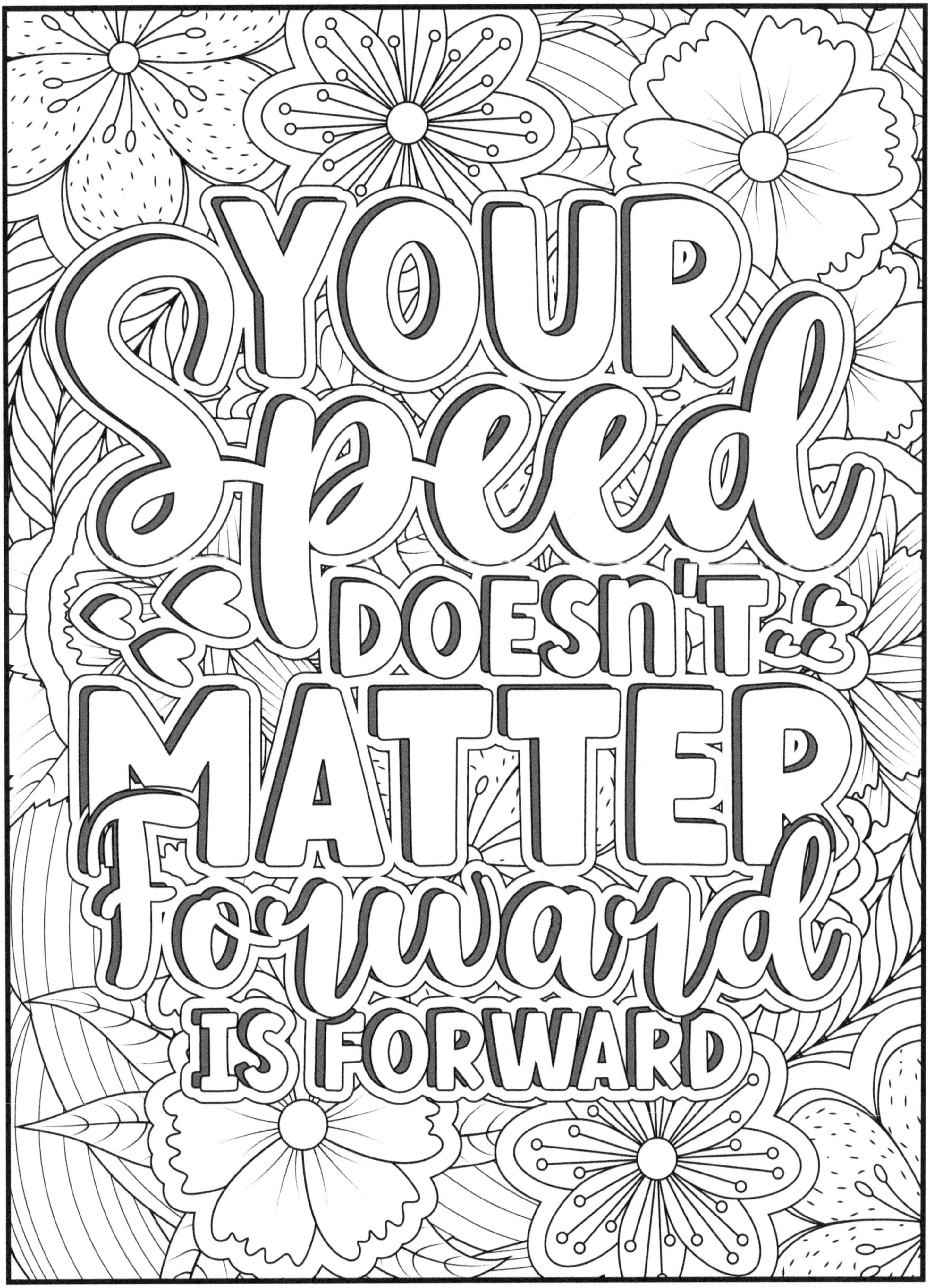
YOUR
Speed
DOESN'T
MATTER
forward
IS FORWARD

www.ingramcontent.com/pod-product-compliance
Lightning Source LLC
Chambersburg PA
CBHW082209290526
45794CB00009B/3483
* 9 7 9 8 8 7 1 6 7 6 7 9 0 *